THE

HANDY

CIVICS

ANSWER

BOOK

How to Be a Good Citizen

David L. Hudson, Jr., J.D.

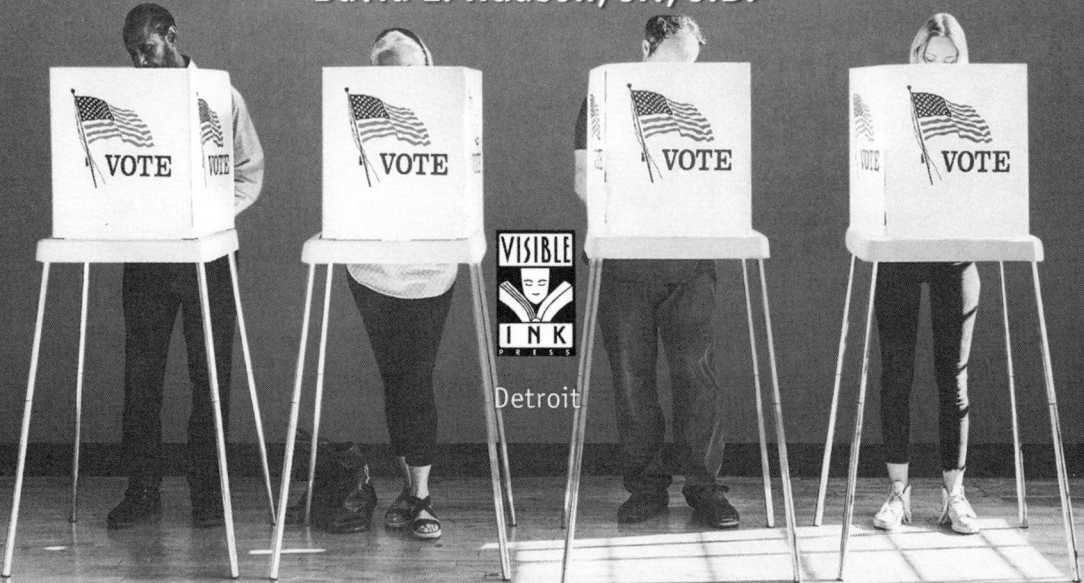

VISIBLE
INK
PRESS

Detroit

Visible Ink Press®
43311 Joy Rd., #414
Canton, MI 48187-2075

Visible Ink Press is a registered trademark of Visible Ink Press LLC.

Most Visible Ink Press books are available at special quantity discounts when purchased in bulk by corporations, organizations, or groups. Customized printings, special imprints, messages, and excerpts can be produced to meet your needs. For more information, contact Special Markets Director, Visible Ink Press, www.visibleink.com, or 734-667-3211.

Managing Editor: Kevin S. Hile
Art Director: Mary Claire Krzewinski
Page Design: Cinelli Design
Typesetting: Lumina Datamatics
Proofreaders: Larry Baker and Shoshana Hurwitz
Indexer: Larry Baker

Cover images: Shutterstock.

ISBN: 978-1-57859-811-3 (paperback)
ISBN: 978-1-57859-861-8 (ebook)
ISBN: 978-1-57859-860-1 (hardbound)

Cataloging-in-Publication Data is on file at the Library of Congress.

Printed in the United States of America.

10 9 8 7 6 5 4 3 2 1

About the Author

David L. Hudson Jr., J.D., is an attorney and law professor at Belmont University's College of Law, where he teaches courses in Constitutional Law, First Amendment Law, and bar exam preparation. He speaks widely on Constitutional Law and school law issues. In 2022, Belmont awarded him its University Faculty Scholarship Award. He previously taught classes at Vanderbilt Law School and the Nashville School of Law, where, in 2018, he was awarded its Distinguished Faculty Award. He also served as a senior law clerk for the Tennessee Supreme Court and earned his undergraduate degree from Duke University and his law degree from Vanderbilt Law School. He is an author, co-author, or co-editor of more than 50 books, including Visible Ink Press's *The Constitution Explained: A Guide for Every American* and *The Handy Supreme Court Answer Book: The History and Issues Explained.* He writes regularly for the American Bar Association's *Preview of United States Supreme Court Cases and ABA Journal.* He lives in Nashville, Tennessee.

Also from Visible Ink Press

The Handy Accounting Answer Book
by Amber Gray, Ph.D.
ISBN: 978-1-57859-675-1

The Handy African American History Answer Book
by Jessie Carnie Smith
ISBN: 978-1-57859-452-8

The Handy American Government Answer Book: How Washington, Politics, and Elections Work
by Gina Misiroglu
ISBN: 978-1-57859-639-3

The Handy American History Answer Book
by David L. Hudson Jr.
ISBN: 978-1-57859-471-9

The Handy Anatomy Answer Book, 2nd edition
by Patricia Barnes-Svarney and Thomas E. Svarney
ISBN: 978-1-57859-542-6

The Handy Answer Book for Kids (and Parents), 2nd edition
by Gina Misiroglu
ISBN: 978-1-57859-219-7

The Handy Armed Forces Answer Book
by Richard Estep
ISBN: 978-1-57859-743-7

The Handy Art History Answer Book
by Madelynn Dickerson
ISBN: 978-1-57859-417-7

The Handy Astronomy Answer Book, 3rd edition
by Charles Liu, Ph.D.
ISBN: 978-1-57859-419-1

The Handy Bible Answer Book
by Jennifer Rebecca Prince
ISBN: 978-1-57859-478-8

The Handy Biology Answer Book, 2nd edition
by Patricia Barnes Svarney and Thomas E. Svarney
ISBN: 978-1-57859-490-0

The Handy Boston Answer Book
by Samuel Willard Crompton
ISBN: 978-1-57859-593-8

The Handy California Answer Book
by Kevin S. Hile
ISBN: 978-1-57859-591-4

The Handy Chemistry Answer Book
by Ian C. Stewart and Justin P. Lamont
ISBN: 978-1-57859-374-3

The Handy Christianity Answer Book
by Steve Werner
ISBN: 978-1-57859-686-7

The Handy Civil War Answer Book
by Samuel Willard Crompton
ISBN: 978-1-57859-476-4

The Handy Communication Answer Book
By Lauren Sergy
ISBN: 978-1-57859-587-7

The Handy Diabetes Answer Book
by Patricia Barnes-Svarney and Thomas E. Svarney
ISBN: 978-1-57859-597-6

The Handy Dinosaur Answer Book, 2nd edition
by Patricia Barnes-Svarney and Thomas E. Svarney
ISBN: 978-1-57859-218-0

The Handy Engineering Answer Book
by DeLean Tolbert Smith, Ph.D.; Aishwary Pawar; Nicole P. Pitterson, Ph.D.; and Debra Butler, Ph.D.
ISBN: 978-1-57859-770-3

The Handy English Grammar Answer Book
by Christine A. Hult, Ph.D.
ISBN: 978-1-57859-520-4

The Handy Forensic Science Answer Book: Reading Clues at the Crime Scene, Crime Lab, and in Court
by Patricia Barnes-Svarney and Thomas E. Svarney
ISBN: 978-1-57859-621-8

The Handy Geography Answer Book, 3rd edition
by Paul A. Tucci
ISBN: 978-1-57859-576-1

The Handy Geology Answer Book
by Patricia Barnes-Svarney and Thomas E. Svarney
ISBN: 978-1-57859-156-5

The Handy History Answer Book: From the Stone Age to the Digital Age, 4th edition
by Stephen A. Werner, Ph.D.
ISBN: 978-1-57859-680-5

The Handy Hockey Answer Book
by Stan Fischler
ISBN: 978-1-57859-513-6

The Handy Investing Answer Book
by Paul A. Tucci
ISBN: 978-1-57859-486-3

The Handy Islam Answer Book
by John Renard, Ph.D.
ISBN: 978-1-57859-510-5

The Handy Law Answer Book
by David L. Hudson, Jr., J.D.
ISBN: 978-1-57859-217-3

The Handy Literature Answer Book
By Daniel S. Burt and Deborah G. Felder
ISBN: 978-1-57859-635-5

The Handy Math Answer Book, 2nd edition
by Patricia Barnes-Svarney and Thomas E. Svarney
ISBN: 978-1-57859-373-6

The Handy Military History Answer Book
by Samuel Willard Crompton
ISBN: 978-1-57859-509-9

The Handy Mythology Answer Book
by David A. Leeming, Ph.D.
ISBN: 978-1-57859-475-7

The Handy New York City Answer Book
by Chris Barsanti
ISBN: 978-1-57859-586-0

The Handy Nutrition Answer Book
by Patricia Barnes-Svarney and Thomas E. Svarney
ISBN: 978-1-57859-484-9

The Handy Ocean Answer Book
by Patricia Barnes-Svarney and Thomas E. Svarney
ISBN: 978-1-57859-063-6

The Handy Personal Finance Answer Book
by Paul A. Tucci
ISBN: 978-1-57859-322-4

The Handy Philosophy Answer Book
by Naomi Zack, Ph.D.
ISBN: 978-1-57859-226-5

The Handy Physics Answer Book, 3rd edition
By Charles Liu, Ph.D.
ISBN: 978-1-57859-695-9

Photo Sources

AgnosticPreachersKid (Wikicommons): p. 420.

Americaslibrary.gov: p. 43.

Americasroof (Wikicommons): p. 362.

Artsy.net: p. 25.

Associated Press: p. 330.

Brooklyn Museum: p. 134.

Chappel, Alonzo. *National Portrait Gallery of Eminent Americans from Original Full Length Portraits by Alonzo Chappel.* Vol I, New York: Johnson, Fry & Co. 1862: p. 196.

CIR Online: p. 363.

The Clarion-Ledger/Jack R. Thornell: p. 353.

Collection of the Maryland State Archives: p. 148.

Cooper, W. D. "Boston Tea Party." *The History of North America.* London: E. Newbury, 1789: p. 5.

Ellis, Edward Sylvester. *The People's History of the World*, Vol VI, 1902: p. 15.

Executive Office of the President of the United States: pp. 50, 60, 124, 376, 411.

Forbes.com: p. 20.

Fordlibrarymuseum.gov: p. 126.

Fresno Bee: p. 350 (right).

Harry S. Truman Presidential Library and Museum: pp. 118, 328.

Harvard Law School Library Legal Portrait Project: p. 205.

Eli Hiller: p. 249.

HomeTreasury.gov: p. 172.

The Indian Reporter: p. 23.

J. Paul Getty Museum: p. 100.

JFKlibrary.org: p. 129.

Jonathunder (Wikicommons): p. 65.

Library of Congress: pp. 2, 55, 111, 138, 187, 199, 202, 208, 212, 215, 220, 319, 323, 334, 338, 346, 350 (left), 352.

Metropolitan Museum of Art: p. 30.

National Archives and Records Administration: p. 39.
National Archives at College Park: p. 246.
National Portrait Gallery: p. 142.
NPS.gov: p. 32.
Oyez.org: p. 35.
Phil Roeder: p. 189.
Brad Sherman: p. 243.
Shutterstock: pp. 10, 13, 47, 68, 71, 73, 78, 80, 84, 87, 89, 92, 95, 104, 112, 114, 121, 153, 240, 253, 255, 262, 264, 267, 270, 271, 274, 278, 282, 286, 288, 292, 296, 306, 309, 311, 313, 378, 385, 392, 395, 403, 407, 412, 415, 419, 426, 428, 431.
Gage Skidmore: p. 258.
John Mathew Smith & www.celebrity-photos.com: pp. 341, 370.
Some Random Serbian (Wikicommons): p. 225.
State Archives of North Carolina: p. 356.
Supremecourthistory.org: p. 161.
Supreme Court of the United States: pp. 76, 159, 175, 192, 232.
U.S. Army: p. 181.
U.S. Congress: pp. 57, 133, 344.
U.S. Department of Justice: pp. 230, 388.
U.S. Federal Government: pp. 178, 399.
U.S. National Archives: p. 358.
Web.archive.org: p. 386.
WhiteHouse.gov: p. 165.
White House Historical Association: p. 107.
Wikipedia Loves Art: p. 26.
Yale University Art Gallery: p. 27.
Public domain: pp. 8, 237, 400.

Table of Contents

Introduction

Civics is all about understanding government and what rights and responsibilities we have as citizens in the United States of America. Civic education has never been more vital in the United States than today when political polarization has risen and coarsened discourse. Selfishness has at times overtaken the common good.

At its root, civics means having a good core understanding of the work and functions of the three different branches of the federal government—legislative, executive, and judiciary. Accordingly, *The Handy Civics Answer Book* examines each of these branches of government in separate chapters. There is a chapter on Congress, a chapter on the Presidency, a chapter on the U.S. Supreme Court, and another on landmark rulings.

But civics includes far more than issues impacting the federal government. Therefore, this book also examines state governments. Other chapters address the Bill of Rights: the part of the U.S. Constitution that provides protections for constitutional rights such as the right to freedom of speech and religion under the First Amendment, the right to keep and bear arms under the Second Amendment, and the right to be free from unreasonable searches and seizures under the Fourth Amendment.

Civics also relates to citizenship and what it takes to be a good citizen in the modern world. Thus, this book also includes a chapter on citizen rights and responsibilities as well as a chapter on how one obtains citizenship, and it discusses the immigration system we have in this country.

Finally, we will take a look at one of the most defining times in modern American history: the Civil Rights Movement of the 1950s and 1960s, which ultimately led to a society that rejected the abject evils of racial segregation and gave birth to such landmark pieces of civil rights legislation as the Civil Rights Act of 1964, the Voting Rights Act of 1965, and the Fair Housing Act of 1968.

In the words of Dr. Martin Luther King, Jr. in his famous "Letter from a Birmingham Jail," "the time is always ripe to do right."

Doing right means that more and more citizens understand and appreciate the study and nurturing of civics and good civic education.

It is the author's hope that this book will help citizens be even more informed about their government, their laws, their freedoms as citizens of the "Land of the Free and the Home of the Brave."

Acknowledgments

I would like to thank Roger Jänecke of Visible Ink Press for giving me another opportunity to contribute to his "Handy Answer Book" series. He is a publishing genius for whom I have immense respect. I also would thank expert editor Kevin Hile, who always improves every manuscript.

Thanks to my family at Belmont Law School, which has given me the chance to explore my scholarship interests and my passion for teaching. Of course, I send heartfelt gratitude to my students from whom I learn on a daily basis.

I also would like to thank my civic education family. This consists of a broad group of people, and I am afraid I will leave someone out if I start listing my names, but you know who you are. I do have to mention Janis Kyser, who is also known as "The Queen of Civic Education." Without her, I would not have met so many amazing people.

Finally, I would like to thank my family, particularly my parents and my wife. They have always been there for me, and I remain eternally grateful.

Dedication

To Roger Desrosiers and Kelley Brown, civic education champions and good friends.

The Formation of the United States

Why did the British colonies in America become disenchanted with the British government?

King George III (1738–1820) was one of Great Britain's longest-serving monarchs in British history. He had many successes as monarch, including territorial advances made in the continent across the Atlantic Ocean—what we now call North America. He and his armed forces enjoyed military successes in the Seven Years' War, the conflict with French emperor Napoleon Bonaparte (1769–1821), and such.

However, King George began to impose more control and economic tightening over the American colonies. He supported many of these economic measures because the colonies were generating income and the British Empire needed money to support their worldwide causes.

What was the Stamp Act?

The Stamp Act of 1765 was a direct tax imposed by the British Parliament upon the American colonists. Under it, the colonists had to pay taxes on everything written or printed. The measure generated revenue but inspired much opposition from the colonists. Many colonists viewed the Stamp Act as oppressive and unfair. It inspired the revolutionary-minded phrase "taxation without representation."

Colonists from several states sent representatives to a meeting in New York known as the Stamp Act Congress. This body approved a resolution stating that only the colonial legislatures could tax the colonists. One of the measures read: "That is inseparably essential to the freedom of a people, and

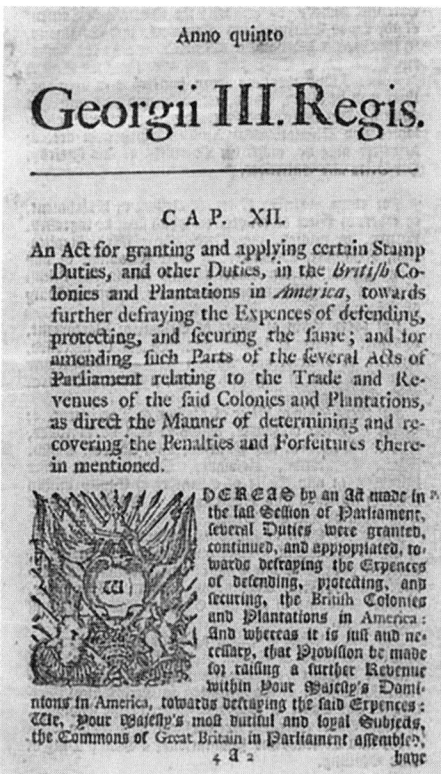

The Stamp Act of 1765 imposed an extra expense on American colonists, requiring official documents to be printed on British paper that included a stamp. There was no logical reason for the requirement, of course, other than to impose another tax on Americans without their consent.

the undoubted rights of Englishmen, that no taxes should be imposed upon them, but with their own consent, given personally, or by their own representatives."

Parliament repealed the Stamp Act in 1766, causing widespread celebration in the colonies, but the British Parliament then passed the Declaratory Act, which reaffirmed Parliament's resolve to pass other tax measures on the colonies. Parliament also passed the Townshend Acts.

What was the previous British policy of "salutary neglect"?

Salutary neglect was the name given to the long-standing British policy of taking a hands-off approach to the American colonies. That policy lasted from the early seventeenth century through the bulk of the eighteenth century—until the 1760s, when the British Crown needed revenue to pay for the expense of fighting wars in North America.

The term is traced to Edmund Burke (1729–1797), a political theorist who served for many years in the House of Commons. In a 1775 speech, Burke said that "through a wise and salutary neglect, a generous nature has been suffered to take her own way to perfection." Historians explain that salutary neglect in part contributed to the Revolutionary War because for many years, colonists had been able to govern themselves largely free from the Crown's influence or direct control. When the British Parliament began to impose laws directly controlling the colonists, they reacted unfavorably. Burke urged his colleagues in Parliament to treat the colonists with respect or face armed rebellion. "Great empires and little minds go ill together," said Burke.

What were the Intolerable Acts?

The so-called Intolerable Acts, also known as the Coercive Acts, were five laws passed by the British Parliament early in 1774. Intended to assert British authority in the Massachusetts colony, the measures were seen as punishment for the Boston Tea Party (December 1773). In brief, the laws enacted the following: closure of the port of Boston; an English trial for any British officer or soldier who was charged with murder in the colonies; the change of the charter of Massachusetts such that the council had to be appointed by the British and that town meetings could not be held without the (British-appointed) governor's permission; the requirement that the colonists house and feed British soldiers; and the extension of the province of Quebec southward to the Ohio River.

While the British intention was to bring the Massachusetts colony under control (and the fifth act was not intended to have any punitive effect on the colony), the result was instead to unite all the colonies in opposition to British rule. In this regard, the acts are seen as a precursor to the American Revolution (1775–1783).

Who started the Boston Tea Party?

Many believe that on December 13, 1773, it was patriot Samuel Adams (1722–1803) who gave the signal to the men, who may have numbered more than 100 and were dressed as Indians, to board the ships in Boston Harbor and dump the tea overboard. Whether or not it was Adams who started the Tea Party, about this there can be no doubt: He was most certainly a leader in the agitation that led up to the event. The show of resistance was in response to the recent passage by the British Parliament of the Tea Act, which allowed the British-owned East India Company to "dump" tea on the American colonies at a low price and also required that the colonists pay a duty for said tea. Colonists

Americans throwing the Cargoes of the Tea Ships into the River, at Boston

A 1789 engraving printed in London depicts the Boston Tea Party. Note that the illustration shows, accurately, that only some of the colonists were dressed as Indians.

feared the act would put local merchants out of business and that if they conceded to pay the duty to the British, they would soon be required to pay other taxes as well.

Once the ships carrying the tea had arrived in Boston Harbor, the colonists tried to have them sent back to England. But when Governor Thomas Hutchinson (1711–1780) of Massachusetts refused to order the return of the ships, patriots organized their show of resistance, which came to be known as the Boston Tea Party.

Why were there two Continental Congresses?

Both meetings were called in reaction to British Parliament's attempts to assert its control in the American colonies. When colonial delegates to the First Continental Congress met, they developed a plan but were obviously prepared for it not to work, since even before dismissal, they agreed to reconvene if it were necessary to do so. In short, the first Congress developed Plan A; the second resorted to Plan B (which was one last appeal to the king) and then to Plan C (finally declaring independence from Britain).

The First Continental Congress convened on September 5, 1774, in Philadelphia, Pennsylvania. The meeting was largely a reaction to the so-called Intolerable Acts (or the Coercive Acts), which British Parliament had passed in an effort to control Massachusetts after the rebellion of the Boston Tea Party (December 1773). Sentiment grew among the colonists that they would need to band together to challenge British authority. Soon, 12 colonies dispatched 56 delegates to a meeting in Philadelphia. (The thirteenth colony, Georgia, declined to send representatives but agreed to go along with whatever plan was developed.) Delegates included Samuel Adams (1722–1803), George Washington (1732–1799), Patrick Henry (1736–1799), John Adams (1735–1826), and John Jay (1745–1829). Each colony had one vote, and when the meeting ended on October 26, the outcome was this: The Congress petitioned the king, declaring that the British Parliament had no authority over the American colonies, that each colony could regulate its own affairs, and that the colonies would not trade with Britain until Parliament rescinded its trade and taxation policies. The petition stopped short of proclaiming independence from Great Britain, but the delegates agreed to meet again the following May—if necessary.

But King George III was determined that the British Empire be preserved at all costs; he believed that if the empire lost the American colonies then there may be a domino effect, with other British possessions encouraged to also demand independence. He feared these losses would render Great Britain a minor state rather than the power it was. With Britain unwilling to lose control in America, in April 1775, fighting broke out between the redcoats and patriots at Lexington and Concord, Massachusetts. So, as agreed, the colonies again sent representatives to Philadelphia, convening the Second Continental Congress on May 10.

Delegates—including George Washington, John Hancock (1737–1793), Thomas Jefferson (1743–1826), and Benjamin Franklin (1706–1790)—organized and prepared for the fight, creating the Continental army and naming Washington as its commander in chief. With armed conflict already underway, the Congress nevertheless moved slowly toward proclaiming independence from Britain: On July 10, two days after issuing a declaration to take up arms, Congress made another appeal to King George III, hoping to settle the matter without further conflict. The attempt failed, and the following summer, the Second Continental Congress approved the Declaration of Independence, breaking off all ties with the mother country.

What does the Declaration of Independence say?

The Declaration of Independence, adopted July 4, 1776, has long been regarded as history's most eloquent statement of the rights of the people. In it, not only did the 13 American colonies declare their freedom from Britain, but they also addressed the reasons for the proclamation (naming the "causes which impel them to the separation") and cited the British government's violations of individual rights, saying "the history of the present King 'George III' of Great Britain is a history of repeated injuries and usurpations," which aimed to establish "an absolute Tyranny over these States."

The opening paragraphs go on to state the American ideal of government, an ideal that is based on the theory of natural rights. The Declaration of Independence puts forth the fundamental principles that a government exists for the benefit of the people and that "all men are created equal." As the chairman of the Second Continental Congress committee that prepared the Declaration of Independence, it was Thomas Jefferson who wrote and presented the first draft to the Second Continental Congress on July 2, 1776.

The passage that is most frequently quoted is this:

> We hold these truths to be self-evident, that all men are created equal, that they are endowed by their Creator with certain unalienable Rights, that among these are Life, Liberty and the pursuit of Happiness. That to secure these rights, Governments are instituted among Men, deriving their just powers from the consent of the governed, That whenever any Form of Government becomes destructive of these ends, it is the Right of the People to alter or to abolish it, and to institute new Government, laying its foundation on such principles and organizing its powers in such form, as to them shall seem most likely to effect their Safety and Happiness.

The famous 1819 John Trumbull oil painting *Declaration of Independence* shows Thomas Jefferson, Benjamin Franklin, John Adams, Robert R. Livingston, and Roger Sherman presenting the historic document to the Second Continental Congress.

Who are considered the Founding Fathers of the United States?

The term is used to refer to a number of American statesmen who were influential during the revolutionary period of the late 1700s. Though definitions vary, most include the authors of the Declaration of Independence and the signers of the U.S. Constitution among the nation's Founding Fathers.

Of the 56 members of the Continental Congress who signed the Declaration of Independence (July 4, 1776), the most well known are John Adams and Samuel Adams of Massachusetts, Benjamin Franklin of Pennsylvania, John Hancock of Massachusetts, and Thomas Jefferson of Virginia.

The 39 men who signed the U.S. Constitution on September 17, 1787, include notable figures such as George Washington, who would go on, of course, to become the first president of the United States; Alexander Hamilton, who, as a former military aid to Washington, went on to become the first U.S. secretary of the treasury; and James Madison, who is called "the Father of the Constitution" for his role as negotiator and recorder of debates between the delegates. At 81 years of age, Franklin was the oldest signer of the Constitution and was among the six statesmen who could claim the distinction of signing both it and the Declaration of Independence; the others were George Clymer (1739–1813), Robert Morris (1734–1806), George Read (1733–1798), Roger Sherman (1721–1793), and James Wilson (1742–1798).

Patriots and politicians conspicuous by their absence from the Constitutional Convention of 1787 were John Adams and Thomas Jefferson, who were performing other government duties at the time and would each go on to become U.S. president; Samuel Adams and John Jay (1745–1829), who were not appointed as state delegates but continued in public life, holding various federal and state government offices (including governor of their states); and Patrick Henry (1736–1799) of Virginia, who saw no

Why did John Hancock go down in history as the most notable signer of the Declaration of Independence?

Most Americans know that when they're putting their "John Hancock" on something, it means they're signing a document. It's because, of the 56 men who signed their names to the historic document, it was Hancock who, as president of the Second Continental Congress, signed the declaration first.

The events were as follows: On July 2, 1776, Thomas Jefferson presented a draft of the declaration to the Second Continental Congress, which had convened in Philadelphia, Pennsylvania, more than a year earlier (on May 10, 1775). The congressional delegates of the 13 colonies then deliberated and debated the draft, making some changes: A section was deleted that condemned England's King George III for encouraging slave trade. Other changes were cosmetic in nature. On July 4 the final draft of the declaration was adopted by Congress, and it was then that Hancock signed it. The document was then printed. A few days later, on July 8, the declaration was read to a crowd who assembled in the yard of the state house. On July 19 the Congress ordered that the Declaration of Independence be written in script on parchment. It is that copy that in early August was signed by all 56 members of the Second Continental Congress. The Declaration of Independence is housed, along with the U.S. Constitution (1788) and the Bill of Rights (1791), in the National Archives Building in Washington, D.C., where it is on display to the public. John Hancock went on to become governor of Massachusetts from 1780 to 1785 and from 1787 to 1793.

need to go beyond the Articles of Confederation (1777) to grant more power to the central government. Henry's view on this issue foreshadows the discontent that crested nearly 100 years later when 12 southern states (including Virginia) seceded from the Union, causing the Civil War (1861–1865) to break out.

Adams, Franklin, Hancock, Jefferson, Washington, Hamilton, Madison, Jay, and Henry: These are the names that most come to mind when the words "Founding Fathers" are uttered. Each of them had a profound impact in the political life of the United States—even beyond their starring roles as patriots and leaders during the American revolutionary era. However, it's important to note that in many texts and to many Americans, the term *Founding Fathers* refers only to the men who drafted the U.S. Constitution since it is that document that continues—more than 200 years after its signing—to provide the solid foundation for American democratic government.

What were the Articles of Confederation?

This American document was the forerunner to the U.S. Constitution (1788). Drafted by the Continental Congress at York, Pennsylvania, on November 15, 1777, the Articles of Confederation went into effect on March 1, 1781, when the last state (Maryland) ratified them. The Articles had shortcomings that were later corrected by the Constitution: they provided the states with more power than the central government, stipulating that Congress rely on the states both to collect taxes and to carry out the acts of Congress.

It is largely thanks to Alexander Hamilton that the Articles were thrown out: realizing they made for a weak national government, Hamilton led the charge to strengthen the central government—even at the expense of the states. Eventually, he won the backing of George Washington, James Madison, John Jay, and others, which led to the convening of the Philadelphia Constitutional Convention, where the ineffectual Articles of Confederation were thrown out and the Constitution was drafted.

One lasting provision of the Articles of Confederation was the Ordinance of 1787. Signed in an era of westward expansion, the Ordinance set the guidelines for how a territory could become a state: a legislature would be elected as soon as the population had reached 5,000 voting citizens (which were men only), and the territory would be eligible for statehood once its population had reached 60,000.

What were the weaknesses of the Articles of Confederation?

The Articles of Confederation created a weak central government, as the central feature of the Articles of Confederation was that "each state retain its sovereignty, independence, and freedom." It created no judicial or executive branches. More troubling was that the Articles did not provide Congress with sufficient authority to deal with foreign nations. Great Britain had closed off trade with the states. It refused to leave the Great Lakes Area. Meanwhile, the Spanish controlled key portions of the Mississippi River. In 1784, Spain closed New Orleans and the lower Mississippi to American navigation.

The Articles allowed individual states to thwart action that would have been for the common good, or the good for most states. On many important matters, nine of the 13 states would have to approve a matter before it could become law. Under the Articles of Confederation, the Confederation Congress could not force state governments to raise monies for the federal government. The Confederation Congress could declare war, but it could not supply an army. The states had to do that. Alexander Hamilton wrote to a colleague: "The fundamental defect is a want of power in Congress."

In sum, the Articles of Confederation created a relatively weak central government that was not equipped to deal with intrastate rivalries and conflicts.

What did James Madison think of the Articles of Confederation?

James Madison, who was called "the Father of the Constitution," was very concerned about the lack of a strong, central government. He knew the Articles of Confederation was wanting. These problems caused many of our leaders to recognize the need for greater central authority. In a letter to James Monroe (1758–1831), Madison wrote of the need for a stronger central government. He wrote that "the defects of the federal system should be amended ... because I apprehend danger to its very existence from a continuance of defects which expose a part if not the whole of the empire to severe distress."

Washington, Madison, and others became convinced that the Articles of Confederation had to be modified. America needed a

James Madison, who later served as president from 1809 to 1817, helped draft the Constitution and championed it and the Bill of Rights.

DID YOU KNOW!?

Which states were the original 13?

In order of admission, they are Delaware, Pennsylvania, New Jersey, Georgia, Connecticut, Massachusetts, Maryland, South Carolina, New Hampshire, Virginia, New York, North Carolina, and Rhode Island. Vermont was the fourteenth and the first free state (the first state without slavery).

central government that could command respect internally and externally.

What was the Annapolis Convention?

The Annapolis Convention was a meeting of representatives from five states—Virginia, Pennsylvania, New Jersey, Delaware, and New York—who met to talk about mutual problems and the need for a stronger central government.

The delegates used the Annapolis Convention to promote the idea for a more national government. The commissioners petitioned Congress to call a meeting of all the states to be held in May 1787 in Philadelphia, Pennsylvania, to discuss how to create a government that could better serve the interests of the country. The exact language, drafted by Alexander Hamilton, asked Congress to allow the states to send representatives to "devise such further provisions as shall appear to them necessary to render the constitution of the Federal Government adequate to the exigencies of the Union."

The commissioners wrote that the Articles of Confederation contained defects, which led to many "embarrassments which characterize the present State of our national affairs, foreign and domestic." Chief Justice Warren Burger (1907–1995) once wrote that the meeting in Annapolis was "the most successful failure in American history" because it led to another meeting in Philadelphia.

What was Shays' Rebellion?

Shays' Rebellion was an uprising of farmers in Massachusetts that led many to believe that there truly was the need for a stronger central government. In 1786, hundreds of farmers, upset that they were taxed and in debt, marched in armed rebellion toward county courthouses. They wanted the courts to cancel their debts.

Shays' Rebellion was an uprising to protest taxes imposed in the state of Massachusetts. About 4,000 citizens protested violently that their civil and economic rights were being violated.

Daniel Shays (1747–1825), a former Revolutionary War hero turned indebted farmer, organized the uprising. Shays led his forces to an attack on the federal arsenal in Springfield, Massachusetts. Though General Benjamin Lincoln (1733–1810) and other government militia stopped Shays' Rebellion, the incident showed many leaders that they need a stronger central government because the states are virtually powerless to stop such violence. Shays' Rebellion provided clear evidence that there needed to be change in the national government.

THE U.S. CONSTITUTION

What was the Philadelphia Convention?

The Philadelphia Convention was the convention from May to September 1787 that created the U.S. Constitution. The original stated purpose was not to create an entirely new constitution. The stated goal was to "revise the Articles of Confederation."

Thus, the delegates were only given the task of proposing revisions to the Articles of Confederation. Instead, they created a whole new Constitution and system of government. Historian Fred Rodell writes that "it might perhaps be said that the writing of the Constitution was unconstitutional."

But that did not stop James Madison and the other delegates from going to the Constitutional Convention.

What was the thinking of James Madison?

James Madison was a political scientist. He studied governments and knew the art of political persuasion. It is no accident that he is called "the Father of the Constitution." A month before the Convention, Madison wrote "Vices of the Political Systems of the United States." The document detailed problems with the existing government and the Articles of Confederation.

According to Madison, the states had too much "independent authority" that was "fatal" to the "present System" of government. Madison pointed out that the states disobeyed federal authority by making their own treaties with the Indians or between each other. Madison pointed out that different states had violated the country's peace treaties with other countries. If different states violated treaties, other countries would violate the treaties.

Madison pointed out that the states were violating the rights of the other states and were not cooperating in matters of common interest. He cited the "practice of many States in restricting the commercial intercourse with other States."

Madison also pointed out that the states would not even fulfill their duties during the Revolutionary War. He wrote: "Even during the war, when external danger supplied in some degree the defect of legal & coercive sanctions, how imperfectly did the States fulfil their obligations to the Union?" He also noted that the Articles of Confederation had never been ratified by the people.

James Madison came to believe that the Articles had to be changed into an entirely new form of government. As can be seen by reading his "Vices," Madison also had little regard for state governments. Madison wanted to create a powerful central government that could command respect and unite the differing interests of the states.

Because he was a great political scientist, Madison knew that he could gain advantages for his pro-central government approach if he planned ahead. Because he was an experienced politician, Madison knew he had to raise the first issues.

The delegates from Virginia arrived early and crafted a plan of government that would become known as the Virginia Plan, or the Randolph Plan.

What was the Virginia Plan?

It was the famous plan, drafted by James Madison, put forth by the Virginia delegates to the Constitutional Convention, which convened on May 25, 1787. After taking a few days to set the ground rules and elect officers, on May 29 the delegation from Virginia, led by Edmund Jennings Randolph (1753–1813), proposed a plan to write an all-new constitution rather than attempt to revise and correct the weak Articles of Confederation. There was opposition (sometimes called the New Jersey Plan), and the issue was debated for weeks. Eventually, a majority vote approved the Virginia Plan, and the delegates began work drafting a document that would provide a strong national government for the United States.

What was the Pinckney Plan?

The Pinckney Plan was another plan of government introduced by Charles Pinckney (1757–1824) of South Carolina. The plan was similar to the Randolph Plan. Some historians suspect that James Madison gave little mention to Pinckney's plans in his notes because he did not want the Pinckney Plan to receive credit. Some historians argue that Madison "suppressed" the Pinckney Plan.

Pinckney's plan also argued for a strong national government. The Convention as a whole never debated Pinckney's plan. However, it was referred to a later committee, the Committee of Detail, which made use of it, and many of his ideas ended up in the final text of the Constitution.

Pinckney made many speeches during the Convention in which he argued for the delegates to think about a central government. Historian Charles Warren writes that on June 25, Pinckney made a particularly passionate speech: "Into the debates which had so largely turned on devotion to the States, Pinckney now breathed a spirit of Americanism."

What was the New Jersey Plan?

On June 15, William Paterson (1745–1806) from New Jersey introduced the New Jersey Plan, sometimes called the Paterson Plan. "Can we, as representatives of independent states, annihilate the essential powers of independency?" Proponents of this plan wanted a weaker central government.

The New Jersey Plan contained many features, including a single-bodied, or unicameral, legislature and a multiperson executive. Under the New Jersey Plan, Congress could only legislate on certain matters. Congress would elect the members of the federal executive. Congress could remove the persons of the federal executive if a majority of state leaders voted such action necessary.

Interestingly, the New Jersey Plan contained language that said the laws of the U.S. Congress "shall be the supreme law of the respective States." This formed the basis for the Supremacy Clause of the U.S. Constitution.

What was the Hamilton Plan?

On June 18, 1787, New York delegate Alexander Hamilton introduced his own plan. Hamilton, perhaps more than any other delegate at the Convention, desired a strong federal government. Hamilton greatly admired the British government. He said: "I believe the British government forms the best model the world ever produced."

He spoke for six hours when introducing his plan. Under his plan, the members of the Senate and the leader of the executive branch would serve life terms as long as they engaged in "good behaviour." Hamilton proposed that a one-person "governor" would serve as what we now call the president.

Alexander Hamilton, who would later serve under Washington as Secretary of the Treasury, led the Annapolis Convention to replace the Articles of Confederation.

What were the key differences between the two major plans?

The two major plans were the Virginia Plan and the New Jersey Plan. The Virginia Plan was favored by the larger states, while the New Jersey Plan was favored by many of the smaller states. The biggest area of disagreement between the two plans focused on representation in Congress.

The larger states, such as Virginia, wanted representation in Congress based on the population of the state. This is called proportional representation. The smaller states, such as Delaware, opposed proportional representation. They advocated the position of the New Jersey Plan—equal representation.

Proportional representation would favor the larger states because they had greater populations. Equal representation would favor the smaller states because they would have an equal voice with their larger neighbors. This issue nearly led to a premature ending of the Convention.

What were the fears of the smaller states?

Many of the delegates from the smaller states feared the power of the larger states. They tried to ensure that each state would possess equal power under the new constitution. Gunning Bedford (1747–1812), a delegate from Delaware, expressed his concerns: "I do not, gentlemen, trust you. If you possess the power, the abuse of it could not be checked; and what then would prevent you from exercising it to our destruction?" Bedford went so far as to suggest that the smaller states would "find some foreign ally of more honor and good faith who will take them by the hand and do them justice."

Many of the smaller states wanted each state to have the same number of representatives in Congress. They did not want proportional representation. Under a system of proportional representation, a state would have a certain number of representatives based on its population. This would obviously favor the larger states.

Historian Catherine Drinker Bowen said, "There was an ever-present danger that the Convention might dissolve and the entire project be abandoned." Delegate Luther Martin (1748–1826) of Maryland said later that "we were on the verge of dissolution scarce held together by the strength of a hair."

However, many of the delegates recognized that they must come to some agreement. If the delegates could not agree, their country could fall prey to foreign powers. Elbridge Gerry (1744–1814) said: "If we do not come to some agreement among ourselves, some foreign sword will probably do the work for us."

Who exactly was James Madison and why was he so prominent at the Convention?

Though he stood only 5 feet, 2 inches tall, James Madison stood tall at the Constitutional Convention. He had been described as "no bigger than half a piece of soap." He spoke in a very low voice.

He graduated from the College of New Jersey (now Princeton University) and lived to the age of 85. He had originally studied to be a minister but had a lifelong career in politics. Though he is largely responsible for the finest legal document in the world, Madison never received a law degree. He had devoted large amounts of time to studying governments and politics. He had played a large role in drafting Virginia's state constitution when he was only 25. At the time of the Convention, he was only 31 years of age.

He would go on to have an illustrious political career. He served as Thomas Jefferson's secretary of state. Then, he would go on to serve two terms as president of the United States from 1809 until 1817.

Madison had a major role in the Convention, as he was the principal draftsman of the Virginia Plan and he was the delegate who took the most detailed notes of the Convention. Historians and all Americans owe a great deal of debt to Madison because he produced a set of detailed notes about the Convention. The Convention had an official secretary named William Jackson (1759–1828), but he did little more than simply record votes. New York delegate Robert Yates's (1738–1801) notes on the debates were published in 1821, but they were not as comprehensive as Madison's. Yates left the Convention in early July, while Madison participated as much as any delegate until the conclusion of the Convention in September.

Madison instructed that his detailed notes of the Convention were not to be released until the last delegate at the Convention died. Ironically, that last delegate was Madison, who died in 1836 at the age of 85.

Why was George Washington so important at the Philadelphia Convention?

George Washington (1732–1799) was the undisputed leader of the Convention even though he rarely spoke. Washington achieved public fame for his leadership during the Revolutionary War. For his bravery during the war, Washington has been called "the Father of Our Country."

Washington was not only a larger-than-life figure, but he was also a large man, standing 6 feet, 3 inches tall. He became a surveyor and explored the Shenandoah Valley over the Blue Ridge

George Washington (at right, standing beside the desk in artist Howard Chandler Christy's 1940 painting *Scene at the Signing of the Constitution of the United States*) was a war hero and natural leader, so he was a favored choice to lead the Philadelphia Convention.

Mountains. His familiarity with exploration landed him a job in command of some troops during the French and Indian War in the 1750s.

After serving in the French and Indian War, Washington became a gentleman farmer for many years. He became a leading figure in Virginia politics. He achieved his great fame when he went as a Virginia delegate to the Second Continental Congress in Philadelphia in May 1775 in his old army uniform.

When the leaders of the Continental Congress discussed who to select to lead the army, Washington was a natural choice. He was a veteran of the French and Indian War, had a commanding presence, and showed up in an army uniform. He got the job.

Washington's leadership during the Revolutionary War was legendary. To many, he had miraculously defeated the British during the Revolutionary War. After the war, he retired from public life—or so he thought.

Other leaders recognized his value as a leading American. James Madison once wrote him, pleading with him to attend the Philadelphia Convention. Madison wrote: "It was the opinion of every judicious friend whom I consulted that your name could not be spared from the Declaration to the Meeting in May in Philadelphia."

On the first day of the Convention, Robert Morris (1734–1806) nominated Washington as president of the Convention. No one else was nominated. Washington was so quiet that he did not speak in the debates until the last day of the convention on September 17, 1787. "His presence kept the Philadelphia Convention together, kept it going, just as his presence had kept a struggling, ill-conditioned army together throughout the terrible years of war."

Who was Gouverneur Morris?

Gouverneur Morris (1752–1816) graduated from Columbia College at age 16. He was 34 years old at the time of the Convention and was considered one of the best lawyers of the day. He had a wooden leg but did not let that stop him from taking an active role in politics. Some historians write that he spoke more frequently than any other delegate at the convention.

Morris served on the Committee of Style near the end of the Convention. He took the lead role in that committee, which crafted the wording of the Constitution. Morris took 23 articles or resolutions and condensed them into seven articles. James Madison, who also served on the Committee of Style, credited Morris with writing the final form of the Constitution.

Founding Father Gouverneur Morris wrote the Preamble to the Constitution, helped foster the idea of America being one nation instead of 13 colonies, and was opposed to slavery being allowed by the Constitution.

What's the story behind Gouverneur Morris' wooden leg?

In his younger days, Gouverneur Morris was apparently quite the ladies' man. While the official story about how he lost his leg was that it happened in a carriage accident, the juicier tale is that he gravely injured himself leaping from a second-story window to escape being caught sleeping with a married woman. Oh, and the wooden leg (pictured) can be seen on display at the New York Historical Society.

Who was Roger Sherman?

Roger Sherman (1721–1893) was a politician from Connecticut who played an influential role in the Convention. It was he who created the Great Compromise that saved the Convention and the Constitution. Under Sherman's measure, one house of Congress would be represented equally among the states and in the other house, states would have proportional representation based on their population.

Sherman has the distinction of signing the early great American documents—the Declaration and Resolves of 1774, the Declaration of Independence, the Articles of Confederation, and finally the U.S. Constitution.

Like Washington, Sherman was a surveyor. From being appointed surveyor at age 23 until his death at the age of 72, Sherman held various political offices.

How did the Convention members work on creating a Congress?

The different states were very divided over how to distribute power in the new legislature. Historian Catherine Drinker Bowen writes: "The practical matter of how the national legislature should be elected was to take up half the summer."

The delegates quickly determined that Congress would consist of two branches. On May 31, the Committee of the Whole voted in favor of the third resolve in the Randolph Plan: "That the national legislation ought to consist of two branches."

The problem for the delegates was deciding how to determine representation in each branch of the legislature.

Among the Founding Fathers, Roger Sherman was the only one who signed the Continental Association papers, the 1774 Petition to the King, the Declaration of Independence, the Articles of Confederation, *and* the Constitution.

On June 11, delegate Roger Sherman from Connecticut first proposed a measure that would eventually save the Constitution. He proposed that one house of Congress be selected by population, while each state would have an equal voice in the other house of Congress. This proposal reflects our current system. In the House of Representatives, states have representatives based on the state's population. In the Senate, each state has two senators.

However, Sherman's proposal was voted down 6–5 when it was first introduced. The delegates continued to argue over the issue of proportional versus equal representation. On July 2, the states voted 5–5 on the question of equal representation in the Senate. The states of Connecticut, New York, New Jersey, Delaware, and Maryland favored equal representation. The states of Massachusetts, Pennsylvania, Virginia, North Carolina, and South Carolina opposed equal representation. The state of Georgia could have broken the tie, but the two Georgia delegates present, William Houstoun (1746–1813) and Abraham Baldwin (1754–1807), split.

Four delegates from Georgia were present at the Convention. However, two of the members, William Few (1748–1828) and William Pierce (1753–1789), left the convention for New York to vote on pressing matters in Congress. Few and Pierce would have voted against equal representation.

The small states would have lost the question of equal representation on this day if it were not for the vote of Abraham Baldwin. Baldwin had lived in Connecticut virtually his whole life, having moved to Georgia only three years before the Convention. Some argue that "Baldwin saved the Convention" because he split the Georgia votes and saved the small states from defeat. They argue that Baldwin voted the way he did because he knew the small states would collapse the Convention if they lost the equal representation question in the Senate.

The Convention then agreed to allow a committee of one person from each of the 11 states to be formed to explore the question. The states voted 10–1 in favor of such a committee. The committee was composed primarily of individuals who were in favor of a senate chosen by equal representation.

On July 5, the committee read its report to the entire delegation. The report called for proportional representation in the House and equal representation in the Senate. Many of the delegates who had wanted proportional representation in both houses had conceded this issue, realizing that the delegates from the small states might leave if they did not get their way on this issue.

What was the Great Compromise?

The Great Compromise was a proposal that ultimately saved the Constitution. On July 16, the delegates approved of the Great Compromise originally introduced by Roger Sherman a month earlier. Under this proposal, each state would have equal representation in the Senate, and each state would have one representative in the House for every 40,000 people.

The Convention adopted the Great Compromise by a vote of five to four with Massachusetts being evenly divided. Historian Charles Warren writes: "The acceptance of the compromise was not only essential to the continuance of the Convention; but it also had the important effect of converting the representatives from Connecticut, New Jersey, and Delaware into ardent supporters of the new Constitution."

Delegates from the smaller states, after they had representation in the new government, now pushed hard for a stronger central government.

What did the Convention members do with regard to the executive branch?

Some delegates feared that creating a single-person executive would be dangerous and lead to a monarch, such as George III. Ironically, most of the delegates assumed that their own George—George Washington—would become the country's chief executive.

For this reason, James Madison wrote to Thomas Jefferson that it was "peculiarly embarrassing" to have the delegates arguing about whether they could trust a single executive. It was "embarrassing" because Washington sat quietly while this discussion continued.

George Mason (1725–1792) from Virginia proposed that there be a three-person executive branch. He said that one individual would come from the North, one from the South, and the other from the middle states.

While some Americans of the country wanted Washington to be a new king, others feared that the executive branch would be too powerful. Fortunately, Washington had no desire to be a monarch.

The delegates disagreed about whether to create a strong independent executive or an executive who would be far less powerful than Congress. The delegates also changed their positions on the length of the president's term. The Committee of Detail originally proposed in its August 6 report that the president would be elected by the legislature for one seven-year term.

Finally, on August 31, another committee—the so-called Committee of Eleven—proposed that the president be chosen by electors. Each state would have the number of electors "equal to the whole number of senators and representatives of the House of Representatives."

Was the issue of federal versus state government a major issue?

Yes, it was, as many of the Founding Fathers had a deep-seated distrust of one central power. They preferred for power to reside in their state governments. However, many others realized that one general government was needed to deal with foreign nations. Delegate John Dickinson (1732–1808) of Pennsylvania offered the following explanation of the power between a general government and various state governments:

> Let our government be like that of the solar system. Let the general government be like the sun and the states and the planets, repelled yet attracted, and the whole moving regularly and harmoniously in their several orbits.

On July 10, two delegates from New York, John Lansing Jr. (1754–1829) and Robert Yates (1738–1801), left the convention. They believed that the convention delegates had strayed too far from its original purpose and were creating too strong of a central government.

The issue of how to divide power between the federal and state governments was an issue of utmost concern throughout the Convention.

How did the Convention delegates deal with the issue of slavery?

Many of the Southern delegates argued that slavery must be protected. The plantation economy of the South thrived on the labor of slaves. James Madison had warned that the biggest obstacle to overcome at the Convention was between the Northern and Southern states. The North and the South had different economies and attitudes. The divisions between the two regions that eventually culminated in the Civil War in the 1860s was already present at the time of the Convention.

Charles Pinckney of South Carolina represented the view of many Southern and other Convention delegates when he said: "If slavery be wrong, it is justified by the example of all the world.... In all ages one half of mankind had been slaves."

Charles Pinckney of South Carolina served as a U.S. senator and also as governor of his state. He justified slavery as a practice that had a history going back to ancient times.

A few delegates spoke out against slavery. George Mason of Virginia, who himself owned slaves, said: "Every master of slaves is born a petty tyrant. They bring the judgment of heaven on a country."

What did the delegates think about admitting new states in the future?

Many of the delegates were also concerned with how Congress would admit new states into the Union. Many members of the Convention viewed the people on the Western frontier with "paternal suspicion of her own alien young."

Elbridge Gerry made a motion that the Constitution set a limit on the number of Western states that could enter the Union. He proposed that the admission of new states be limited "in such a manner that they should never be able to outnumber the Atlantic states." However, other delegates argued that it would be unfair to deny peoples in other parts of the country their opportunity to apply for statehood. Roger Sherman of Connecticut pointed out: "Besides, we are providing for our posterity, for our children and grandchildren, who would be as likely to be citizens of new Western states as of the old states."

James Madison also argued in favor of admission of other states without too many conditions. When Gouverneur Morris spoke in favor of limiting the admission of Western states, Madison responded: "Did the gentleman then determine the human character by the points of the compass?"

However, the vast majority of the delegates did not want to dissolve the Union to contest the slavery issue. Many members from the Southern states would leave the Convention rather than agree to the abolition of slavery. The issue of slavery was closely tied to the question of representation in Congress. The Southern states wanted to count slaves in their population numbers because they would obtain more seats in the House of Representatives. The Northern states did not want to count slaves for purposes of legislative representation.

The delegates eventually agreed to tie taxation to representation and count slaves as three-fifths of a person. Some historians contend that the Convention agreed to this compromise over slavery and representation in exchange for the exclusion of slavery in the Northwest Ordinance of 1787.

The Northern and Southern delegates bargained over the issues of slavery and trade well into the month of August. On August 24, the so-called Committee of Eleven issued a report that contained four provisions: (1) Congress could prohibit the exportation of slaves until 1800; (2) Congress could tax imported slaves; (3) exports could not be taxed; and (4) Congress could pass navigation acts with a simple majority.

The Constitution would extend the date to allow the importation of slaves until 1808. The Constitution also contained a clause, called the Fugitive Slave Clause, which allowed Southerners to go into Northern states to recover runaway slaves. Unfortunately, the Fugitive Slave Clause enabled the capture of free blacks in Northern territory by Southern slaveowners.

Surely, the inclusion of slavery into the Constitution is not a proud moment in American history. Because the Constitution implicitly approved of slavery, the famed abolitionist William Lloyd Garrison (1805–1879) said the Constitution was a "covenant with death and an agreement with hell."

But many historians have concluded that the delegates had no choice. Christopher and James Collier explain: "In sum if the North had pressed for the abolition of slavery, there would have been no Constitution, and everybody at the Convention knew it." Furthermore, the Northern delegates were not willing to risk the Union to protect African Americans.

James Madison spoke about the inclusion of the Slave Trade Clause in the Constitution at the Virginia ratification convention. Madison said: "The southern states would not have entered into the union of America, without the temporary possession of that trade." However, Madison pointed out that under the Articles of Confederation, the slave trade could have continued forever, but "by this clause an end may be put to it after twenty years."

What was the Committee of Detail and what did it do?

On July 23, the Convention appointed a small committee called the Committee of Detail to put into place the various measures that had been voted and approved. This committee consisted of Edmund Randolph (1753–1813), James Wilson (1742–1798), Nathaniel Gorham (1738–1796), Oliver Ellsworth (1745–1807), and John Rutledge (1739–1800). The committee made a report on

John Rutledge, who would go on to serve as governor of South Carolina and as a U.S. Supreme Court justice, chaired the Committee of Detail.

August 6. This committee produced a report from which the entire Convention would debate. The results of those debates would lead to the final product called the United States Constitution.

The rest of the Convention adjourned while the members of the Committee of Detail worked to produce their report. The Committee used much of the terminology that we recognize today. For example, the committee used the term "Congress" instead of "Legislature of the United States." The first branch became "the House of Representatives" and the second branch became "the Senate." The committee also listed the necessary qualifications for persons serving as members of Congress. Many of these, such as age and years of citizenship, were taken from similar provisions in state constitutions.

Perhaps even more significantly, the Committee of Detail decided to list or enumerate the specific powers of Congress rather than give it a general grant of power. The Committee listed 18 different powers of Congress. In its draft, the committee also inserted several limitations on Congress's powers. For example, the Committee limited Congress's power to levy export taxes on the states. Many of these limitations appeared in the final form of the Constitution in Article I, Section 9.

From August 7 until the end of the Convention, the delegates debated the draft produced by the Committee of Detail. For much of August, the Committee debated the 18 grants of powers to Congress that it included in its report. On August 20, Congress debated the so-called Necessary and Proper Clause, which provides: "to make all laws that shall be necessary and proper for carrying into execution the foregoing powers, and all other powers vested, by this Constitution, in the Government of the United States, or in any department or officer thereof."

Opponents of this clause during the ratification debate would refer to it as the "sweeping clause" because it gave broad powers to Congress. Historian Charles Warren writes: "That it did not arouse any discussion in the Convention was probably due to the fact that the delegates understood that this clause, in reality, added nothing to the powers already granted."

On August 22, the Convention debated the restraints on the power of Congress. That day, Representative Elbridge Gerry of Massachusetts introduced a measure that would prohibit Congress from passing any bill of attainder or ex post facto law. This provision made it to the Constitution in its final form. Bills of attainder refer to laws that declare a person guilty of a crime with a trial. Ex post facto laws are laws that make an act a crime after the fact.

What was the Committee of Style?

On September 5, five men were chosen to form a so-called Committee of Style and Arrangement. These five were William Samuel Johnson (1727–1819), Alexander Hamilton (1755–1804), Gouverneur Morris (1752–1816), James Madison (1751–1836), and Rufus King (1755–1827). The duty of this committee was to "revise the style of and arrange the articles which had been agreed to by the House."

The Committee of Style had to condense 23 different articles. They eventually condensed the document into seven articles. Morris did the bulk of the work. Madison wrote, "The finish given to the style and arrangement . . . fairly belongs to the pen of Mr. Morris."

The delegates signed and submitted the document to Congress on September 17, 1787. Near the end of their debates, the delegates had to decide whether the Constitution should be ratified by the state legislatures or at state conventions. The delegates voted 9–1 in favor of popular conventions. On September 28, 1787, Congress submitted the Constitution to the various states. This began the process of ratification.

DID YOU KNOW!?

On August 31, delegates at the full Convention debated how they were going to ratify the new Constitution. Some delegates argued that the new Constitution must be ratified by all 13 states. However, many delegates recognized that not all 13 states may ratify. The tiny state of Rhode Island, for example, refused to send delegates to the Constitutional Convention.

Who actually wrote the U.S. Constitution?

In spirit, the U.S. Constitution was created by all 55 delegates at the meeting that convened on May 25, 1787, in Philadelphia's Independence Hall. Thomas Jefferson (1743–1826) called the Constitutional Convention "an assembly of demi-gods," and with good cause: The delegates were the young nation's brightest and best. When the states had been called upon to send representatives to the meeting, 12 states answered by sending their most experienced, most talented, and smartest men; Rhode Island, which feared the interference of a strengthened national government in state affairs, sent no one to Philadelphia.

Even in such stellar company, the document did have to be written. While many had a hand in this process, it was New York lawyer and future American politician and diplomat Gouverneur Morris who took on the task of penning the Constitution, putting into prose the resolutions reached by the convention. Morris had the considerable help of the records that James Madison of Virginia had kept as he managed the debates among the delegates and suggested compromises. In that capacity and because he designed the system of checks and balances among the legislative (Congress), the executive (the president of the United States), and the judicial (Supreme Court) branches, Madison had considerable influence on the document's language, quite rightfully earning him the designation "the Father of the Constitution."

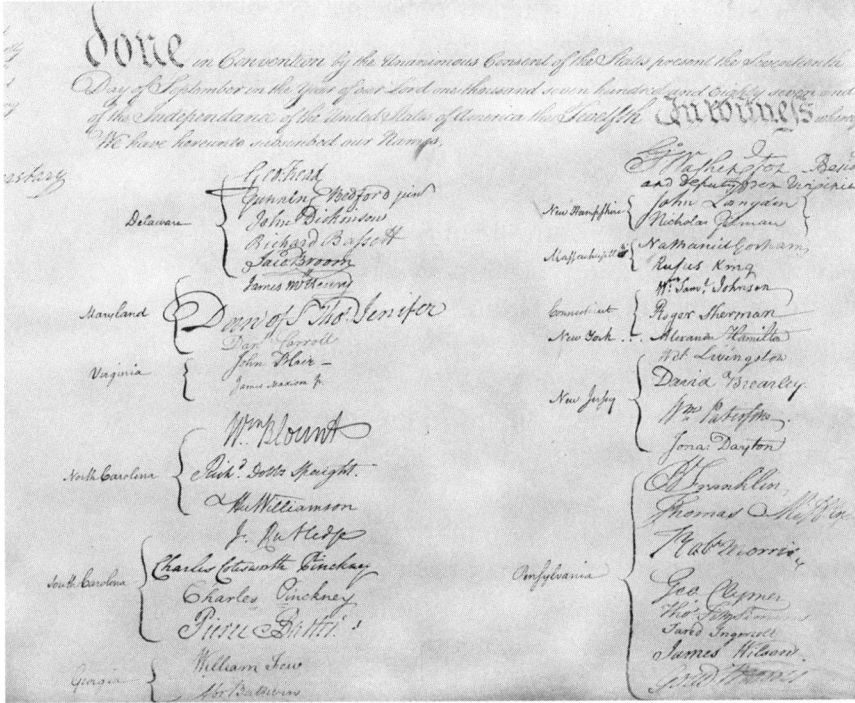

Thirty-nine of the delegates of the Convention signed the U.S. Constitution, with three refusing because at that time, it still lacked a Bill of Rights. They also objected that the document had essentially been composed in secret without the knowledge of the people.

The original document, drafted by Morris, is preserved in the National Archives Building in Washington, D.C. While the Constitution has been amended by Congress, the tenets set forth therein have remained with Americans for more than two centuries, and they have provided proof to the countries of the world that a constitution outlining the principles and purposes of its government is necessary to good government.

Who signed and did not sign the Constitution at the end of the Convention?

Thirty-nine of the 42 delegates present at the end signed the Constitution on September 17, 1787. The respected Benjamin

Franklin (1706–1790) called upon all his fellow delegates to sign the Constitution even if they disagreed with various portions of it. Franklin urged them to "on this occasion doubt a little of his own infallibility—and to make manifest our unanimity, put his name to this instrument."

Of the 42 members present at the end, all but three signed the document. These three were Elbridge Gerry of Massachusetts, George Mason of Virginia, and Edmund Randolph of Virginia. Both Gerry and Mason opposed the Constitution in large part because it did not contain a bill of rights. A few days earlier, Mason had said: "I would sooner chop off my right hand than put it to the Constitution."

Mason honestly believed that the system of government would produce either a "monarchy or a corrupt oppressive aristocracy." He also contended that the "Constitution has been formed without the knowledge or idea of the people."

Ironically, Randolph, whose name bears the title of the chief plan introduced during the Convention, also refused to sign the Constitution. He said that the states should be allowed to offer amendments, which should then be discussed by a second "General Convention." The Convention unanimously rejected Randolph's call for a second convention.

Legend has it that Franklin wept as he signed the document. Franklin made his famous remark that when he looked at the picture of a sun on Washington's chair, he could tell it was a rising, not a setting, sun. He said:

> Painters have found it difficult to distinguish in their art a rising from a setting sun. I have often and often in the course of the session, and the vicissitudes of my hopes and fears as to its issue, looked at that behind the president without being able to tell whether it was rising or setting. But now at length I have the happiness to know that it is a rising and not a setting sun.

Was ratification easy in the states?

No, ratification in the states was a difficult battle. There were many who were opposed to this new constitution for different reasons. Some believed it created a too powerful central government. Others felt that the absence of a Bill of Rights was fatal.

On September 17, 1987, 39 delegates at the Constitutional Convention in Philadelphia signed the U.S. Constitution. The Constitution contains seven sections called articles. Article VII provides: "The ratification of the conventions of nine states shall be sufficient for the establishment of the Constitution between the states so ratifying the same."

The debates at the Philadelphia Convention were not easy. Some delegates never showed up, others left early, and still a few others refused to sign the document in the end. The delegates had to compromise on many issues. But the crafting of the document and the signing of the document did not end the matter.

The "real fight" came on the convention floor, where delegates contemplated whether to ratify the Constitution. Many merchants, businesspeople, and big plantation owners in the South favored the Constitution. They knew the new Constitution would help commercial interests. They wanted the government to protect their business interests.

On the other side were many small farmers who did not want to sacrifice their individual freedom. "They were the men who then controlled most of the state legislatures, and helped themselves with paper money and other 'levelling laws.'"

Ratification was not an easy process. Political leaders were split on the issue of ratification. Supporters of the new Constitution with its strong central government called themselves Federalists. Opponents of the Constitution were known as Anti-Federalists. Many of the Anti-Federalists opposed the Constitution because it failed to provide for a bill of rights and gave too much power to the federal government at the expense of the state governments.

What were the principal objections of the Anti-Federalists to the Constitution?

The Anti-Federalists were particularly concerned with the so-called "Necessary and Proper Clause" of the new Constitution. Article I, Section 8, provided Congress with the power to "make all Laws which shall be necessary and proper" for executing its powers vested in the Constitution. Other Anti-Federalists were concerned with the Supremacy Clause in Article VI. Many Anti-Federalists viewed this clause as wiping out the powers of state governments.

Many Anti-Federalists also argued that the Constitution gave too much power to the president. Some feared that the president and the Senate would unite to become like the king of England and the upper house of the English Parliament, the House of Lords. The king of England and the House of Lords represented aristocrats, the upper class of society, and tended to ignore the interests of regular people.

In what states was the ratification debate of the Constitution closest and most intense?

Ratification was most difficult in the populous states of Massachusetts and Virginia. The debate in Massachusetts was particularly intense. Massachusetts ultimately voted 187–168 in favor of the Constitution on February 6, 1788, only after the Federalists agreed to recommend amending the Constitution to include protections for individual liberties.

What were the Federalist Papers?

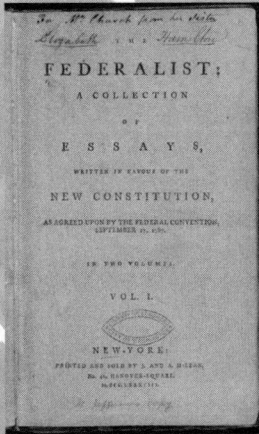

The Federalist Papers were a series of 85 essays written by James Madison (1751–1836), Alexander Hamilton (1755–1804), or John Jay (1745–1829) that argued for the new Constitution during the intense ratification struggle.

These 85 essays, written under the pen name Publius, are still considered the definitive work on the Constitution. Thomas Jefferson (1743–1826) once called them "the best commentary on the principles of government which ever was written."

These articles discussed the framework of the Constitution, including the principles of checks and balances and separation of powers among the three branches of government. Hamilton, Jay, and Madison sought to persuade the readers that the newly designed government was the best course of action for the young country. Hamilton wrote that the nation faced a "crisis." He wrote that if the country voted against the new Constitution, that decision would "deserve to be considered as the general misfortune of mankind."

Massachusetts became the first state to officially recommend amendments to the Constitution during the ratification process. Though the nine proposed amendments bear little resemblance to the final U.S. Bill of Rights, they were an important precursor to the Bill of Rights.

When was the U.S. Constitution ratified?

The Constitution was ratified by the required nine states on June 21, 1788. It went into effect the following year, superseding the Articles of Confederation (1781).

What is the structure of the Constitution?

The Constitution is composed of seven articles (and now 27 amendments). The first three articles discuss the features of the three branches of government: legislative, executive, and judicial. The fourth article deals with the states and the admission of new states. The fifth article discusses the process of amending the Constitution. The sixth article provides that the Constitution and federal laws are the "supreme law of the land." The seventh article provides that the Constitution will go into effect when it is ratified by nine states.

How can the Constitution be amended?

Article V provides how the Constitution can be amended. Congress can propose amendments by a two-thirds vote in each house of Congress. Then, the proposed amendment must be approved of by three-fourths of the state legislatures to become law.

There is another method that has been used far less often in the history of the United States. Congress can call a "convention

What are three defining concepts important to understanding the Constitution?

The Constitution contains three great principles that distinguish it from other documents. These are federalism, separation of powers, and checks and balances.

for proposing amendments" when two-thirds of the state legislatures call for them. Then, the proposals must be approved by three-fourths of the states.

The article also provided that the Constitution could not be amended to outlaw the slave trade until 1808.

FEDERALISM

Federalism refers to a system of government in which power is divided between a nation and its states. The general or federal government possesses ultimate control over many matters, but the various state governments retain many other powers. The concept seems natural to Americans of the twenty-first century. But it was very difficult for many Americans to accept in 1787 and 1788. Well-known lawyer, legal scholar, solicitor general, and Watergate special prosecutor Archibald Cox (1912–2004) wrote: "The key idea was extraordinarily imaginative two hundred years ago. Even today those who grow up in other countries find the concept difficult to comprehend."

Disputes over the relationship of power between the federal and state governments continue to this day. Some Americans believe that the federal government plays too large a role and intrudes on the power of the states. Other Americans believe that the federal government should take a more active role. However, nearly all Americans accept the political reality that their lives are affected and governed by state and federal governments.

What exactly is separation of powers?

The Framers understood that dividing power among the different branches of government would ensure that no one branch would become too powerful. This concept is known as the separation of powers. Many of the Founding Fathers understood the importance of separating powers between the branches of government. Many of them had read French philosopher Baron de Montesquieu's *L'Esprit des Lois*, which talked about this principle.

In the Federalist Papers, James Madison described Montesquieu as "the oracle who is always consulted and cited on this subject." Madison described the principle: "The accumulation of all powers, legislative, executive and judiciary, in the same hands, whether of one, a few, or many, and whether hereditary, self-appointed, or elective, may justly be pronounced the very definition of tyranny."

Separation of powers is a philosophy in which each branch has its own powers. U.S. Supreme Court justice Anthony Kennedy (1937–) explains: "Separation of powers was designed to implement a fundamental insight: Concentration of power in the hands of a single branch is a threat to liberty."

Our Constitution adheres to this principle. The powers of Congress are described in Article I, the powers of the executive branch are detailed in Article II, and the powers of the judicial branch are listed in Article III.

Sometimes, one branch will encroach on territory that the other branch considers is its own power. This occurred in the 1950s when President Harry S. Truman (1884–1972) issued an executive

LEGISLATIVE

EXECUTIVE

The Founding Fathers wisely divvied up the government's power between three branches of government: one to make the laws, one to enforce them, and one to interpret them.

JUDICIAL

order, seizing the country's steel mills and placing them under the control of the federal government. Truman claimed he had the authority as commander in chief to ensure that the steel mills would continue to produce products necessary for the war effort.

Several steel companies, including Youngstown Sheet & Tube Company, challenged the president's actions in federal court. These companies claimed that Truman had acted arbitrarily in violation of the Constitution. In *Youngstown Sheet & Tube Co. v. Sawyer*, the U.S. Supreme Court ruled 6–3 in favor of the steel companies. Justice Hugo Black (1886–1971) wrote: "If the President had the authority to issue the order he did, it must be found in some provision of the Constitution." The court determined that the president violated the separation of powers principle by

What is the concept of "checks and balances"?

Closely related to the separation of powers principle is the notion of checks and balances. The Constitution grants each branch of government the power to check certain actions by the other branches of government. For example, the president is the commander in chief of the armed forces, but Congress has the power to declare war. Congress can pass legislation, but the president has a veto power. The legislature can pass laws, but the judicial branch has the power to declare those laws unconstitutional.

Federal judges hold their positions for life terms, but they are appointed by the president and confirmed by the Senate.

committing a legislative act. In other words, the high court ruled that the seizure of the steel mills was a legislative act that must be done by Congress.

What is the legacy of the U.S. Constitution?

The legacy of the U.S. Constitution is profound. The Framers of the Constitution crafted a document that created a strong national government. Without this strong government, the United States of America might never have survived. Even with the Constitution, this country plunged into a bloody civil war during the 1860s.

However, the Constitution has stood the test of time. It has become the world's oldest continuing constitution. Two-thirds of the world's governments have constitutions that date back to

1970. Our Constitution dates back much further, to 1787. The Constitution has allowed this country to develop as a nation of laws and to grow and achieve social progress.

The Framers had to compromise to create a constitution. The Northern and Southern states compromised on the issue of slavery. Those who favored a nationalist point of view had to compromise with those of a more states' rights point of view. As historian Charles Warren writes: "Each had been obliged to sacrifice part of its demands and to subordinate its own advantage to the welfare of the whole country."

The Framers also compromised on the issue of representation between the larger and smaller states. This battle between those with a more nationalist point of view and those with a more states' rights point of view nearly broke up the Convention in Philadelphia. The Framers compromised by creating a system of proportional representation in the House of Representatives and a system of equal representation in the Senate.

The Framers balanced power between the central, federal, government and state governments. The Framers did create a strong central government and made sure that federal law is supreme over state law. But the Framers did not create a government that deprived the states of all its powers.

Today, different states have different state laws. Some states have state income taxes, while others do not. Some states have lotteries, while others do not. Some states have laws empowering school officials to pass dress codes or uniform requirements on public school students, while other states do not. The states still have a great deal of power to decide questions within their borders.

However, the Framers recognized that the states must obey the authority of the federal government. In the 1950s, when Arkansas governor Orval Faubus (1910–1994) threatened to defy federal court orders to desegregate Central High School, President Dwight D. Eisenhower (1890–1969) had to send in the National Guard to enforce federal law.

Many in society disagree over the distribution of power between the federal and state governments. During the time of the Civil Rights Movement in the 1950s and 1960s, many politicians in the South complained that the federal government was exceeding its authority and violated states' rights. In the present day, politicians and citizens debate whether the federal government has gone too far or not far enough in providing social services.

People disagree about how to interpret the Constitution. Some argue for a literal interpretation of the words in the Constitution. This method often asks what was the "Framers intent" or what was the original intent.

Others criticize this model, claiming that it is a nearly impossible task of determining original intent. For example, attorney Al Knight writes: "Original intent? Whose intent? The fact is that trying to apply the Framers' intent is like trying to breathe the atmosphere of the moon. Whether it is a good idea or a bad one is beside the point—the problem is there is nothing of substance to work with."

In the 2000 presidential election, Democrat candidate and vice president Al Gore (pictured) lost to George W. Bush when the Supreme Court refused to allow a recount of votes in Florida, a state (interestingly enough) governed by Bush's brother, Jeb.

Others argue that judges should interpret the Constitution using contemporary social values. Former U.S. Supreme Court justice William J. Brennan Jr. (1906–1997) said that as a Supreme Court justice, it was his duty to apply the Constitution through the current day. He said: "We current Justices read the Constitution in the only way we can, as twentieth-century Americans. We look to the history of the time of framing and to the intervening history of interpretation. The ultimate question must be, what do the words of the text mean for our time? For the genius of the Constitution rests not in any static meaning it might have had in a world that is dead and gone, but in the adaptability of its great principles to cope with current problems and current needs."

Consider that in 2000, the United States faced a potential constitutional crisis in the presidential election between Democratic candidate Al Gore and Republican candidate George W. Bush. The election hung in the balance when the election was too close to call in the deciding state of Florida. The dispute involved both major political parties, all three branches of government in Florida, and the court of last resort—the U.S. Supreme Court.

Many disagreed with the Court's decision in *Bush v. Gore*. But the country moved forward without a violent revolution. The case proceeded through our court system to the U.S. Supreme Court, which acts as the ultimate arbiter on legal questions under our Constitution. Whether one agrees or disagrees with the Court's decision, at least the question was decided by a judicial decision rather than a bloody civil war. Other countries might have erupted into violence, revolution, or civil war because of a disputed election for the nation's highest office.

The Constitution above all else shows that we are a nation of laws. When the citizens and politicians discover something wrong with our system, they can propose lawful changes.

The genius of the Constitution can be seen in how the Framers crafted language broad enough to apply to later generations. For example, the First Amendment provides that "Congress shall make no law ... abridging the freedom of speech." The Founding

Fathers probably never imagined technology like the Internet, social media, or artificial intelligence. Yet, the First Amendment applies to the Internet just as it does to the printing press. The Founding Fathers wanted to establish a system that would serve later generations as well as solve the practical difficulties of their time.

The Framers knew they had to craft a document with general terms that would last for future generations. Language such as "necessary and proper," "general welfare," and "due process of law" allows later generations to apply the language of the Constitution to changing circumstances and social change.

John Adams (1735–1826), the nation's second president, wrote Convention delegate Rufus King (1755–1827) that the Constitution was "if not the greatest exertion of human understanding, the greatest single effort of national deliberation that the world has ever seen."

U.S. Supreme Court chief justice Warren Burger (1907–1995) said it best: "The Constitution was indeed a watershed in the history of governments and more important, in humanity's struggle for freedom and fulfillment. It behooves all of us to read it, understand it, revere it, and vigorously defend it."

The Legislative Branch

Where are the powers of Congress contained?

The powers of Congress are found in Article I of the U.S. Constitution, by far the longest article in the Constitution. It reflects the Framers' belief that the legislature must be bicameral, consisting of two houses of Congress—the House of Representatives and the Senate. It also reflects the Framers' careful concerns with both checks and balances and separation of powers. It contains qualifications for each house of Congress and then a detailed list of Congress's powers. But the Framers also worried about the legislative branch becoming too powerful, so they included many limitations as well.

What is the Vesting Clause?

The Vesting Clause is the opening sentence in Article I that reads: "All legislative Powers herein granted shall be vested in a

Congress of the United States, which shall consist of a Senate and House of Representatives." This clause provides that all legislative powers found in Article I are found in Congress, a bicameral body with a Senate and a House of Representatives.

Why did the Framers want to limit the powers of Congress?

The Framers wanted to make sure that Congress did not have unlimited powers. They feared the unlimited power of the English Parliament, which passed onerous taxing laws on the colonies that led to the Revolutionary War. Thus, the Framers also created two other branches—the executive and the judicial—that could serve as checks upon Congress and each other.

What are the two houses of Congress?

The two houses of Congress are the U.S. House of Representatives and the U.S. Senate, or the House and Senate for short. The Constitution, thus, provides for a bicameral (two houses) legislature. This is similar to Great Britain, whose Parliament has a House of Commons and a House of Lords.

What are the terms of office for members of the House?

The Constitution provides: "The House of Representatives shall be composed of Members chosen every second Year by the People of the several States...." Thus, members of the House serve two-year terms. The Framers designed the House

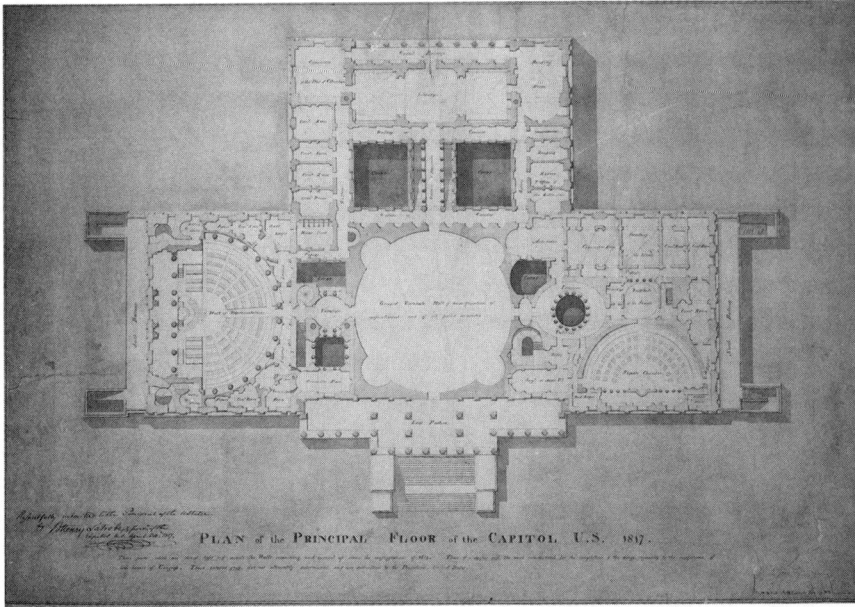

PLAN of the PRINCIPAL FLOOR of the CAPITOL, U.S. 1817.

Congress is divided into two houses: the House of Representatives and the Senate. In the Capitol Building, the House meets in the South Wing (shown at left), and the Senate meets in the North Wing.

of Representatives as the body of Congress most tied to the people. That is why members of the House are far more numerous than members of the Senate. It also explains why members of the House are subject to two-year terms rather than the six-year terms of the senators. The House of Representatives is known as "the People's House."

Do members of the House of Representatives have term limits?

No, the Constitution does not set term limits for members of the House (or Senate, for that matter), unlike the president, who is limited to two terms by the Twenty-third Amendment. This has led to some members of Congress serving for an extremely long time. The longest-serving House member was John Dingell Jr. of Michigan, who served 59 years, from 1955 until 2015.

What are the qualifications for serving in the House?

The Constitution provides: "No Person shall be a Representative who shall not have attained to the Age of twenty-five Years, and been seven Years a Citizen of the United States, and who shall not, when elected, be an Inhabitant of that State in which he shall be chosen." The so-called Qualifications Clause explains who can serve in the U.S. House of Representatives. It requires that members of the House be (1) at least 25 years of age, (2) a U.S. citizen, and (3) live in the state in which they are elected.

Did any persons serve even though they were younger than 25 years of age as the Constitution requires?

Yes, despite the clear constitutional language regarding the required age, William Charles Cole Claiborne (1775–1817) served as a representative beginning in 1797, when he was only 22 years old. Perhaps even more remarkably, he had previously served on the Tennessee Supreme Court when he was 21. Claiborne was elected to a second term in Congress when he was only 24. Claiborne did not seek a third term but instead was appointed by President Thomas Jefferson (1743–1826) to serve as governor of the Territory of Mississippi. He later served as governor of the Orleans Territory and governor of Louisiana.

Who is the leader of the House of Representatives?

The leader of the U.S. House of Representatives is the Speaker of the House. The Speaker is the presiding officer of the

The current, and 56th, speaker of the House is Mike Johnson, a Republican representative from Louisiana.

House and controls the flow and movement of how the House proceeds in its sessions. The Speaker serves as both the political and parliamentary leader of the House. The position of Speaker traces its origins to the British House of Commons, who had a leader as well. The House elects its speakers at the beginning of each term of Congress.

The very first Speaker of the House was Frederick Muhlenberg of Maryland, who served as Speaker during the First (1789–1791) and the Third Congresses (1793–1795). Some of the more influential Speakers in American history include Henry Clay (1777–1852) of Kentucky, Thomas Brackett Reed (1839–1902) of Maine, Joseph Cannon (1836–1926) of Illinois, and the legendary Sam Rayburn (1882–1961) of Texas. In total, 56 different individuals have served as Speaker of the House.

The Speaker traditionally is the head of the Rules Committee and has a large role in the overall agenda of the House. The Speaker is a member of the majority party in Congress. For example, as of late 2023, the Speaker of the House, Mike Johnson

(1972–) of Louisiana, is a Republican, and the Republican Party has a majority in the House of Representatives.

What is the House's role with regard to impeachment?

The House has the sole power to impeach federal officials, including the president of the United States. The House considers articles of impeachment and votes. All that is needed to impeach a federal official is a majority vote. Article II, Section 4, of the Constitution further provides that "the President, Vice President and all Civil Officers of the United States, shall be removed from Office on Impeachment for, and Conviction of, Treason, Bribery, or other high Crimes and Misdemeanors." While the House has the impeachment power, the Senate actually holds the impeachment trials. Thus, the House impeaches and the Senate either convicts or acquits. The power of impeachment is limited to removal of office, but if that happens, they can never serve in that office again. Impeachment is reserved for serious misdeeds. As Alexander Hamilton (1755–1804) wrote in Federalist #65, impeachment applies to "misconduct of public men, or in other words from the abuse or violation of some public trust."

How many members are there in the House?

There are 435 members in the House, set proportionally by population in each state. This does not come from the Constitution but from a federal law.

How has the process of selecting senators changed?

The original language provided that senators were "chosen by the Legislature thereof," meaning that a state legislature elected the senators. However, the Seventeenth Amendment to the Constitution amended the Constitution to provide for the direct election of senators.

How many members are there in the Senate?

Unlike the House, which has 435 members, there are two senators from each state. Since 1959, when the 49th and 50th states, Alaska and Hawaii, entered the Union, the number of senators has been 100. This was determined as a result of "the Great Compromise," developed by Roger Sherman (1721–1793), which saved the Constitutional Convention in 1787 from collapsing.

How long is a term for U.S. senators?

The term for senators is six years. The Senate is considered the more deliberative body of Congress. Like the House, some members of the Senate have served an extraordinarily long time. For example, Robert Byrd (1917–2010) of West Virginia served in the U.S. Senate for more than 51 years, from 1959 until 2010. As of late 2023, the longest currently serving senator is Chuck Grassley of Iowa, who has served nearly 43 years in the Senate.

How are senators chosen in rotational elections?

Article I, Section 3, also provides that elections in the Senate are spaced out in three categories. That means every two years, there is a different set of elections for certain Senate seats. The idea here is continuity and stability. If all sitting senators were up for reelection in the same year, there could be a massive change in membership and a loss of necessary experience.

What is the role of the vice president in the Senate?

The Constitution provides: "The Vice President of the United States shall be President of the Senate, but shall have no Vote, unless they be equally divided." Article I, Section 3, also provides that the vice president shall be president of the Senate. This

Vice President Mike Pence is shown here with his daughter, Charlotte, writing a speech after the disruption of the counting of the election results on January 6, 2021, by Trump supporters who wanted to hang him for not betraying his duty in the Senate.

means that the vice president can preside over the Senate. However, if the vice president does not preside over the Senate, that duty devolves to the Senate's president pro tempore, or someone designated by the president pro tempore. The other significant role of the vice president is that of a tie-breaker. For example, if the Senate is tied 50–50, the vice president can cast the deciding vote. Some vice presidents have cast many tie-breaking votes in American history. John C. Calhoun (1782–1850), Andrew Jackson's (1767–1845) vice president, cast 31 different tie-breaking votes from 1825 to 1832. The very first vice president, John Adams (1735–1826), has the second highest number of tie-breaking votes with 29, from 1789 to 1797.

Who is the president pro tempore of the Senate?

The president pro tempore, or president pro tem, presides over the Senate in the absence of the vice president. Because the vice president has many duties in the executive branch—including representing the United States in many foreign countries—the day-to-day activities often fall to the president pro tempore. The Senate elects the president pro tempore. Traditionally, the honor often goes to the longest-serving senator of the majority party. The Senate's president pro tempore is third in line for presidential succession behind the vice president and the Speaker of the House. Aside from being in the line of presidential succession, the president pro tem lacks the authority of the Senate majority and minority leaders.

What is the Senate's role with respect to impeachment?

The Senate is where impeachment trials take place. The Constitution provides: "The Senate shall have the sole Power to try all Impeachments. When sitting for that Purpose, they shall be on Oath or Affirmation. When the President of the United States is tried, the Chief Justice shall preside: And no Person shall be convicted without the Concurrence of two thirds of the Members present."

While the House has the sole power of impeachment, the Senate holds the impeachment trials. The Constitution requires that senators take an oath or affirmation when they preside over impeachment proceedings. This provision also provides that the chief justice of the U.S. Supreme Court presides over the Senate impeachment trials of presidents. Thus, Chief Justice Salmon P. Chase (1808–1873) presided over the impeachment trial of President Andrew Johnson (1808–1875); Chief Justice William H. Rehnquist (1924–2005) presided over the impeachment trial of President Bill Clinton (1946–); and Chief Justice John G. Roberts Jr. (1955–) presided over the first impeachment trial of President Donald J. Trump (1946–). For Trump's second impeachment trial, because he was then a former president, Senator Patrick Leahy (1940–) of Vermont, in his role as president pro tem, presided, rather than Chief Justice Roberts.

The Constitution also requires that the senators must vote by a two-thirds majority to convict a president during the impeachment trial. This has resulted in no president ever being found guilty in an impeachment trial. If a person is impeached, they are removed from office but not subject to further criminal penalties for being impeached. However, the person impeached may be disqualified from holding future office.

Does each house of Congress set its own rules?

Yes, Article I, Section 5, establishes the rules of each body of Congress. It begins with the language that each house of Congress can judge its elections. This means that in a razor-thin election, a losing party might petition Congress and question even the recount in their own state. Perhaps the most notorious example of this was the bitter 1984 House race in Indiana between Democratic incumbent Frank McCloskey (1939–2003) and his Republican challenger, Richard D. McIntyre (1956–2007).

McIntyre had been declared the winner by 34 votes one day after the election and by 418 votes after a state-ordered recount. However, McCloskey petitioned the House, and the General Accounting Office deemed that McCloskey actually won the election by four votes. A three-member task force in the House recommended to the full House that McCloskey be declared the winner. In March 1985, the full House then voted 236 to 190 in favor of the Democratic incumbent McCloskey. Many Republicans stormed out of the House in protest, accusing their Democratic colleagues of "abuse of power" and "legislative tyranny." The Republicans then vowed to institute a series of "McIntyre" reforms to ensure this did not happen again in the future.

Can each house of Congress punish and expel its own members?

Yes, the Constitution provides that "each House may determine the Rules of its Proceedings, punish its Members for disorderly Behaviour, and, with the Concurrence of two thirds, expel a Member." Each House can determine how it operates—what rules of parliamentary proceedings that it adopts. It also means that the House controls the House and the Senate controls the Senate. In other words, one house of Congress cannot dictate to the other house how it operates. The House Rules Committee sets the rules for its members. For example, the House sets time limits for how long its members can speak on the legislative floor.

The provision also provides that each House can punish its members for "disorderly Behaviour." This can take the place of an expulsion, but that requires a two-thirds vote—something unlikely to happen in the current two-party system. Both political parties will not want to lose a member when the balance of power between the two parties is so close.

The Senate has expelled 15 senators. Most of these were for supporting the Confederacy during the time of the Civil War. Several senators have resigned when confronted with expulsion proceedings. For example, Robert W. Packwood (1932–), a Republican senator from Oregon, resigned from office in 1995 for sexual misconduct and abuse of power.

There are less drastic forms of punishment, including a censure. A censure is a significant action that does not lead to expulsion but can lead to a member losing prestigious committee positions. In Senate history, only nine senators have ever been censured. They include the following:

Senator	Date	Reason for Expulsion
Timothy Pickering	1811	reading confidential documents
Benjamin Tappan	1844	releasing a confidential vote to the press
Benjamin R. Tillman and John L. McLaurin	1902	fighting in the Senate
Hiram Bingham III	1929	employing a lobbyist on his staff
Joseph McCarthy	1954	abuse of power
Thomas Dodd	1967	using political campaign funds for personal use
Herman Talmadge	1979	improper financial conduct
David Durenberger	1990	use of campaign money for personal use

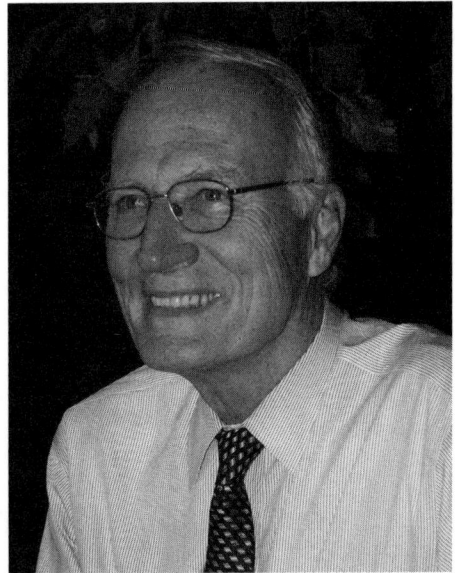

A former Republican senator representing Minnesota, David Durenberger (1934–2023) was expelled from the Senate for using campaign funds for personal use.

The House also has seen its fair share of censures in its history, beginning with the 1832 censure of House member William Stanbery (1788–1873) of Ohio, who was censured for insulting Andrew Stevenson (1784–1857), the Speaker of the House. Stanbery said Stevenson's eye might be "too frequently turned from the chair you occupy toward the White House." Some of the censures appear harsh. Consider that in February 1868, Representative Fernando Wood (1812–1881) of New York was censured for referring to a piece of legislation as "a monstrosity, a measure of the most infamous of the many infamous acts of this infamous Congress." The legendary Charles Rangel (1930–) of New York was censured for misuse of congressional letterhead for fundraising and inaccurate federal tax returns.

The House has an even lesser form of punishment known as a reprimand. It represents a less serious expression of disapproval than a censure. The first known reprimand in House history came in 1976, when the House reprimanded Robert L. F. Sikes (1906–1994) of Florida for using his office for personal gain. Sikes had failed to reveal that he had a financial interest in two companies that did business with the government. Some of the reprimands in House history are for interesting conduct. For example, Barney Frank (1940–) of Massachusetts was reprimanded for fixing parking tickets in 1990, and Joe Wilson (1947–) of South Carolina was reprimanded in 2009 for interrupting President Barack Obama's (1961–) remarks to a joint session of the House and Senate, which was found to be a "breach of decorum and degraded the proceedings of the joint session."

Do the houses work together?

Yes, and that is mainly because the Constitution requires it. The Constitution provides: "Neither House, during the Session of Congress, shall, without the Consent of the other, adjourn for more than three days, nor to any other Place than that in which the two Houses shall be sitting." This last clause in Article I, Section 5, is premised on the concept of efficiency, that Congress will be more effective if both houses are working at the same time in the same general location. They also wanted to avoid certain cagey legislators seeking an adjournment of their House in order to avoid voting on a measure or to engage in dilatory action merely to stall legislation. Furthermore, sometimes there needs to be some synergy between both houses of Congress in making sure that companion bills in the House and Senate are cleaned up.

DID YOU KNOW!?

What is the compensation for serving in Congress?

As of 2024, regular members of Congress receive $174,000 per year. The majority leaders of the House and Senate receive $193,400 per year. The speaker of the House of Representatives, who is third in line to the presidency, receives $223,500.

What is the Speech and Debate Clause?

The Speech and Debate Clause is one of the more interesting ones in the Constitution. Legislative attorney Todd Garvey explains that this clause is a "key pillar" in the concept of separation of powers, shielding members of Congress from intrusions by the executive and judicial branches. Garvey explains: "The Clause, which derives its form from the language of the English Bill of Rights and has deep roots in the historic struggles between King and Parliament, serves chiefly to protect the independence, integrity, and effectiveness of the legislative branch by barring executive or judicial intrusions into the protected sphere of the legislative process."

This measure ensures that members of Congress have absolute immunity from prosecution or questioning for their speeches and comments in Congress. The Clause provides ample room for free debate. Legislators do not have to worry that their speech might lead to prosecution or other sorts of legal trouble. Thus, a key facet of the Speech and Debate Clause is that legislators receive both criminal and civil immunity for their legislative acts— not just their speech but also their work product in Congress.

While there is no disagreement about the scope of the Clause to protect legislators for prosecution for their speech in Congress, lower courts disagree about whether the Speech and Debate Clause extends beyond this to prohibit the disclosure of legislative documents during an investigation. For example, let's say that agents of the FBI raid the office of a member of Congress to look for evidence of criminal wrongdoing. Can the representative assert that any legislative documents are immune from executive branch scrutiny because they are protected by the Speech or Debate Clause? The argument for the legislator would be that they should have the ability, under the Speech and Debate Clause, to examine the documents to determine whether they are covered by the privileges afforded by the Speech and Debate Clause before they are examined by federal agents. Garvey explains, in a report for the Congressional Research Service, that the extent of these privileges has divided lower courts and is "ripe for Supreme Court review."

What is the Origination Clause?

Article I, Section 7, begins with the Origination Clause—that all revenue bills must originate, or begin, in the House of Representatives rather than the Senate. The Framers took the Origination Bill from England, where revenue bills had to originate in the House of Commons rather than the House of Lords. The thinking behind the Origination Clause is that it is better to have revenue bills originate in the House, which is more responsive to the people. Note, however, that the Senate can propose amendments to revenue bills, giving the more deliberate body a say in the process.

What is the Presentment Clause?

Bills that pass Congress must be signed by the president. Usually, this is done without much ceremony, but sometimes an important bill gets more publicity and ceremony, such as in this photo with President Bill Clinton signing the 1997 Balanced Budget bill.

Article I, Section 7, provides that every bill that passes Congress must be presented to the president for signature. The president can sign the bill, in which case the bill becomes law. The president can object to the bill. This act is known as a veto. Interestingly, the term "veto" is not mentioned in the Constitution. The president must identity his objections to the bill when issuing a veto.

The president has ten days to either sign the bill or veto it. The Constitution provides, however, that Congress can override a presidential veto by reconsidering the measure and passing it by a two-thirds supermajority. When Congress passes a bill by a supermajority, the bill does not need to be presented to the president. Thus, Congress by a two-thirds majority can still pass a bill even after a presidential objection or veto.

If the president does not sign the bill or veto within the ten days, then the bill automatically becomes law unless Congress adjourns before the passage of ten days. Such a situation is known as a "pocket veto." The Congressional Research Service explains: "For example, if a bill were to be presented to the President in the 116th Congress, and the bill presentment period extended beyond January 3, 2021, an unsigned bill could not be received by the since-concluded 116th Congress. A new bill and process to pass the measure would have to begin in the 117th Congress for it to become law."

Thus, Congress cannot override a "pocket veto." To avoid this situation, Congress simply must present bills to the president and be available to meet without adjournment after the ten-day presentment period has passed.

What is the Presentment of Resolutions Clause?

The Presentment of Resolutions Clause provides that any measure requiring the affirmance of both houses of Congress must be presented to the president. In other words, Congress cannot avoid the reach of the Presentment Clause by classifying its measure as a resolution or order rather than a bill. For example, when Congress declares war, it does so in the form of a joint resolution. Such a joint resolution must be presented to the president.

The Supreme Court emphasized the importance of this clause in the case *INS v. Chadha* (1983), writing: "Presentment to the President and the Presidential veto were considered so imperative that the draftsmen took special pains to assure that these requirements could not be circumvented. During the final debate on Art. I, § 7, cl. 2, James Madison expressed concern that it might easily be evaded by the simple expedient of calling a proposed law a 'resolution' or 'vote,' rather than a 'bill.'"

The Court in *Chadha* ruled unconstitutional a provision in an immigration law that allowed one house of Congress to veto an action by the attorney general of the United States. The Court reasoned that under the Constitution, the veto power resided with the president, not Congress.

It bears mentioning that in the *Chadha* case, those defending the immigration measure that allowed for one-house veto power emphasized that it was much more efficient than the cumbersome method provided by the Presentment Clause of Article I, Section 7, and the requirement of bicameralism. The Supreme Court responded with a civics lesson:

> The choices we discern as having been made in the Constitutional Convention impose burdens on governmental processes that often seem clumsy, inefficient, even unworkable, but those hard choices were consciously made by men who had lived under a form of government that permitted arbitrary governmental acts to go unchecked. There is no support in the Constitution or decisions of this Court for the proposition that the cumbersomeness and delays often encountered in complying with explicit constitutional standards may be

avoided, either by the Congress or by the President. See *Youngstown Sheet & Tube Co. v. Sawyer* (1952). With all the obvious flaws of delay, untidiness, and potential for abuse, we have not yet found a better way to preserve freedom than by making the exercise of power subject to the carefully crafted restraints spelled out in the Constitution.

What is the Tax and Spend Clause?

The Tax and Spend Clause contains two of Congress's most important powers in Article I, Section 8. Congress has the broad power of taxation and the power to spend for the general welfare.

The tax power is important. Congress later passed the Sixteenth Amendment, which gave Congress the power to impose an income tax. But the power to tax is truly an awesome power of Congress. After all, Congress is the branch of government that has the power of the purse.

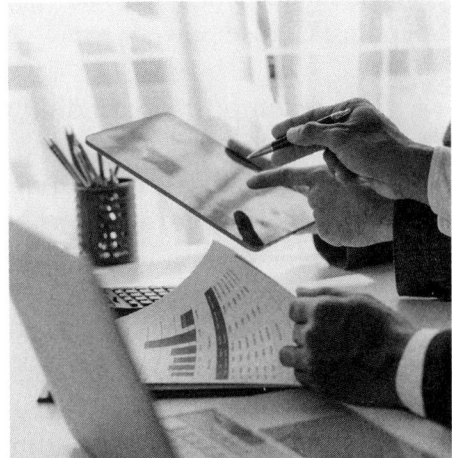

The power of taxation lies with Congress, including the power to impose the income taxes that went into effect in 1913. And, of course, Congress also determines how those taxes are spent.

Congress's taxing power came into prominence in a hotly debated Supreme Court decision, *National Federation of Independent Business v. Sebelius* (2012), often called the ObamaCare case. The Supreme Court narrowly upheld 5–4 a provision of the healthcare law that required persons to purchase health insurance. In his opinion, Chief Justice John G. Roberts (1955–) reasoned that this individual mandate provision (individual mandate to purchase health insurance, or if not to pay a penalty) was a tax and fell within Congress's taxing power. Roberts explained that the individual mandate is calculated like a tax in the sense that it is based on a percentage of a person's income.

Congress also has the power to spend money for the general welfare of the country. Generally, Congress has broad power to spend money however it wants provided that it does not violate another provision of the Constitution. The Supreme Court ruled in *Steward Machine Co. v. Davis* (1937) that Congress could under the Social Security Act provide for unemployment compensation. The Court identified this as falling within Congress's Spending Clause powers.

Similarly, Congress had the authority under its Spending Clause powers to provide for an older-age pension program in the Social Security Act. The Supreme Court upheld this part of the Social Security Act as yet another example of Congress's Spending Clause powers.

The reach of the Spending Clause powers extends to congressional conditions on grants to state governments. In other words, Congress has the ability to place conditions on grants to state and local governments as long as the conditions are clear, there is a relationship to the purpose of the spending programs, and they are not too coercive.

The breadth of Congress's Spending Clause powers can be seen through the Supreme Court decision in *South Dakota v. Dole* (1987). South Dakota at the time allowed people to purchase

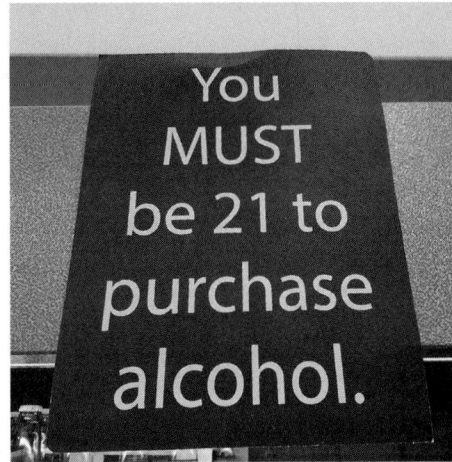

The U.S. Supreme Court ruled that Congress can impose federal laws overriding state laws when it is best for the general welfare of the people, such as the age limit for serving alcohol.

alcohol if they were at least 19 years old. In 1984, Congress passed a federal law directing the secretary of transportation to withhold a percentage of federal highway funds from those states that allowed persons under 21 years of age to purchase alcohol.

South Dakota then sued the United States, contending that the federal law violates the constitutional limitations of Congress's Spending Clause powers and violates the Twenty-first Amendment of the Constitution, which empowers states to regulate the sale of alcoholic beverages.

The U.S. Supreme Court upheld the federal law as a valid exercise of congressional authority under the Spending Clause. First, the Court determined that the law was in pursuit of the general welfare. Writing for the majority, Chief Justice William Rehnquist (1924–2005) found that the law easily served the general welfare. He also found that the law had a clear purpose, writing that "the condition imposed by Congress is directly related to one of the main purposes for which highway funds are expended—safe interstate travel."

What is the Commerce Clause?

The Commerce Clause, which reads "To regulate Commerce with foreign Nations, and among the several states, and with the Indian tribes," is probably Congress's most expansive power. The Commerce Clause has been used to justify federal civil rights laws, federal criminal laws, securities laws, environmental laws, and many others. Constitution law expert Erwin Chemerinsky writes that "[f]rom the perspective of constitutional law, the commerce clause has been the focus of most of the Supreme Court decisions that have considered the scope of congressional power and federalism."

Under the Commerce Clause, Congress can regulate the channels of interstate commerce, the instrumentalities of interstate commerce, and activities that substantially affect the flow of interstate commerce. For example, the channels of interstate commerce would include highways, waterways, and air channels—the methods by which goods move through the country. The instrumentalities of interstate commerce concern things such as ships, boats, railways, and airplanes. The third category focuses on activities—even if seemingly of a state or local nature—that have a substantial effect on interstate commerce.

How did Congress use the Commerce Clause to protect civil rights?

Congress has construed its Commerce Clause powers to justify federal civil rights laws, such as the Civil Rights Act of 1964. The Heart of Atlanta Motel, which practiced racial segregation, contended that Congress did not have the authority to pass a law that regulated how it conducted its business. The motel had 216 rooms and was located only a few blocks from two major interstates. However, 75 percent of the guests at the motel were from outside of Georgia, a key fact the Court relied on to talk about the flow of interstate commerce.

The Court in *Heart of Atlanta Motel v. United States* (1964) recounted the extensive congressional testimony that African Americans faced much discrimination and many burdens when traveling through parts of the country that practiced segregation. The Court also noted that much testimony showed that the discrimination was across the United States, not just in the South, and that such uncertainty in obtaining suitable lodging had a real, discernible impact on many African Americans, who forewent travel to avoid such problems.

The Supreme Court explained that "the determinative test of the exercise of power by the Congress under the Commerce Clause is simply whether the activity sought to be regulated is 'commerce which concerns more States than one' and has a real and substantial relation to the national interest." The Court had little trouble in finding that segregated hotel practices had a national impact on commerce and the economy.

The Heart of Atlanta Motel argued that it was a local business that only impacted local affairs, not national matters. The Court was not persuaded. Instead, the Court found ample evidence about the harmful impact that racial discrimination had upon the flow of interstate commerce. The motel also argued that Congress primarily seemed focused on moral wrongs, not economic ones, in passing the Civil Rights Act of 1964.

The Court also rejected this argument, saying that while Congress was concerned with moral wrongs too, Congress had established through its hearings and debates that the moral wrong of racial discrimination had very real and negative impacts on interstate commerce.

On the very same day, the Supreme Court also upheld the application of the Civil Rights Act of 1964 to a restaurant in Birmingham, Alabama, Ollie's Barbecue, that contended that it had the right to exclude African Americans from its main seating

U.S. Supreme Court justice Tom C. Clark, ruling on the case of an Atlanta restaurant discriminating against black customers, ruled that its activities were not merely local in nature because much of the food came from out of state.

area. The restaurant allowed African Americans to order food and pick it up from the back of the restaurant, but African Americans were not allowed to dine in the restaurant.

The owners of the restaurant argued that their activities were local in nature and that Congress could not reach their local activities through the Commerce Clause. The Court noted that evidence showed that nearly half of the meat procured by the restaurant came from out of state. "The record is replete with testimony of the burdens placed on interstate commerce by racial discrimination in restaurants," Justice Tom C. Clark (1899–1977) wrote for the Court. "A comparison of per capita spending by [African Americans] in restaurants, theaters, and like establishments indicated less spending, after discounting income differences, in areas where discrimination is widely practiced." He concluded:

> The power of Congress in this field is broad and sweeping; where it keeps within its sphere and violates no express constitutional limitation it has been the rule of this Court, going back almost to the founding days of the Republic, not to interfere. The

Civil Rights Act of 1964, as here applied, we find to be plainly appropriate in the resolution of what the Congress found to be a national commercial problem of the first magnitude. We find it in no violation of any express limitations of the Constitution and we therefore declare it valid.

How expansive has the Commerce Clause power been interpreted by the Supreme Court?

Since the New Deal era, the Supreme Court has interpreted the Commerce Clause quite broadly, giving Congress a wide berth when it came to passing laws premised on its Commerce Clause powers. In fact, from 1937 until 1995, the Supreme Court did not rule a single federal law as exceeding Congress's powers under the clause.

That finally changed in *United States v. Lopez* (1995), a case involving a 12th-grade student at Edison High School in San Antonio, Texas, who was charged with violating a federal law known as the Gun-Free School Zones Act of 1990. The law prohibits an individual from knowingly carrying a firearm within 1,000 feet of a school. Alfonso Lopez Jr. was found with a concealed .38 caliber handgun and five bullets. He said he needed the gun for self-defense.

But federal authorities prosecuted him for violating the Gun-Free School Zones Act. Lopez waived his right to a jury trial. At a bench trial, the judge found him guilty and sentenced him to six months imprisonment and two years of supervised release.

Lopez's attorney challenged the constitutionality of the Gun-Free School Zones Act and lost in the lower courts. But the U.S. Supreme Court reversed in a stunning victory. Writing for a five-justice majority, Chief Justice William Rehnquist identified the operative question as whether the regulated activity in this case—gun possession—substantially affects interstate commerce. Rehnquist reasoned that the law is a "criminal statute that by its terms has nothing to do with 'commerce' or any sort of economic enterprise."

Rehnquist reasoned that possession of a handgun "in a local school zone is in no sense an economic activity that might, through repetition elsewhere, substantially affect any sort of interstate commerce." He noted Lopez was a local student at a local school and there was no evidence that Lopez had traveled out of state with the gun.

Ultimately, Rehnquist reasoned that this was a matter for state or local regulation, not federal regulation. In a concurring opinion, Justice Anthony Kennedy (1936–) noted that more than 40 states already had laws on the books prohibiting the possession of guns at or near schools. Justice Clarence Thomas (1948–) would have gone even further than his colleagues in the majority. He called for the Court to "temper our Commerce Clause jurisprudence" and reject the substantially effect interstate commerce test, which he viewed as "an innovation of the 20th century." Thomas worried most about what he called "the aggregation principle." Under the aggregation principle, a single item may not substantially affect interstate commerce, but when one considers that product in

The Gun-Free School Zones Act of 1990 prohibits anyone from carrying a loaded or unsecured gun into an area known to be a designated school zone.

aggregation across multiple state lines and in multiple locations, it might have a substantial impact on interstate commerce.

The Court reached a similar result in *United States v. Morrison* (2000), a case examining a federal law known as the Violence Against Women Act, which provided a federal civil remedy for victims of gender-related violence. Christy Brzonkala, a student at Virginia Tech University, alleged that two members of the Virginia Tech football team, Antonio Morrison and James Crawford, assaulted and raped her. She filed a complaint under the school's sexual assault policy.

Morrison admitted that he had sexual contact with Brzonkala, and a school judicial committee suspended him for two semesters. Morrison indicated that he intended to challenge this process in federal court, and the school held a second hearing at which Morrison was only found to have committed the offense of "using abusive language." Virginia Tech's administration set aside Morrison's punishment, and Brzonkala dropped out of school.

She later sued Morrison, Crawford, and Virginia Tech in federal court under the Violence Against Women Act of 1994. Once again, the Supreme Court found that Congress had exceeded its powers under the Commerce Clause in passing this federal law that had no substantial impact on the economy. "We accordingly reject the argument that Congress may regulate noneconomic, violent criminal conduct based solely on that conduct's aggregate effect on interstate commerce," Chief Justice Rehnquist wrote for the majority.

Is the Supreme Court today more deferential when it comes to the Commerce Clause?

Yes, since 2005, it appears that the Supreme Court has been more deferential to Congress's broad powers under the Commerce Clause. The Court, for example, in *Ashcroft v. Raich,*

The Supreme Court ruled in a 2005 case that the federal government *can* regulate intrastate commerce in marijuana even though it is legal in some states.

upheld the application of the federal Controlled Substances Act, which criminalizes marijuana. This federal law conflicted with a California law, called the Compassionate Use Act of 1996, which allowed for the medicinal use of marijuana. Two women, Angel McClary Raich and Diane Monson, who needed marijuana to combat crippling physical pain, filed a federal lawsuit, challenging the application of the federal Controlled Substances Act to their in-state use and growth of a few marijuana plants.

The U.S. Supreme Court upheld the federal law, noting that "Congress had a rational basis for concluding that leaving home-consumed marijuana outside federal control would similarly affect price and market conditions." The Court applied the aggregation principle to find that Congress had a rational basis for passing the law and applying it to even home consumption of marijuana.

What is the Dormant Commerce Clause?

The Dormant Commerce Clause is a negative inference from the Commerce Clause itself, meaning that states cannot pass laws that unduly restrict the free flow of interstate commerce. The Commerce Clause is a positive grant of power to Congress to pass federal legislation that substantially impacts commerce. But the Commerce Clause has another power—it limits state laws that unduly restrict the free flow of interstate commerce. This is what is known as the Dormant Commerce Clause.

The Dormant Commerce Clause prohibits states from passing laws rooted in economic protectionism that restrict the free flow of goods. Under the Dormant Commerce Clause, if a state law discriminates against out-of-state actors or nonresident economic actors, then it is constitutional only if the law is narrowly drawn to serve a very important state interest.

An example of a law deemed to violate the Dormant Commerce Clause was a Tennessee law that imposed a two-year residency requirement on all individuals and businesses who seek to sell liquor. The Supreme Court viewed this as a protectionist

What is Congress's power with regard to naturalization?

The Naturalization Clause gives Congress the power to decide naturalization—the process by which a person can become a citizen of the United States. The Court back in 1892 defined naturalization as "the act of adopting a foreigner, and clothing him with the privileges of a native citizen. Immigration law is a massive body of law that deals not only with whether and how a person can become a citizen but also with when Congress can deport a noncitizen, or alien."

DID YOU KNOW!?

measure that discriminated against non-Tennesseans. The Court concluded that the law violated the Dormant Commerce Clause.

What is the Copyright Clause?

The Copyright Clause of Article I, Section 8—which reads "To promote the Progress of Science and useful Arts, by securing for limited Times to Authors and Inventors the exclusive Right to their respective Writings and Discoveries"—means that Congress can regulate the law of copyrights, patents, and trademarks. In other words, copyright laws are federal laws, not state laws. Another way of explaining this is that the area of intellectual property is largely governed by federal law, not state law. The Framers intended for the Copyright Clause to be an engine of free expression, giving inventors protection for their own original creative works. However, when a copyright law restricts speech or prohibits speech from entering the public domain, some argue that such copyright laws infringe on the First Amendment.

Some inherent degree of tension exists between the First Amendment and copyright. Copyright allows creators of expressive conduct to control the flow of certain information and expression, while the First Amendment ensures the free flow of information and expression. The primary purpose of copyright law is to provide protection for the creator of an expressive work. The main purpose of the First Amendment is to ensure public access to information. Copyright protection reduces access to some information by limiting the extent to which it can be copied by others.

Copyright creates property rights for the creators of certain works. This is why copyright, along with patent and trademark law, is labeled under the rubric of intellectual property. If a person copies another's work without permission, that person has trespassed on the creator's property, or copyrighted expression. This is called copyright infringement. If a person directly copies another's expression, that person has committed direct copyright infringement. If a person or company enables others to commit copyright infringement, they have committed contributory or vicarious infringement.

Copyright exists to increase knowledge. It does so by providing creators with an economic incentive to produce work. Copyright protects "original works of authorship fixed in any tangible medium of expression." It protects books, artwork, sculptures, paintings, musical compositions, and many other forms. The U.S. Supreme Court has written: "It should not be forgotten that the Framers intended copyright itself to be an engine of free expression."

How is copyright an engine of free expression?

The theory is that copyright law already has built-in free-expression principles that ensure its compatibility with the First Amendment and free expression. These are the fair use doctrine and the idea/expression dichotomy.

Fair use means that there are times when someone can use someone else's copyrighted work without it constituting infringement. Fair use became an important part of the common, or judge-made, law. The Copyright Act of 1976 incorporated, or codified, the common-law concept of fair use. Section 107 of the 1976 copyright law begins with a preamble: "The fair use of a copyrighted work … for purposes such as criticism, comment, news reporting, teaching (including multiple copies for classroom use), scholarship, or research, is not an infringement of copyright." For example, a book reviewer could quote portions of a book in writing her review without committing copyright infringement. The book reviewer's quotations would qualify as fair use.

Copyright law lists four nonexclusive factors as especially relevant in determining fair use:

1. The purpose and character of the use, including whether such use is of a commercial nature or is for nonprofit educational purposes.

2. The nature of the copyrighted work.

3. The proportion of material that was copied.

4. The effect of the potential market for or value of the copyrighted work.

The idea/expression dictomony recognizes that if copyright law is too rigid, then there will be a dramatic reduction in the public's access to information. Copyright law attempts to resolve this dilemma to a degree by distinguishing between expression and ideas. This is called the idea/expression dichotomy.

The Supreme Court has been very reluctant to find copyright laws violative of the First Amendment. The Court tends to reason that copyright law already has these built-in protections for free speech—the idea/expression dichotomy and the fair use doctrine.

Copyright laws are designed to protect content creators from having their work essentially stolen by others for profit. Since the advent of AI programs creating text and art, this has become an increasingly problematic issue.

The Supreme Court upheld Congress's Copyright Clause power to pass the Copyright Term Extension Act of 1998, a law that extended the terms of copyright protection by 20 years. The Court, in an opinion by Justice Ruth Bader Ginsburg (1933–2020), did not see the law as an incursion into free-speech principles. "Copyright law contains built-in First Amendment accommodations," she wrote, noting the fair use doctrine and the idea/expression dichotomy.

Similarly, Ginsburg wrote the Court's majority opinion in *Golan v. Holder* (2012), rejecting a First Amendment challenge to a U.S. copyright law that extended copyright protection to some foreign works that had previously been in the public domain. Ginsburg viewed the law as an attempt for the United States to join international copyright law protections rather than a denial of viewpoint or a violation of other generally applicable First Amendment principles. Once again, she viewed copyright law's built-in First Amendment accommodations as sufficient.

What is Congress's power with regard to lower federal courts?

The Constitution gives Congress the power "To constitute Tribunals inferior to the supreme Court." The Constitution calls for one supreme court and such lower courts as Congress deems necessary. Article I, Section 8, further explains that Congress has the power to create lower courts or tribunals. The federal court system is composed of three levels: (1) the federal district court level; (2) the federal circuit court of appeals level; and (3) the United States Supreme Court.

The federal district courts are the trial courts in the federal system. There are 94 federal judicial districts in the United States. Some states only have one, while other states have three judicial districts. A party that loses before a federal district court can then appeal to the federal circuit court of appeals. These are the intermediate appellate courts in the federal system. In 1891, Congress created the so-called Evarts Act, which established nine federal circuit courts of appeals. Currently, there are 13 federal U.S. circuit courts of appeals. There are 11 numbered circuits (from the First Circuit to the Eleventh Circuit), the D.C. Circuit, and the so-called Federal Circuit.

The power to create inferior tribunals means that Congress can create additional federal judicial district courts (the trial courts in the federal system) and additional federal circuit courts of appeals (the intermediate appellate courts in the federal judicial system). In 1982, Congress created the 11th Circuit because the Fifth Circuit was considered too large.

The current debate is whether Congress should create a 12th U.S. Circuit Court of Appeals—making the total number 14—because the Ninth Circuit is too large. For several years, proposals have been introduced into Congress to break up the Ninth Circuit into two circuits. In June 2021, the Ninth Circuit Court of Appeals Judgeship and Reorganization Act of 2021 was introduced. Under this proposal, federal courts from the states of Alaska, Arizona, Idaho, Montana, Nevada, Oregon, and Washington would become the 12th U.S. Circuit Court of Appeals instead of the 9th Circuit.

What is the piracy power?

The Constitution's piracy power reads: "To define and punish Piracies and Felonies committed on the high Seas, and Offences against the Law of Nations." When the Framers created the Constitution, the fledgling nation needed to ensure that its ships were protected on the high seas and oceans. The British Navy was still the dominant force in the world, and other countries, such as Spain and France, had significant naval forces as

Piracy was more of an issue for the young America in the eighteenth century than it is today, the Constitutional provision to punish pirates is still in effect.

well. Although piracy is generally not considered one of the grave threats facing the nation in the twenty-first century, it was a significant problem in the late eighteenth century.

What is Congress's power with regard to war?

The Constitution gives Congress the power to declare war. This is called the "war-making power." Congress has issued formal declarations of war pursuant to this power in five different wars in American history: the War of 1812 with Great Britain, the war with Mexico in 1846, the War with Spain in 1898, the First World War, and the Second World War. In each case, the president, as commander-in-chief, had sought a formal declaration of war from Congress, and Congress ruled in favor of such a declaration.

Congress also has passed different joint resolutions that offer the authorization of the use of force to defend American interests. For example, Congress never formally declared war in either the Korean War or the Vietnam War. Instead, it was the president who committed American troops to battle. However, Congress did pass a joint resolution in 1964, known as the Gulf of Tonkin Resolution, that "promote[d] the maintenance of international peace and security in southeast Asia." Congress ultimately repealed the resolution in 1971 in the wake of increasing unrest and dissension over the Vietnam War.

In 1973, Congress passed the War Powers Act that purportedly limits the president's power to declare war. Under this law, the president must give notice to Congress of military deployments and to remove troops after 60 days if Congress does not authorize the use of military force. The Supreme Court has never ruled on whether the War Powers Act is constitutional or not.

A somewhat similar occurrence happened in response to the terrorist attacks on U.S. soil on September 11, 2001, when planes crashed into the Twin Towers of the World Trade Center in New York City and one in Washington, D.C. President George W. Bush consulted with leaders of Congress, which overwhelmingly passed a joint resolution sanctioning the president with the ability to take appropriate measures to deal with those responsible for such terrorist attacks. The resolution authorized President Bush:

> to use all necessary and appropriate force against those nations, organizations, or persons he determines planned, authorized, committed, or aided the terrorist attacks that occurred on September 11, 2001, or harbored such organizations or persons, in order to prevent any future acts of international terrorism against the United States by such nations, organizations or persons.

The unusual thing about this resolution was that it authorized military force not only against offending countries but also "organizations or persons." This was because the terrorist group Al-Qaeda was behind the terrorist attacks and that organization was not a nation-state. Thus began the so-called War on Terror, which ultimately led to numerous legal conflicts that led to several U.S. Supreme Court decisions.

What is Congress's power over the armed forces?

The Constitution provides in the so-called Army and Navy Powers: "To raise and support Armies, but no Appropriation of Money to that Use shall be for a longer Term than two Years" and "to provide and maintain a Navy."

Article I, Section 8, empowers Congress to maintain a professional military service in the form of an army and a navy. During the Revolutionary War, a standing army was of grave concern to the colonists. They feared that the standing army would consist of loyalists—those more loyal to the king of England than the individual colonies.

Congress has the power to raise and maintain a professional military for the country's defense, with new appropriations budgets requiring approval every two years. This initially involved just the U.S. Army and Navy but now includes the Air Force, Marines, and Space Force, as well as the Coast Guard.

During the time of the framing, there was no air warfare. The Framers knew that war was fought on land and sea. Thus, there was a need for an army and a navy. However, the advent of air warfare in World War I showed the need for an air force. This falls under an implied power of Congress under these two provisions. There is a branch of the U.S. military called the United States Marine Corps. Its origins owe to the so-called "Continental Marines" that fought during the Revolutionary War. In 1834, Congress approved of the Marines as following under a branch of the United States Navy. Federal law provides three main statutory duties of the Marines, including:

- Seizure or defense of advanced naval bases and other land operations to support naval campaigns

- Development of tactics, technique, and equipment used by amphibious landing forces in coordination with the Army and Air Force, and

- Such other duties as the president or Department of Defense may direct.

These clauses also give Congress the power to approve of various reserve components to the armed forces, such as the U.S. Army Reserves. There are seven components to the armed reserves, including:

- Army National Guard

- Army Reserve

- Navy Reserve

- Marine Corps Reserve

- Air National Guard

- Air Force Reserve

- Coast Guard Reserve

What is the Necessary and Proper Clause?

The Necessary and Proper Clause is the so-called "elastic clause" or the "sweeping clause" because it gives Congress many implied powers to carry out its other stated powers in Article I, Section 8. In other words, the Necessary and Proper Clause supplements Congress's other listed powers in the Constitution.

Chief Justice John Marshall (1755–1835) gave a broad reading of the Necessary and Proper Clause in the celebrated case of *McCullough v. Maryland* (1819), which asked the fundamental question of whether Congress had the authority to create a national bank. Marshall explained:

> Is this the sense in which the word "necessary" is always used? Does it always import an absolute physical necessity so strong that one thing to which another may be termed necessary cannot exist without that other? We think it does not. We find that it frequently imports no more than that one thing that is convenient, or useful, or essential to another. To employ the means necessary to an end is generally understood as employing any means calculated to produce the end, and not as being confined to those single means, without which the end would be entirely unattainable … A thing may be necessary, very necessary, absolutely or indispensably necessary.

What is Congress's role with regard to habeas corpus?

Article I, Section 9, provides: "The Privilege of the Writ of Habeas Corpus shall not be suspended, unless when in Cases of

Rebellion or Invasion the public Safety may require it." Habeas corpus, known as "the Great Writ," essentially means that the government may not hold someone unconstitutionally or arbitrarily arrest someone. Prisons often file a writ of habeas corpus in federal court, contending that their constitutional rights were violated somewhere along the way in their criminal proceedings, often in state criminal court proceedings.

The provision suggests that habeas corpus may be suspended during times of rebellion or invasion. President Abraham Lincoln (1809–1865) suspended the writ of habeas corpus, except that he did it without congressional approval beforehand, though Congress did ratify his actions. The Supreme Court ruled in *Ex parte Milligan* (1866) that though the suspension of the writ of habeas corpus was lawful, a civilian could not be tried via military tribunals. The Court noted that though "there should be a power somewhere of suspending the writ of habeas corpus, [the

Several presidents have suspended (or tried to suspend) habeas corpus. Abraham Lincoln did so first during the U.S. Civil War, and so did Ulysses S. Grant during the period of Reconstruction. During World War II, Franklin D. Roosevelt suspended it, but when George W. Bush tried to with regard to Guantanamo Bay detainees, the Supreme Court prevented it.

Constitution] does not say that after a writ of habeas corpus is denied a citizen … shall be tried otherwise than by the course of the common law."

During the War on Terror, the Supreme Court ruled in a series of cases that even enemy combatants detained at Guantanamo Bay, Cuba, had a right to access the courts through a writ of habeas corpus.

What does the Constitution say are two types of laws that Congress (or state legislatures) cannot pass?

The Constitution provides in Article I, Section 10, of the Constitution that "no Bill of Attainder or ex post facto laws shall be passed." The Constitution, therefore, prohibits both. Bills of attainders are laws in which a legislature targets a person or group of persons and imposes punishment without a trial. The U.S. Supreme Court defined ex post facto laws in *Calder v. Bull* (1798) as "that [which] makes an action done before the passing of the law, and which was *innocent* when done, criminal; and punishes such action" or "that *aggravates* a *crime*, or makes it *greater* than it was, when committed." Thus, an ex post facto law increases the penalty for an existing crime to the detriment of a person who already had committed the crime. Another version of an ex post facto law is a law that makes criminal what was innocent conduct when the person committed the action. Many sex offender registration and notification laws have been challenged as ex post facto laws, but the Supreme Court generally has held that they are not primarily punitive and deemed them not to be ex post facto laws.

How does Article I limit Congress's taxing power?

The Constitution provides that "No Tax or Duty shall be laid on Articles exported from any State." It also provides that "No Preference shall be given by any Regulation of Commerce or Revenue to the Ports of one State over those of another; nor shall Vessels bound to, or from, one State, be obliged to enter, clear, or pay Duties in another." These two provisions try to ensure that Congress treats states fairly and not tax them to death like the English Crown. The first provision bans export taxes. The idea here is that it would be unfair for Congress to impose a tax on a particular crop grown mainly in one state. For example, this provision prohibited Congress from imposing export taxes on tobacco, which would really hurt Virginia disproportionately, or on cotton, which might hurt Mississippi disproportionately. The second provision tries to promote the free flow of interstate commerce and not allow a preference to be given to one state over another state when it comes to navigation and trade. In a sense, Congress agreed to not discriminate or pick favorites among states when it came to commerce.

How does Congress actually get its work done?

Congress gets its work done through committees—standing committees, joint committees, and special or select committees. Both the House and Senate have these different types of committees. Standing committees regularly meet with the same members and are considered permanent. Joint committees hold members of both the House and Senate together. Finally, special or select committees are assembled for a specific purpose, and they are not as permanent as standing committees.

The committees may then establish smaller groups called subcommittees. The committee process enables members of Congress to become subject matter experts on issues important to the American public and body politic. Committees hold different types of hearings—oversight hearings, investigative hearings, and confirmation hearings.

Oversight hearings allow members of Congress to oversee the operations of the executive branch—specifically the review of how administrative agencies in the executive branch are performing their duties. Oversight hearings also are used when a program under its purview is about to expire and needs to be reauthorized to continue.

Investigative hearings are different. These often involve allegations of wrongdoing or abuse, and Congress holds an investigative hearing to determine whether there is a need for a legislative remedy to help address the problem. These hearings are more confrontational and often involve both witnesses and subpoenas.

Congress organizes committees in order to get specific work done for the government. For example, the Judicial Committee—shown here in a 2006 confirmation hearing—typically has the duty of reviewing bills involving the Civil Code, Code of Civil Procedure, Evidence Code, Family Code, and Probate Code.

Finally, confirmation hearings are held in the Senate following presidential nominations for different positions. Recall that Article II of the Constitution authorizes the president to nominate certain government officials with the "advice and consent" of the Senate. Hearings are normally held only for higher positions, such as federal judicial nominees. For example, Supreme Court nominees participate in highly watched hearings.

What is a committee markup?

A committee markup is the key formal step in which committee members offer changes to a bill and mark up the language of a bill before sending it to the House or Senate floor. During the markup session, the committee may be examining a bill referred from another committee or examining a revised draft of a bill. At this meeting, which is typically open to the public, committee members consider possible changes to the proposal by offering and voting on amendments to it, including possibly a complete substitute for its text.

DID YOU KNOW?

What is a floor amendment?

A floor amendment is an amendment to a piece of legislation that is offered by a senator or member of the House on the floor of the actual chamber when the body is considering the measure. Floor amendments are different than committee amendments. A committee amendment is offered while a House or Senate committee is meeting. But a floor amendment is presented in the actual chamber in front of the whole body—or at least the members who are present.

What is a conference committee?

A conference committee is a temporary, ad-hoc committee consisting of members of both houses of Congress (the House and Senate) for the purpose of reconciling differences between versions of bills that passed both houses. In other words, the House passes a bill and the Senate passes a nearly identical bill. However, there are some differences between the two. Thus, a conference committee is formed to examine and iron out those differences.

The Executive Branch

How long does the president serve?

American presidents serve four-year terms. This was a major issue during the Constitutional Convention of 1787, as different members of the Convention argued on issues such as the length of term and whether the president should consist of a single individual or perhaps a group of three individuals. When Pennsylvania delegate James Wilson (1742–1798) suggested that the executive office should be held by one person, a lengthy silence followed at the Convention. The delegates each had their own conceptions of executive power, and they were leery of granting too much control to a powerful executive who could usurp legislative authority and engage in tyrannical actions. The Framers eventually decided upon a single executive, primarily because they felt conflicts would be more easily avoided if there were only one person in the nation's highest office. Also, they believed that Congress could more carefully watch and check a single executive. Thus, ultimately, the Founders determined that the president should consist of a single chief executive who serves a term of four years.

In fact, Article II, Section 1, of the Constitution opens with the following language: "The executive power shall be vested in a President of the United States of America. He shall hold his Office during the term of four years...."

Originally, there was no limit in the Constitution on how many terms the president could serve. However, President Franklin Delano Roosevelt (1882–1945) was elected to four consecutive terms, though he died early in his fourth term. Many feared that this was a bad precedent, as the president could become too powerful. Thus, Congress passed the Twenty-second Amendment in 1951, which provides: "No person shall be elected to the office of the President more than twice, and no person who has held the office of President, or acted as President, for more than two years of a term to which some other person was elected President shall be elected to the office of the President more than once."

President Franklin D. Roosevelt was elected to four terms in office, after which Congress, fearful that a lack of term limits would give the Executive Branch too much power, passed the Twenty-second Amendment.

What are the duties of the president of the United States?

The president's chief duty is to protect the U.S. Constitution and enforce the laws made by Congress. However, they also have a host of other responsibilities tied to their job as the nation's leader. These include: recommending legislation to Congress, calling special sessions of Congress, delivering messages to Congress, signing or vetoing legislation, appointing federal judges, appointing heads of federal departments and agencies and other principal federal officials, appointing representatives to foreign countries, carrying on official business with foreign nations, acting as commander in chief of the armed forces, and granting pardons for offenses against the United States.

What are the implied constitutional powers of the president?

The president possesses certain powers that are not enumerated or listed in the U.S. Constitution. For example, although the Constitution does not grant the president the expressed power to remove administrators from their offices, as the chief executive the president holds power over executive branch officials, unless such removal power is limited by public law. Another implied constitutional power is derived from the president's authority as commander in chief. Although Congress has the explicit power to declare war, the president holds the responsibility to protect the nation from sudden attack and can initiate military activities overseas without a formal declaration of war. Through the War Powers Resolution of 1973, Congress sought to define more clearly the conditions under which presidents unilaterally can authorize military action abroad.

What is the Vesting Clause?

The Vesting Clause is the first sentence in Article II of the Constitution that provides that "the executive power shall be vested in a President of the United States." The Vesting Clause establishes the office of the presidency. Others contend that this clause does much more, giving the president executive powers, which include various implied powers that are not given explicitly in other provisions of Article II.

For example, some scholars argue that the Vesting Clause gives the executive a great deal of power. For example, law professor John Yoo writes in his book *The Powers of War and Peace* (2005) that "Article II's Vesting Clause requires that we construe any ambiguities in the allocation of power in favor of the President." This school of thought is associated with the term *unitary executive*—meaning that the president often has the sole authority to act in certain circumstances.

Have there been proposals to amend or repeal the Twenty-second Amendment limiting the terms of the presidency?

Yes, there have been several through the years. Periodically, a member of Congress will introduce a measure to repeal the Twenty-second Amendment. This usually occurs when a member of Congress is in the same political party as a sitting two-term president and wishes that that person could run for a third term. For example, Democratic Representative Barney Frank (1940–) introduced a measure to repeal the Twenty-second Amendment in 1999, toward the end of Democratic president Bill Clinton's

(1946–) second term. Representative Steny H. Hoyer (1939–), a Democrat, introduced a measure to repeal the Twenty-second Amendment in 2005 as Democratic president Barack Obama (1961–) was entering his second term. However, such attempts are sometimes bipartisan. In 1995, Republican senator Mitch McConnell (1942–) and Democratic senator Harry Reid (1939–) introduced a joint resolution calling for the repeal of the Twenty-second Amendment.

How are presidents elected?

Presidents are elected through the process involving the Electoral College. The Constitution provides: "Each State shall appoint, in such Manner as the Legislature thereof may direct, a Number of Electors, equal to the whole Number of Senators and Representatives to which the State may be entitled in the Congress but no Senator or Representative, or Person holding an Office of Trust or Profit under the United States, shall be appointed an Elector."

The electoral votes from each state go to the winner of the vote in that state. Thus, if Candidate A wins the vote in a certain state, then the electors cast their ballots for Candidate A. Some states have many more electoral votes than others. For example, California has 55 electoral votes, as it has two senators and 53 representatives. Thus, this state carries much more force than, say, the state of Tennessee, which has only 11 electoral votes.

While many criticize the Electoral College, it has its defenders, who argue that the Electoral College ensures that voters from every state have a meaningful say in the election.

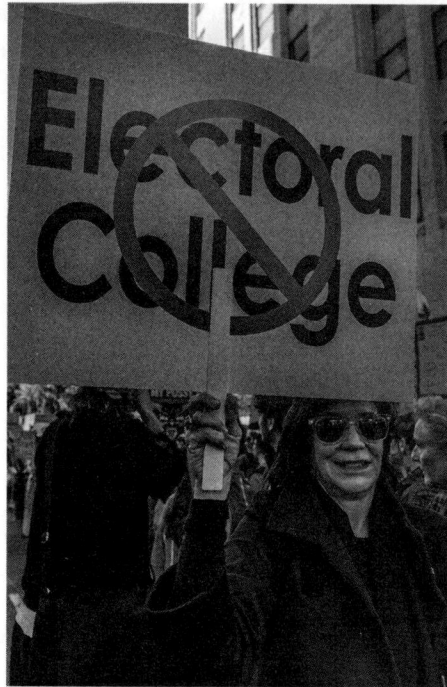

Recent contentious elections for the president have inspired a growing movement of citizens who would like to see the end of the Electoral College in favor of election by popular vote.

Why was the Electoral College created?

The Founding Fathers established the Electoral College as a compromise between election of the president by Congress and election by popular vote. They were attempting to create a blueprint that would allow for the election of the president without political parties, without national campaigns, and without disturbing the carefully designed balance between the presidency and Congress, and between the states and the federal government. It sought to meet a number of democratic needs, including providing a degree of popular participation in the election process, giving the less populous states some additional leverage in the election process, and generally insulating the election process from political manipulation.

How many electoral votes does a candidate need to win the presidency?

Because there are 538 electoral votes, a candidate needs a majority of 270 electoral votes to win the presidency. Sometimes, presidential elections are razor close. Consider the presidential election of 2000 between Republican candidate George W. Bush (1946–) and Democratic candidate Al Gore (1948–). Bush captured 271 electoral votes to narrowly capture the presidency over Gore.

How are electoral votes tabulated?

Electoral votes are counted and certified by a joint session of Congress, held on January 6 of the year succeeding the election in November. A majority of electoral votes is required to win. If no candidate wins a majority, then the president is elected by the House of Representatives, and the vice president is elected by the Senate, a process known as a contingent election.

How are electors chosen?

The U.S. Constitution left the method of selecting electors up to the states, so methods vary. Generally, the political parties nominate electors at their state party conventions (in 36 states) or by a vote of the party's central committee in each state (in ten states). Aside from members of Congress and employees of the federal government, who are prohibited from serving as an elector in order to maintain the balance between the legislative and executive branches of the federal government, anyone may serve as an elector. Since electors are often selected in recognition of their service and dedication to their political party, they are often state-elected officials, party leaders, or persons who have a personal or political affiliation with the presidential candidate. Today, all states choose their electors by direct statewide election, except for Maine and Nebraska.

What is a "faithless elector"?

A faithless elector is the term used to describe an elector in the electoral college who does not follow the will expressed by the popular vote in a presidential election. Instead, they cast an electoral vote for another candidate. For example, in the presidential election of 1976, Republicans carried the state of Washington; however, one Republican elector from that state refused to vote for the Republican presidential nominee, incumbent Gerald Ford (1913–2006). Another example occurred in 1988, when a Democratic elector for West Virginia voted for Lloyd Bentsen (1921–2006) for president and Michael Dukakis (1933–) for vice president—instead of the other way around. However, the vote of a faithless elector has never influenced the results of a presidential election. Although most states legally require electors to vote for the candidates for whom they are pledged, the U.S. Constitution allows electoral discretion in the voting process.

The U.S. Supreme Court upheld a Washington state law allowing states to punish faithless electors in *Chiafalo v. Washington* (2020). That case involved a situation in Washington state when three electors refused to cast their electoral votes for Democratic candidate Hillary Clinton (1947–) in the 2016 presidential election. "Article II and the Twelfth Amendment give States broad power over electors, and give electors themselves no rights," Justice Elena Kagan (1960–) wrote for the Court. "Early in our history, States decided to tie electors to the presidential choices of others, whether legislatures or citizens."

What happened in the election of 1800 that required a shift in presidential elections?

By 1800, the fledgling Federalist and Democratic-Republican parties had begun to take shape. (The Democratic-Republican Party was actually known as the Republican Party at that time, but historians retroactively added "Democratic" to its name to differentiate it from the modern Republican Party.) The Democratic-Republican Party ran incumbent vice president Thomas Jefferson (1743–1826) as its presidential candidate and Aaron Burr (1756–1836) as its vice presidential candidate. The Federalist Party ran incumbent president John Adams (1735–1826) and diplomat Charles C. Pinckney (1746–1825) as their candidates.

However, an equal number of electors voted for both Jefferson and Burr. While their intentions were to elect Jefferson as president and Burr as vice president, the vote showed that each man was tied for the presidency, having received the same number of electoral votes. Burr seized the opportunity to become president,

Thomas Jefferson butted heads with the Electoral College system when he found himself in a tie with Aaron Burr for the presidency in 1800, a complication that led to the passage of the Twelfth Amendment.

and the Federalist Party seized the opportunity to help defeat Jefferson and claim the presidency. Amid bitter infighting, the election was thrown into the House of Representatives—where each of the states had one vote—to decide the fate of the election. Before Jefferson finally received a majority of the votes, the House voted 36 times, casting ballots over a period of six days. In the end, ten states voted for Jefferson and four states voted for Burr. As the runner-up, Burr became vice president.

The election of 1800 exposed the flaws of the early electoral system and led to the adoption of the Twelfth Amendment, which was ratified by the states in September 1804. According to this amendment, electors cast separate ballots for president and vice president. The amendment also says that if no candidate receives an absolute majority of electoral votes, then the House of Representatives selects the president among the top three contenders—with each state casting only one vote and an absolute majority needed to claim the presidency.

What are the criticisms of the Electoral College?

Detractors of the Electoral College tend to be proponents of the popular vote and often mention the fact that the Electoral College can result in a president being elected, as in the election of 1824 and four others, with fewer popular votes than his opponent. Opponents also point to the risk of faithless electors, although there has never been an election decided by one. Depressed voter turnout is another reason that critics cite when mentioning the institution of the Electoral College. They maintain, for example, that because each state is entitled to the same number of electoral votes regardless of voter turnout, there is no incentive for states to encourage their citizens to go to the polls at election time. Another key criticism is that the results of the Electoral College election can fail to accurately reflect the popular will.

Have any presidential candidates won the popular vote but lost the election?

Yes, five times in American history, a presidential candidate has won the popular vote but lost the presidency. In 1824, Democrat-Republican Andrew Jackson (1767–1845) won the popular vote but lost the election to Democratic-Republican John Quincy Adams (1767–1848). In 1876, Democrat Samuel Tilden (1814–1866) won the popular vote but lost the election to the Republican candidate Rutherford B. Hayes (1822–1893). In 1888, incumbent Democratic president Grover Cleveland (1837–1908) won the popular vote but lost the election to Republican candidate Benjamin Harrison (1833–1901). In 2000, Democratic candidate Al Gore won the popular vote but lost the election to Republican candidate George W. Bush. In 2016, Democratic candidate Hillary Clinton won the popular vote but lost the election to Republican candidate Donald Trump (1946–).

Have there been proposals to abolish the Electoral College?

Yes, there have been numerous proposals to abolish the electoral college. Most recently, Democratic representative Steve Cohen (1949–) of Tennessee and eight cosponsors introduced a measure in the U.S. House of Representatives to abolish the Electoral College. Cohen and his colleagues introduced H.J. Resolution 14 in January 2021, calling for a constitutional amendment for the direct election of the president and vice president.

DID YOU KNOW!?

Which states have the fewest electoral college votes?

The states of Alaska, Montana, North Dakota, South Dakota, Vermont, and Wyoming only have three electoral college votes—as does the District of Columbia.

Which president received all of the electoral votes?

President George Washington (1732–1799) received all 69 electoral votes in the election of 1789. This was no surprise, as leaders nearly unanimously wanted Washington to serve as president. This continued in the presidential election of 1792, when Washington received all 132 electoral votes.

How did the Twelfth Amendment bring more clarity to the presidential election process?

The Twelfth Amendment ensured that candidates run exclusively for president or vice president and that a person running for vice president cannot in the same election challenge the president. The Constitution originally provided that the person receiving the highest number of electoral votes would be president, and the person receiving the second highest number of electoral votes would be vice president. This presented quite a problem in the election of 1796, when two former members of President George Washington's cabinet ran against each other—Washington's vice president, John Adams, ran against Washington's first secretary of state, Thomas Jefferson. In the election of 1796, Adams edged out Jefferson in the electoral college 71 to 68. This produced the most unusual result that Adams of the Federalist Party was president and his political enemy, Jefferson of the Democratic-Republican Party, was vice president.

Congress addressed this anomaly by enacting the Twelfth Amendment to the U.S. Constitution. This amendment—although quite wordy—essentially separates the president and vice president. A person runs exclusively for president or vice president. The result of the Twelfth Amendment is that a president and vice president run together for the same political party on the same ticket. This avoids the thorny problem of having a president and vice president from opposite political parties.

What are the qualifications for being president?

The Constitution provides in Article II, Section 1: "No Person except a natural born Citizen, or a Citizen of the United

Theodore Roosevelt was the youngest person to assume the office of president, which he did at the age of 42 after President William McKinley's assassination in 1901.

States, at the time of the Adoption of this Constitution, shall be eligible to the Office of President; neither shall any person be eligible to that Office who shall not have attained to the Age of thirty five Years, and been fourteen Years a Resident within the United States." Thus, there are three requirements for the presidency: (1) that a person be a natural-born citizen; (2) that the person be at least 35 years of age; and (3) that the person reside in the United States for at least 14 years.

What is the presidential oath?

The oath of office for the president is outlined in Article II, Section 1, of the U.S. Constitution and reads as follows: "I do solemnly swear (or affirm) that I will faithfully execute the office of President of the United States, and will, to the best of my ability, preserve, protect, and defend the Constitution of the United States." Usually, the chief justice of the Supreme Court administers the oath, although there is no provision made for this in the Constitution. In fact, throughout American history, other judges have administered the oath at times of unexpected presidential succession.

President Bill Clinton is shown here in 1993 taking the oath of office in which he must swear to defend, protect, and preserve the Constitution.

What does it mean to be commander in chief?

Article II, Section 2, begins with one of the more frequently invoked phrases in American constitutional law and popular culture alike—that the president is "commander in chief." This means that the president is the leader of the armed forces of the United States—the Army and Navy by text and the Marines and Air Force by extension. Harold Baynton (1903–1978), an acting U.S. assistant to the attorney general, wrote in a 1947 memo that "the phrase 'Army and Navy' is used in the Constitution as a means of describing all the armed forces of the United States." Thus, the president of the United States is the leader of the most powerful military in the world. That is an awesome responsibility.

The Founding Fathers wanted the president in charge of the armed forces even over the military commanders. Recall that the Founding Fathers were quite concerned about standing armies and the potential ability of the military to overthrow the government. The Constitution gives Congress the power to declare war, but oftentimes, presidents have acted quickly in case of military conflict or when military force is necessary. Founding Father James Madison (1751–1836) had warned that the president, more so than Congress, might be more prone to declare war than a more deliberative body. In other words, according to Madison, the president was "most interested in war & most prone to use it."

What is the pardon power?

The pardon power means the president can pardon anyone of federal offenses. The Constitution's pardon power provides: "and he shall have Power to grant Reprieves and Pardons for Offenses against the United States, except in Cases of Impeachment."

Article II, Section 2, contains the president's pardon power, a power traced back to early Greece and Rome and, in more modern times, English law and early colonial law. The pardon power extends only to federal crimes, not state crimes. Furthermore, the president cannot pardon impeachment convictions. Furthermore, a presidential pardon cannot be issued to cover conduct that has not yet been committed. But the pardon power otherwise is plenary, or quite broad. Critics have charged that it is too broad.

There are different types of pardons, including full pardons for individuals, amnesties for groups of persons, and commutations, which reduce the penalties associated with convictions. Note that the Constitution itself speaks of "Reprieves and Pardons." There are also remissions of fines and forfeitures and reprieves.

The full pardon—what Chief Justice John Marshall (1755–1835) in 1833 called "an act of grace"—is by far the most expansive type of pardon. It releases the person from wrongdoing and restores the person's civil rights without qualification. This means that a person pardoned of a felony offense can vote in elections or possess a firearm. The Supreme Court explained in *Ex parte Garland* (1866) that "a pardon reaches both the punishment

A Thanksgiving tradition formed from the power of the pardon in which the president "pardons" a turkey, saving it from becoming dinner (President Ronald Reagan pictured in 1984).

prescribed for the offense and the guilt of the offender; and when the pardon is full, it releases the punishment and blots out of existence the guilt, so that in the eye of the law the offender is as innocent as if he had never committed the offense."

What have been some of the most controversial presidential pardons?

Throughout American history there have been some very controversial pardons. Perhaps the most controversial was President Andrew Johnson (1808–1875), a Southerner from Tennessee, issuing a blanket pardon to all Confederate troops who were willing to pledge their allegiance to the United States of America.

In 1974, President Gerald Ford (1913–2006) pardoned former president Richard Nixon (1913–1994) for Nixon's involvement in the Watergate scandal. Ford said the pardon was necessary to allow the bitterly divided nation to move on after the Watergate scandal.

In 1977, President Jimmy Carter (1924–) issued a pardon to many persons who dodged the draft in order to avoid military service during the Vietnam War. The next year, Carter issued a posthumous pardon to former Confederate president Jefferson Davis (1808–1889), saying that the country needed to heal.

In 2001, President Bill Clinton (1946–)—in his last day in office—pardoned his half brother Roger Clinton (1956–), who had a cocaine trafficking conviction from the 1980s. But it was Clinton's pardon of billionaire financier Marc Rich (1934–2013) on Clinton's last day in office that shocked many people across the political spectrum. The *New York Times* called the pardon "a shocking abuse of presidential power."

Can a president issue a self-pardon?

It is not clear whether a president can pardon themself, though the issue became relevant during the presidency of Donald Trump, who was impeached twice. In 2018 Trump stated that he had "the absolute right" to issue a self-pardon. Trump's presidency was not the only time this discussion took place, as the topic surfaced during the presidencies of both Nixon (who was nearly impeached) and Clinton (who was impeached).

What is the treaty power?

The Treaty Clause provides that presidents can enter into treaties or international agreements with other countries but that such treaties must be approved by a two-thirds Senate vote to be approved. The clause's "advice and consent" language seems to indicate that the Senate has an "advice" role before the president enters into a treaty. However, in practice, the Senate's role primarily has been one of approving or rejecting a treaty entered into by a president.

The great majority—90 percent according to experts—of international agreements entered into by presidents, however, are not treaties but rather so-called executive agreements. Such international agreements are not submitted to the Senate for its advice and consent. Presidents have entered into such executive agreements with far greater frequency in the post–World War II era.

What is the appointment power?

The president can nominate and appoint various officers to the federal government, including ambassadors, public ministers and consuls, judges of the Supreme Court, U.S. attorneys, and all other officers of the United States. The Senate then confirms these presidential appointments. Congress does have the power to appoint so-called inferior officers—a subject that has led to much litigation over who falls into that category. In other words, there has been significant debate over who is a principal officer and who is an inferior officer.

This represents a key example of the separation of powers concept dividing power between the president and Congress. Some early presidents often took the language more literally— "the advice and consent" language referring to senatorial power. For example, President George Washington (1732–1799) believed that prenomination advice from the Senate was allowable but not required. Some presidents through the years have informally sought advice from members of Congress, but by far, the more standard model has been the president nominating and the Senate confirming. In other words, the term "advice and consent" has really devolved into just the word "consent" or the lack of consent.

What is the removal power?

The Constitution does not specifically mention that the president may remove officers, but this power has been deemed to be a corollary of the Appointment Clause. The thinking is that if the president can appoint an officer, the president can remove that officer, too. The U.S. Supreme Court explained this removal power in 2020 by invoking President Harry Truman's (1884–1972) famous line that "the buck stops" with the president: "Without such power, the President could not be held fully accountable for discharging his own responsibilities; the buck would stop somewhere else."

The Supreme Court addressed the reach of the president's removal power in a case involving an agency created by Congress called the Consumer Financial Protection Bureau. Under the structure of this agency, Congress provided that the director of this bureau could not be removed by the president absent inefficiency, neglect, or malfeasance.

The Court reasoned that Congress violated the principle of separation of powers by creating an independent agency and installing a director who essentially was free from the reach of the president, the head of the executive branch. Chief Justice John Roberts Jr. (1955–) reasoned that "[s]uch an agency lacks a foundation in historical practice and clashes with constitutional structure by concentrating power in a unilateral actor insulated from Presidential control."

President Harry Truman kept a sign on his desk that said, "The Buck Stops Here," meaning he was ultimately responsible for the actions of his administration.

What are recess appointments?

Presidents can make "recess appointments" when the Senate is not in session. This clause was not considered controversial by the Framers at the 1787 Convention. Presumably, the idea was that there needs to be an additional way to make sure that the government operates smoothly and if the Senate is not in session, something must be done. Alexander Hamilton (1755–1804) advanced this idea of recess appointments in the Federalist Papers, indicating that they were necessary to ensure the government operated efficiently.

Sometimes, however, presidents have used the recess power strategically. For example, a president could use the recess power to put in place a person that they think the Senate would not approve. Some presidents used the recess power quite frequently. President Bill Clinton made 139 recess appointments, while his successor, President George W. Bush, made 179.

A recess is a break in Senate or House proceedings. The Twentieth Amendment says that Congress shall begin its session on January 3 of each year. It may end some time in the fall. Thus, there may be a so-called "intersession recess" between when Congress formally ends its session and when it begins a new session. But there are also smaller breaks called "intrasession recesses," when Congress breaks for shorter periods of time.

In 2014, the U.S. Supreme Court examined the president's recess powers to examine whether several recess appointments by President Barack Obama were constitutional. The Court held that recess appointments include both intersession and intrasession recesses. The Court determined that a recess period occurs only when the Senate is not in session for 10 days or longer. President Obama had sought to use the recess power to make appointments during Senate breaks of as few as three days. Congress deemed this unconstitutional. Congress also held that for purposes of the Recess Appointments Clause, "the Senate is in session when it says it is, provided that, under its own rules, it retains the capacity to transact Senate business."

Presidents use the recess power to fill all types of positions. Some of the more high-profile uses of recess appointments concern appointments to the federal bench. For example, President George W. Bush used his recess appointment power to nominate Charles W. Pickering (1937–) to the U.S. Court of Appeals for the Fifth Circuit in 2004. Pickering had previously served as a federal district court judge since 1990. Bush used the recess power because earlier, when he had tried to nominate Pickering to the Court of Appeals, the Democrats in the Senate had strongly opposed Pickering for his views on abortion and because of opposition from some civil rights groups. Ultimately, Pickering retired from the bench just before his recess appointment ended.

What is the State of the Union Address?

The president's State of the Union Address consists of a summary of the year's developments, often focusing on the positive, and a recommendation to Congress for certain proposals that the president thinks necessary or beneficial for the public. Presidents George Washington and John Adams delivered their State of the Union addresses before Congress. Washington gave his initial address on January 8, 1790. Such addresses were known as "the Annual Address."

However, the third president, Thomas Jefferson, balked at this practice and sent his State of the Union addresses in written form. Jefferson felt the practice of having the president deliver an address before Congress was akin to the British practice of a "speech from the throne." Subsequent presidents followed Jefferson's practice until President Woodrow Wilson (1856–1924) appeared before Congress in 1913.

President George H. W. Bush is shown here in 1992 giving his last State of the Union Address to the Joint Session of Congress.

President Franklin Delano Roosevelt also appeared before Congress and delivered his message to the nation. This has become common practice for presidents to deliver the State of the Union message before both houses of Congress in either January or February of each year. Since 1947, when President Harry Truman delivered a State of the Union Address, the addresses have been televised.

Some presidents do not deliver a State of the Union Address in their first year on the job because it falls so closely to their Inauguration Address, and some presidents do not give a State of the Union Address right before they leave office in late January. President William Henry Harrison (1773–1841), the ninth president, did not give a State of the Union Address because he died 32 days after his inauguration. The only other president not to give a State of the Union Address was James Garfield (1831–1881), who was assassinated in his first year in office.

In 1982, President Ronald Reagan (1911–2004) started a tradition by acknowledging federal employee Lenny Skutnik (1953–), who was cheered for saving the life of Priscilla Tirado, a passenger on an airplane that had crash-landed in the icy Potomac River. Since Reagan's heartwarming gesture, subsequent presidents have honored a variety of humanitarians and other inspiriting figures. These individuals are sometimes called "the Lenny Skutniks." President Clinton pointed to civil rights heroine Rosa Parks (1913–2005), the woman who started the Montgomery Bus Boycott in the late 1950s by refusing to give up her seat to a white passenger.

Since 1966, there has been a tradition of a so-called "Opposition Response" to the president's State of the Union Address. This began when Senator Everett Dirksen (1896–1969) and Representative Gerald Ford, both Republicans, delivered a message contrary to the message offered by then Democratic president Lyndon Baines Johnson (1908–1973).

Can the president convene Congress?

Yes, presidents have the power under the Constitution to convene Congress—either house or both of them—on "extraordinary occasions." This usually occurs when the president has called on Congress to declare war, declare an emergency, or consider important appointments. U.S. Supreme Court justice Joseph Story (1779–1845) wrote in his influential *Commentaries on the Constitution of the United States* that "the power to convene congress on extraordinary occasions is indispensable to the proper operations, and even safety of the government." In 1948, President Harry Truman convened both houses of Congress to consider thorny questions of inflation and foreign aid.

It was more common in early American history for the president to convene Congress, or at least the Senate. President George Washington convened the Senate to consider several of his appointments. He also convened the Senate to consider the Jay Treaty.

The last clause grants the president the authority to adjourn Congress whenever the chambers cannot agree when to adjourn. Congress has agreed when to adjourn nearly all the time over the years. Thus, this is a presidential power that has never been exercised.

What is the Take Care Clause?

The Take Care Clause is one of the more controversial clauses in the Constitution in the sense that it is subject to widely varying interpretations. It has a Janus-like character (two-faced) because some view it primarily as a limitation on presidential power, while other scholars and historians view it as a major source of presidential power.

The limitation view interprets the clause as saying that the president should enforce the laws that Congress makes. In other words, the president must follow the directives of Congress in ensuring that the law is enforced. However, the more expansive view interprets the Clause as empowering the president to enforce federal law.

The Supreme Court has seemingly emphasized that the Take Care Clause means that the president cannot alter the law but has a constitutional obligation to make sure that the executive department follows the law. The Court at least implied this during its seminal opinion *Marbury v. Madison* (1803), when the Court reasoned that when the executive branch fails to enforce the law or perform a duty, that a person can file a writ of mandamus, ordering the executive official, even the president, to comply with the law.

The interpretation of the clause comes into focus, or becomes a major issue, when the executive branch decides not to enforce certain federal laws. For example, during the Obama administration, federal prosecutors were instructed not to enforce the Controlled Substances Act when it came to the criminalization of marijuana and not to enforce certain aspects of the nation's immigration laws. The Obama administration believed that marijuana should not be prosecuted, particularly when used for medicinal purposes. The administration also believed that the immigration laws should not be used to deport those individuals who came to the United States when they were children and had not run afoul of the criminal laws. These were examples of the executive branch exercising its prosecutorial discretion under the power of the Take Care Clause. Critics charged that it was an example of the executive branch flouting the will of Congress and a segment of the population. For example, Todd Garvey of the Congressional Research Service writes in a white paper that "some Members of Congress have asserted that these unilateral Presidential nonenforcement determinations upset the separation of powers, harm Congress as an institution and a coordinate branch of government, and are in direct violation of the President's constitutional obligation to 'take Care that the Laws be faithfully executed.'"

Does the Constitution mention executive orders?

Although President Trump (pictured) gave the appearance of signing a lot of executive orders, he only signed 220 during his time in office, fewer than many presidents. The record holder is Franklin D. Roosevelt, who issued 3,721, although he was in office for four terms, including during World War II, which necessitated such orders for quick action.

No, the Constitution does not mention executive orders, but presidents have utilized them sometimes quite extensively. All presidents except William Henry Harrison (who only served in office about 30 days) starting from George Washington to Joe Biden (1942–) have issued executive orders. It is considered a part of what is termed inherent presidential power. Much of that inherent power derives from the Take Care Clause.

Executive orders must derive either from one of the president's Congressional powers (such as the Take Care Clause) or from a statutory directive from Congress. In other words, its authority must stem from the Constitution or an act of Congress. Thus, an executive order can exceed the president's power if not rooted or closely connected to one of the president's Article II powers either singularly or in the aggregate, or at the direction of Congress. Like laws and statutes, the courts can review the constitutionality of executive orders. For example, the Supreme Court invalidated President Harry Truman's executive order that he issued seizing the nation's steel mills in *Youngstown Sheet & Tube Company v. Sawyer*.

Some presidential executive orders are quite famous or infamous in American history, such as President Franklin Delano Roosevelt's Executive Order 9066 in 1942, which created internment camps on American soil for Japanese American citizens or President Truman's Executive Order 9981 in 1948, which ordered the desegregation of the American armed forces. Truman contended that the authority for this executive order stemmed from his authority as commander in chief.

Presidents can sometimes modify or revise previous executive orders with new executive orders. This sometimes happens when a new president takes office and has fundamentally different policy ideas or preferences than his predecessor. Many believe that presidents have issued too many executive orders, arrogating themselves the ability to issue executive orders to address a wide range of issues. Cato Institute scholar Michael Tanner refers to it as "Presidents Gone Wild—with Executive Orders."

What is executive privilege?

Another power of the presidency not found in the Constitution is executive privilege—the ability of the president to keep secret conversations or written memos from advisors. Presidents have claimed the need for executive privilege to give and receive candid advice from advisors and members of the cabinet. Presidents also have claimed that executive privilege is necessary for national security issues.

Probably the most infamous example of executive privilege occurred in the wake of the Watergate scandal. In June 1972, a burglary occurred at the headquarters of the Democratic National Headquarters at the Watergate building in Washington, D.C. The burglars were connected to the Committee for the Re-election of the President, and it was eventually revealed that high-level White House officials were also involved. During Senate committee hearings, presidential aide Alexander Butterfield (1926–) revealed that there was a secret taping system in the White House. This caused Attorney General Elliot Richardson (1920–1999) to appoint a special prosecutor, Archibald Cox (1912–2004), to investigate.

Cox then issued a subpoena for the White House tapes, which President Richard Nixon (1913–1994) resisted on the grounds of

President Richard Nixon eventually had to relent and release the Watergate tapes after it became clear he could not protect himself with the argument that executive privilege gave him the right not to hand over evidence.

executive privilege. This led to Nixon demanding that Attorney General Richardson fire Cox. Richardson and his number two in command, William Ruckelshaus (1932–2019), refused to fire Cox and instead resigned from office in an event called "the Saturday Night Massacre."

Eventually, a new special prosecutor, Leon Jaworski (1905–1982), sought a grand jury indictment of several White House officials, and President Nixon was named an "unindicted co-conspirator." Jaworksi issued a subpoena duces tecum (a subpoena to produce documents) to hand over the tapes. Once again, Nixon claimed executive privilege and sought to quash the subpoena.

Ultimately, the case went to the U.S. Supreme Court, which unanimously ruled that the president did not have an absolute privilege to withhold the tapes. Chief Justice Warren Burger (1907–1995) wrote the opinion for the Court denying the privilege and ordering that the subpoena must be followed. Chief Justice Burger emphasized that the president's invocation of executive privilege was not tied to "military or diplomatic secrets"—areas that might justify executive privilege. Instead, the president's "generalized interest in confidentiality" was trumped by the particularized need for this evidence in a criminal case. Burger wrote that "the allowance of the privilege to withhold evidence that is demonstrably relevant in a criminal trial would cut deeply into the guarantee of due process of law and gravely impair the basic function of the courts." He concluded that the president's generalized interest in confidentiality "cannot prevail over the fundamental demands of due process of law in the fair administration of criminal justice."

What is Inauguration Day?

Inauguration Day marks the beginning of a president's new term. The Oath of Office is the main focus of the day and the only activity required by law. As mandated by the language in Article II, Section 1, the president-elect takes the oath and states: "I do solemnly swear (or affirm) that I will faithfully execute the office of President of the United States, and will to the best of my ability preserve, protect, and defend the Constitution of the United States."

George Washington added the words "so help me God," and most presidents have followed suit. President Washington also set the precedent of kissing the Bible after taking the oath, although not all presidents have followed this custom. Washington also followed his swearing-in with the nation's first inaugural address, a tradition most presidents have adopted. Since the early days of Washington, each president has added his own stamp on the day's events, so Inauguration Day reflects the personality and tastes of the incoming chief executive.

On what date is Inauguration Day held?

Inauguration Day originally took place on March 4, giving electors from each state nearly four months after Election Day to cast their ballots for president. In 1933, the Constitution's Twentieth Amendment officially changed the date to January 20 to expedite the change in presidential administrations. Franklin D. Roosevelt's second inauguration in 1937 was the first to take place on this new January 20 date.

What were the most memorable inaugural addresses?

To inspire Americans, inaugural addresses have been carefully composed and edited by presidents and their trusted advisors. Abraham Lincoln's (1809–1865) first inaugural address made no mention of the Republican Party platform, which clearly

President John F. Kennedy gave his inaugural address on January 21, 1961, which is remembered by many for his famous speech.

condemned slavery. Against a backdrop of succession and strife, Lincoln instead admonished listeners: "In your hands, my dissatisfied fellow-countrymen, and not in mine, is the momentous issue of civil war." Until the final draft, Lincoln's address had ended with a question for the South: "Shall it be peace or sword?" However, the famous concluding paragraph ended instead on a less contentious note: "We are not enemies, but friends." Lincoln's second inaugural address, in which he pled for peace and reconciliation, is considered among his best speeches. He called on Americans to "finish the work we're in, to bind up the nation's wounds."

John F. Kennedy's (1917–1963) 1961 inaugural address challenged Americans to live up to the nation's ideals and outlined his ideas for foreign policy. He famously concluded, "Ask not what your country can do for you—ask what you can do for your country." Kennedy's inauguration also included Robert

Frost (1874–1963) reading his poem "The Gift Outright." Thirty years later, Bill Clinton paid homage to Kennedy when he asked poet Maya Angelou (1928–2014) to read her poem "On the Pulse of Morning" at his 1993 inauguration.

Have presidents faced impeachment?

Yes, a few presidents have faced impeachment, which represents the ultimate check against the president and other civil officers of the United States. It is a crucial check to ensure that the president and other officials comport themselves within the confines of the law. As we read in the last chapter, Article I provides that the House has the sole power of impeachment, and impeachment trials are held in the Senate. Article I, Section 3, provides that "no Person shall be convicted without the Concurrence of two thirds of the Members present."

Impeachment has a long history in law. The English Parliament used the power of impeachment to police political offenses against the government. The American colonies also had impeachment as a tool at their disposal. It normally was confined to misconduct committed while in office.

A key textual question is: What are "high crimes and misdemeanors"? It is clear what treason and bribery are, but what rises to the level of such "high crimes and misdemeanors"? Some believe that this means the president must commit a felony-type offense that poses a grave threat to the security of the nation. Others take a much broader view as to what constitutes impeachable offenses.

There is no right to a jury trial in an impeachment proceeding. However, the president or other officials have a legal team that defends and presents evidence before the senators. The chief justice of the U.S. Supreme Court normally presides over these proceedings. The Senate has very broad discretion in setting the procedures to be used during the impeachment proceedings.

Four presidents have faced impeachment: Andrew Johnson (1808–1875), Richard Nixon (1913–1994), Bill Clinton (1946–), and Donald Trump (1946–). Johnson, who assumed the presidency after the assassination of Abraham Lincoln, was the first president to be impeached. Johnson got into hot water for firing Secretary of War Edwin Stanton (1814–1869) in violation of a federal law known as the Tenure in Office Act. Congress had passed this law to prevent Johnson, a Southerner, from firing members of Lincoln's cabinet. Though the Supreme Court declared the Tenure in Office Act unconstitutional, Congress still impeached Johnson, though he was not convicted in the Senate.

There was not another presidential impeachment situation until Richard Nixon. The House Judiciary Committee voted on articles of impeachment on Nixon, but the president resigned before the full House could take up the articles of impeachment.

On December 19, 1998, President Bill Clinton was impeached by the House for obstruction of justice and perjury. Clinton got into trouble after he allegedly lied during a deposition in a civil suit brought by Paula Jones (1966–), who alleged that Clinton had sexually harassed her when he was the governor of Arkansas. During a deposition in the civil case, Clinton told Jones's attorneys that he never had an extramarital affair with White House intern Monica Lewinsky (1973–) and that he did not have sex with her.

Attorney General Janet Reno (1938–2016) appointed Independent Counsel Kenneth Starr (1946–2022) to investigate whether Clinton lied in the deposition and the grand jury. The investigation also examined a wide variety of possible other misdeeds. This led to a behemoth report called "the Starr Report."

The House voted on two articles of impeachment against Clinton. In the Senate, Chief Justice William Rehnquist (1924–2005) presided over the impeachment trial. The Senate did not convict Clinton by the necessary two-thirds majority.

Then came the presidency of Donald J. Trump. The House impeached Trump twice—the first time in December 2019 and then again in January 2021. Each time, there were not enough votes in the Senate to convict Trump. The first impeachment of Donald Trump consisted of two articles: (1) abuse of power and (2) obstruction of Congress. The first impeachment began after there was some evidence that President Trump had enlisted foreign aid from Ukraine during his presidential reelection campaign for the 2020 election. The Senate acquitted Trump of both charges in February 2020. The votes were 48–52 and 47–53.

In an unprecedented move, the House once again impeached Trump on charges of "inciting an insurrection." The allegation was that President Trump had incited a riot on January 6 when he urged many of his supporters to march on the Capitol and make their voices heard. In the months following Trump's loss in the November 2020 election, he had said that the election was "rigged" and stolen by the Democrats. On January 6, Trump told a throng of people: "You don't concede when there's theft involved. Our country has had enough. We're not going to take it any more…. If you don't fight like hell, you're not going to have a country anymore."

While Trump never specifically told his supporters to storm the Capitol and cause a riot, House Democrats believed that he was responsible for fanning the flames of discontent that boiled over on January 6, 2021—the day Congress convened to certify the results of the presidential election—when a mob overran the Capitol and occupied the houses of Congress, committing acts of vandalism.

The second impeachment trial conducted in the Senate led to a final result of 57–43. While a majority of senators voted for the impeachment of President Trump, the vote fell ten votes short of the necessary two-thirds majority. Trump remained defiant after his second acquittal, calling the proceedings "the latest witch hunt in the history of our country."

On January 13, 2021, one week before President Trump left office, Speaker of the House Nancy Pelosi signed his second impeachment papers. Trump is the first U.S. president to have been impeached twice. On August 31, 2023, Trump was indicted for the charges described in this second impeachment—that is, incitement of an insurrection.

The second impeachment trial was unprecedented, as the trial in the Senate took place after President Trump already had left the presidency. Some argue that impeachment proceedings should extend only to those officials who are still in office, as the plain text of the Constitution reads "current officials" can be impeached, not former officials. Others argue that the impeachment process can continue once the official leaves office, as long as the impeachment is for conduct that the official committed while in office.

Ultimately, impeachment remains a highly partisan matter. All four of the presidents who faced impeachment served in highly partisan times.

HISTORIC PRESIDENTS

Who was the first president of the United States?

The first president of the United States was George Washington (1732–1799), who served two terms from 1789 to

George Washington was unanimously respected and admired by the American people for his leadership abilities as both a military commander and president.

1797. Washington is called "the Father of the Country" and was the near-universal choice of his contemporaries and the general public for the high office. This arose primarily because he was the leading American general during the Revolutionary War and is given much credit for the American colonists' successes against the British armed forces.

Washington served two terms as president and received all of the electoral votes in both elections—69 in the election of 1789 and 132 in the election of 1792. Nearly everyone agreed at the time that Washington was the right person to lead the country.

Why is Abraham Lincoln considered one of the greatest, if not *the* greatest, president?

Abraham Lincoln (1809–1865), the country's sixteenth president, is considered arguably the greatest president in history because he guided the country through the U.S. Civil War—the most divisive threat to the stability of the country in history. Many Southern states had seceded from the Union, and it took a bloody four-plus years' war to bring the nation back.

Lincoln also earned the nickname of "the Great Emancipator" because he issued an executive order in September 1862 called the Emancipation Proclamation. It announced his intention to free the slaves from states that had seceded from the Union. In the words of U.S. senator George McGovern of South Dakota (1922–2012) in his biography of Lincoln, the Emancipation Proclamation represented "the beginning of the end of slavery in the United States" and "changed the whole nature of the world."

Lincoln was also famous for some truly great speeches, such as the short Gettysburg Address, which he delivered on November 19,

Why was Franklin Delano Roosevelt considered one of the greatest U.S. presidents?

Franklin Delano Roosevelt (1882–1945), the nation's 32nd president, is considered near the top of the list of greatest U.S. presidents because of his leadership during the travails and tribulations of the Great Depression and World War II. He connected to the people with his famous "Fireside Chats," and he vigorously supported and advocated for various economic laws designed to bring relief and recovery to many of those in the country who were suffering. His leadership in World War II also places him in good stead historically, as he stood—along with British prime minister Winston Churchill (1874–1965)—as a strong leader during the dire threat posed by the Nazi Empire of Germany and its leader, Adolf Hitler (1889–1945).

1863, at the dedication at the Soldiers' National Cemetery in Gettysburg, Pennsylvania, the site of a famous Union victory in the Civil War several months earlier. Lincoln talked about the U.S. Civil War as a human struggle for equality. The address begins with the memorable words: "Four score and seven years ago our fathers brought forth on this continent a new nation, conceived in liberty, and dedicated to the proposition that all men are created equal." It is considered one of the greatest speeches in world history.

What was the New Deal?

The New Deal is the name given to a series of economic programs initiated by Franklin Roosevelt and his administration to improve the American economy that continued to be mired in the Great Depression. In his inaugural address, Roosevelt promised a "new deal" for the "forgotten people."

The New Deal focused on relief, recovery, and reform. It consisted of the creation of the Social Security system, the Federal Deposit Insurance Corporation, and the Civilian Conservation Corps, which gave jobs to many unemployed young men. Another law passed as part of the New Deal was the Fair Labor Standards Act of 1938, which provided better working conditions for laborers.

Roosevelt garnered popular support for many of his New Deal programs through a series of speeches to the American public known as "the Fireside Chats." Roosevelt gave 30 of these "chats" in 1933 and 1934. They contributed greatly to the popularity of the president and showcased his leadership skills.

Why is Thomas Jefferson generally considered a great president?

Thomas Jefferson (1743–1826), the nation's third president, who served from 1801 to 1809, was an effective leader during the early years of the nation's history and his presidency. He also greatly expanded the size of the nation with the famous "Louisiana Purchase" from France. Jefferson approved of this deal to acquire the French colony of Louisiana and the port city of New Orleans for commerce and defense purposes. The 15-million-dollar purchase nearly doubled the size of the United States at the time.

Jefferson also commissioned the exploration of the Western lands that became future territories of the United States by Meriwether Lewis (1774–1809) and William Clark (1770–1838). Their famous trip became known as the Lewis and Clark Expedition.

Jefferson was also famous for his authorship of the Declaration of Independence and for founding the University of Virginia.

What famous quote by a sitting president showed great respect for the incredible intellect of Jefferson?

President John F. Kennedy (1917–1963) told a group of 49 Nobel Peace Prize winners at the White House in 1962: "I think this is the most extraordinary collection of talent and human knowledge that has ever been gathered together at the White House—with the possible exception of when Thomas Jefferson dined alone."

What was historic about the election of Barack Obama?

Barack Obama (1961–), the nation's 44th president, was the first African American president in American history. Many viewed the election of Obama as a sign of racial progress and societal advancement in the United States.

Who was the first person to become president who was not elected to the office?

John Tyler (1790–1862), the tenth president of the United States, assumed the office of the presidency after the death of President William Henry Harrison (1773–1841), who sadly died

Formerly governor of Virginia, John Tyler was vice president under President William Henry Harrison and succeeded him when Harrison died in office.

shortly after he assumed office. Tyler, as the sitting vice president, then assumed the office. He served out the remainder of the term from the years 1841 to 1845. Critics lampooned Tyler as "His Accidency" for the way that he assumed the presidency following the death of Harrison.

What other persons became president without winning a presidential election?

In addition to John Tyler, there were five other presidents who assumed the office without ever winning a presidential election. Vice President Millard Fillmore (1800–1874) assumed the office after President Zachary Taylor (1784–1850) died in office in 1850. Vice President Andrew Johnson (1808–1875) became president in 1865 following the assassination of President Abraham Lincoln. Similarly, Vice President Chester A. Arthur (1829–1886) became president following the assassination of President James Garfield (1831–1881) in 1881; Vice President Theodore Roosevelt became president after President William McKinley (1843–1901) was assassinated. Finally, Vice President Gerald Ford (1913–2006) became president following the resignation of President Richard Nixon (1913–1994) in 1974.

Who was the youngest person to serve as president?

Theodore Roosevelt (1858–1919) was only 42 years old when he assumed the presidency in 1901 following the assassination of President William McKinley (1843–1901). Roosevelt was subsequently reelected to another term. President John F. Kennedy was the youngest elected president, taking office at the age of 43 after defeating Richard Nixon in 1960.

What was unusual about President Donald J. Trump's prior experience before being elected president?

President Donald J. Trump (1946–), the nation's 45th president, is the only president to never hold any sort of public or elected office before becoming president. Instead, Trump was a television star, real estate magnate, casino owner, and was involved in other private business interests.

The Judicial Branch

What federal courts does the Constitution call for?

The U.S. Constitution provides that there shall be "one supreme court" and such "inferior courts" as Congress deems necessary. This means that it is the job of Congress to create the lower federal courts.

How was the U.S. Supreme Court created?

Article III, Section 1, of the U.S. Constitution provided that "the judicial Power of the United States, shall be vested in one supreme Court, and in such inferior Courts the Congress may from time to time ordain and establish." The Constitution was adopted in 1787 and ratified in 1788. However, the Constitution did not create the U.S. Supreme Court.

Instead, the Court was created by Congress passing the Judiciary Act of 1789, which established the Court's jurisdiction. The Judiciary Act of 1789 called for six justices on the Court—a chief justice and five associate justices.

Why is the Judiciary Act of 1789 so important?

This law is so important because it created the federal judicial system in the United States. Justice Sandra Day O'Connor (1930–2023), in her book *The Majesty of the Law: Reflections of a Supreme Court Justice,* writes that the Judiciary Act of 1789 "stands as the single most important legislative enactment of the nation's founding years."

Who was the principal author of the Judiciary Act of 1789?

One of the Framers of the Constitution and a senator from Connecticut, Oliver Ellsworth was the principal author of the Judiciary Act and, later, the third chief justice of the U.S. Supreme Court.

Oliver Ellsworth (1745–1807) of Connecticut was the principal author of the Judiciary Act of 1789. A member of the Philadelphia Convention in 1787, Ellsworth became a U.S senator when the Senate first convened in 1789. He was elected chair of the committee designed to follow the dictates of Article III of the new Constitution to create a federal judiciary. William Paterson (1745–1806) from New Jersey, another member of the 1787 Convention, also assisted in the drafting of the Judiciary Act of 1789.

Both Ellsworth and Paterson later became justices on the U.S. Supreme Court.

What type of federal court system did Congress create in the Judiciary Act of 1789?

Congress created a three-tiered system of federal courts. At the bottom level were federal district court judges. The next level—the intermediate level—are the federal circuit courts of appeals. Finally, there is the highest court, the U.S. Supreme Court.

Today, we still have this three-tiered system of federal courts. There are 94 different federal judicial districts, 13 federal courts of appeals, and one U.S. Supreme Court.

What are the 13 different federal courts of appeals?

There are 11 numbered circuits from the First Circuit to the Eleventh Circuit, the D.C. Circuit, and the Federal Circuit. The Federal Circuit is a bit different from the other federal courts of appeals, as it hears specialized cases, such as patent cases.

Does Article III of the Constitution call for a chief justice?

Ironically, Article III of the Constitution does not mention a chief justice at all. It only mentions that there will be "one supreme court." However, Article I, Section 3, mentions a "Chief Justice" when talking about the impeachment of a president. It reads: "When the President of the United States is tried, the Chief Justice shall preside."

Under the Constitution, who appoints Supreme Court justices?

The Constitution provides that the president has the power to appoint "Judges of the Supreme Court." Article II, Section 2, says that the president has the power to appoint Supreme Court justices and other federal judges but that it shall be done "with the Advice and Consent of the Senate." Thus, the president nominates Supreme Court justices and the U.S. Senate, then confirms or denies the selection.

DID YOU KNOW?

Which Founding Father first proposed how justices would obtain their positions?

Nathaniel Gorham (1738–1796), one of the two Massachusetts members of the Constitutional Convention of 1787 that created the Constitution, first proposed the idea that the president should nominate the justices and the Senate should confirm them. Gorham never served as a federal judge, but he did serve one term as a judge of the Middlesex County Court of Common Pleas.

Does the Constitution explicitly give the power of judicial review to the judiciary?

No, the U.S. Constitution does not mention the concept of judicial review, which is the concept that the judicial branch has the power to declare acts of the legislative and executive branches of government unconstitutional. It is the power of judicial review that gives the U.S. Supreme Court the power to strike down federal and state laws that violate some aspect of the Constitution.

Many Framers assumed that the Court would have the power to declare laws unconstitutional, but it is not specifically mentioned in the Constitution. Several lower courts asserted the judiciary's power of judicial review and, most famously, Chief Justice John Marshall (1755–1835) clearly established the power of judicial review when he wrote in *Marbury v. Madison* (1803): "It is emphatically the province of the judicial department to declare what the law is."

What other provision of the Constitution implies a power of judicial review?

The Supremacy Clause of the Constitution, found in Article VI of the Constitution, provides support for the concept of judicial review—at least according to some legal historians and scholars. Chief Justice John Marshall cited the Supremacy Clause in his *Marbury v. Madison* opinion, writing:

> It also is not entirely unworthy of observation that in declaring what shall be the supreme law of the land, the constitution itself is first mentioned; and

not the laws of the United States generally, but those only when shall be made in pursuance of the constitution, have that rank.

Thus, the particular phraseology of the Constitution of the United States confirms and strengthens the principle, supposed to be essential to all written Constitutions, that a law repugnant to the Constitution is void and that courts, as well as other departments, are bound by that instrument.

What does the Supremacy Clause say?

The Supremacy Clause reads: "This Constitution, and the Laws of the United States which shall be made in Pursuance thereof; and all Treaties made, or which shall be under the Authority of the United States, shall be the supreme Law of the Land and the Judges in every State shall be bound thereby, any Thing in the Constitution or Laws of any State to the Contrary Notwithstanding."

It means that federal law is supreme over state law. This concept is often called preemption.

What does Article III say about life tenure for federal judges?

Article III in effect provides life tenure for federal judges. It does not set a time limit but says that federal judges "shall hold their Offices during good behavior." Article III, Section 4, provides for the removal of "all civil Officers of the United States ...

on Impeachment for, and Conviction of, Treason, Bribery, or other high Crimes and Misdemeanors."

The Framers of the Constitution gave life tenure to federal judges to ensure an independent judiciary, a judiciary that would not bow to the political pressures of the day. Federal judges often have had to make difficult decisions that a significant segment of the public may question quite critically. For this very reason, Alexander Hamilton (1755–1804) wrote in #78 of the Federalist Papers that "the complete independence of the courts of justice is peculiarly essential in a limited Constitution."

Hamilton added:

> If then the courts are to be considered as the bulwarks of a limited constitution against legislative encroachments, this consideration will afford a strong argument for the permanent tenure of judicial officers, since nothing will contribute so much as this to the independent spirit of judges, which must be essential to the faithful performance of so arduous a duty.

Can Supreme Court justices be impeached?

Yes, federal judges—including U.S. Supreme Court justices—can be impeached. The Constitution provides that federal judges "shall hold their Offices during good behavior." They can be impeached for "treason, bribery, or other high crimes and misdemeanors." This means that federal judges, and Supreme Court justices, who receive lifetime appointments can theoretically be removed for really bad behavior.

Have any Supreme Court justices been impeached?

Justice Samuel Chase (1741–1811), who signed the Declaration of Independence and served as the chief judge of Maryland's highest state court, was impeached by the U.S. House of Representatives but not convicted in the Senate.

The U.S. Constitution gives the U.S. House of Representatives the "sole power of Impeachment" and the U.S. Senate "the sole Power to try all impeachments." It takes a two-thirds majority vote in the Senate for someone to be impeached and removed from office.

Chase landed into trouble on the Supreme Court for his conduct during the sedition trial of journalist James Callender

Samuel Chase was a Founding Father, a representative of Maryland, and then an associate justice of the Supreme Court. He was the first justice to be impeached, but he was eventually acquitted.

(1758–1803). Chase apparently conducted himself in a very partisan manner during this trial. Chase also attacked President Thomas Jefferson (1743–1826), saying the president had engaged in "seditious attacks on the principles of the Constitution." Alfred H. Knight wrote in his book *The Wizards of Washington: Triumphs and Travesties of the United States Supreme Court*: "As a target for impeachment and removal, the eccentric Federalist Chase was the answer to a partisan Republican's prayer."

The House of Representatives impeached Chase 72–32 on eight charges in March 1804. However, the Senate acquitted Chase with only a 19–15 vote for conviction on the closest count—but still short of the necessary two-thirds majority, or 24 votes.

Many view the acquittal of Justice Chase as essential to the principle of an independent judiciary.

What justice in modern charges faced an impeachment threat?

Justice William O. Douglas (1898–1980), who served on the Court from 1939 to 1975, faced an impeachment threat in April 1970 when House leader Gerald Ford (1913–2006), a future president, called for the impeachment of Justice Douglas. Ford said that Douglas "was unfit" and "should be removed." He also said that "an impeachable offense is whatever a majority of the House of Representatives considers it to be at a given moment in history."

Several House Democrats responded that such an attempt was "an attack on the integrity and the independence of the United States Supreme Court." Critics charged that Douglas had a connection with the Parvin Foundation. Others criticized his book *Points of Rebellion*, which critics charged fomented youth activists at the time. Others criticized the fact that he had published an article on folk singing that was published by Ralph Ginzburg (1929–2006), who had a pornography case before the U.S. Supreme Court.

Justice Hugo Black (1886–1971) was incensed at the attack on his longtime colleague. According to Bruce Murphy in his biography of Douglas, *Wild Bill*, Black told a group of southern congressmen: "I have known Bill Douglas for thirty years. He's never knowingly done any improper, unethical, or corrupt thing. Tell his detractors that in spite of my age, I think I have one trial left in me. Tell them that if they move against Bill Douglas, I'll resign from the Court and represent him. It will be the biggest, most important case I ever tried."

What happened with the Douglas impeachment effort?

After a six-month investigation, on December 15, 1970, the Impeachment Subcommittee of the Judiciary Committee ruled by a three-to-one vote that there was not substantial grounds for impeachment. Three Democrats voted against impeachment: Emanuel Celler (1888–1981) of New York, Byron G. Rogers (1900–1983) of Colorado, and Jack Brooks (1922–2012) of Texas. One Republican dissented, J. Edward Hutchinson (1914–1985) from Michigan. The other Republican on the subcommittee, William M. McCullough (1901–1980) of Ohio, declined to vote cither way. Douglas told the press after learning of the subcommittee's report: "The Select Committee has now performed its constitutional duties and I will try to continue to perform mine."

Where did the Supreme Court first meet?

The Court met in the Royal Exchange Building on Broad Street in New York City on February 2, 1790. The Court met on the second floor of the building in the afternoons, as the New York

What greeting does the marshal announce when the Court comes into session?

When the Court comes into session, the marshal announces: "Oyez! Oyez! Oyez! All persons having business before the Honorable, the Supreme Court of the United States, are admonished to draw near and give their attention, for the Court is now sitting. God save the United States and this Honorable Court."

state legislature met in the room during the morning hours. The Court met in New York for only one year, meeting in Philadelphia the next year.

Why did many early U.S. Supreme Court justices quit the job?

Many early justices left the job after only a short time because they did not enjoy the practice of circuit-riding. Under the early system, U.S. Supreme Court justices had to "ride circuit," meaning that they had to travel to hear appeals on circuit courts. These appeals consisted of one Supreme Court justice and two district court judges. Twice a year, the Supreme Court justices had to engage in this practice. Justice James Iredell (1751–1799) referred to himself as a "traveling postboy." Justice Thomas Johnson (1732–1819) went even further in his opposition—he simply quit the job.

When the capital moved to Washington, D.C., where did the Supreme Court meet?

When the capital moved from New York City to Washington, D.C., so did the U.S. Supreme Court. The problem was that it did not have a permanent home. From 1801 to 1809, the justices met in different rooms in the basement of the Capitol building. In 1810, the Court also met at Long's Tavern. In 1810, the Court met in a specific room in the Capitol.

In what rented home did the Court meet after the Capitol was burned?

In 1815 and 1816, the U.S. Supreme Court met in Bell's Tavern, a rented home. The Court had to meet there because the Capitol building was burned to the ground by the British during the War of 1812.

When did the Court meet in the old Senate chamber?

The Supreme Court met in the old Senate chamber, on the first floor of the Capitol building, from 1860 until 1935, when it moved into its own building—the Supreme Court Building, where it holds Court today.

When did the Court require attorneys to file written briefs?

In 1821, the Supreme Court began requiring attorneys to file written briefs before the Court. Now, that is customary. Since 2007, attorneys have been required to file their briefs both electronically and in print.

What is the nickname of the Supreme Court Building?

The nickname of the building is the Marble Palace because white marble represents the primary material used in the building. According to the Supreme Court's own website, $3 million worth of marble was used in its construction. Famous attorney

Completed in 1935, the Supreme Court Building was designed by architect Cass Gilbert.

and scholar John Paul Frank (1917–2002) published a book about the U.S. Supreme Court in 1958 entitled *Marble Palace: The Supreme Court in American Life.*

What famous cases did John Paul Frank argue before the Court?

In addition to being a Supreme Court scholar, John Paul Frank was a first-rate attorney. He represented Ernesto Miranda (1941–1976) in the famous *Miranda v. Arizona* case decided by the Warren Court in 1966. In *Miranda*, the Court declared that police must give suspects warnings before placing them under arrest and in custodial interrogation. Frank also argued for the Arizona State Bar in the attorney advertising case *Bates v. State Bar of Arizona* (1977). In that decision, the Court ruled that Arizona attorneys John Bates and Van O'Steen (1946–) had a First Amendment right to publish a newspaper ad publicizing their prices for routine, low-cost legal services.

Is the police's failure to read Miranda rights itself a violation of the Fifth Amendment?

The U.S. Supreme Court ruled in *Vega v. Tekoh* (2022) that the police's failure to read a suspect his Miranda rights is not in and of itself a Fifth Amendment violation. Instead, the Court reasoned that *Miranda* and subsequent cases established a prophylactic rule instead of something that is absolutely mandated by the Constitution. A prophylactic rule is one that is judicially created and is not necessarily required by the Constitution.

In this context, the U.S. Supreme Court majority in *Vega v. Tekoh* used that description of *Miranda* as a prophylactic rule to mean that just because the police fail to read a suspect his Miranda rights it does not mean that the suspect can then turn around and sue the police officer for a violation of his Fifth Amendment right to be free from compelled self-incrimination.

The case itself involved a police officer named Carlos Vega, who interrogated Terence Tekoh, a certified nursing assistant, over allegedly inappropriately touching a female patient. After the interrogation, Tekoh apparently confessed but had not been read his Miranda rights. After a first trial ended in a mistrial, a second jury found Tekoh not guilty. Tekoh then sued Vega for a violation of his First Amendment rights. The specific legal question that came up during this civil rights trial was Vega's failure to adhere to *Miranda:* Did that failure establish a Fifth Amendment violation?

Ultimately, the U.S. Supreme Court said no. Writing for the majority, Justice Samuel Alito concluded: "In sum, a violation of *Miranda* does not necessarily constitute a violation of the Constitution, and therefore such a violation does not constitute the deprivation" of a constitutional right.

Justice Elena Kagan wrote a dissenting opinion in which she stressed that the Court's 1966 ruling in *Miranda* derives from the Constitution.

Who was the architect of the new Supreme Court Building?

Cass Gilbert (1859–1934), who also designed the Customs House and the U.S. Chamber of Commerce Building in Washington, D.C., was the architect of the new Supreme Court Building. Unfortunately, Gilbert died before the completion of the building, which was then handled by his son, Cass Gilbert Jr. (1894–1975).

DID YOU KNOW?

THE TERM

When does the U.S. Supreme Court meet?

The U.S. Supreme Court convenes the first Monday of October for the start of its new term. The Court's term usually ends at the end of June. Federal law, codified at 28 U.S.C. §2, provides: "The Supreme Court shall hold at the seat of government a term of court commencing on the first Monday in October of each year and may hold such adjourned or special terms as may be necessary."

When did the Court first begin its terms on the first Monday of October?

The U.S. Supreme Court first began its term on the first Monday in October 1917. Congress had passed a law effectuating such a change in a 1916 statute. In the mid-nineteenth century, the Court was beginning its term in December and meeting through March. However, the Court's docket exploded in growth, as the Court was hearing many more cases. To accommodate this expanding docket, Congress allowed the Court in 1866 to set its own starting point for its terms. The Court moved its starting time to October. In 1873, Congress formalized this development by passing a law that moved the Court's term from the first Monday in December to the second Monday in October. It remained there until 1917.

When did the Court originally begin its new terms?

The Judiciary Act of 1789 provided that the Court's terms shall begin the first Monday of February and the first Monday of August. The first meeting of the Court occurred on February 2, 1790.

When does the Court generally conclude its work?

The Supreme Court usually finishes all its opinions by the end of June. It is quite rare for a Supreme Court opinion to be released after June 30.

Does the Court ever meet outside of its traditional term time?

Yes, the Court sometimes holds special sessions in important cases. For example, the Court held a special session on July 19, 1942, to hear the case of *Ex parte Quirin* to determine whether alleged German saboteurs were entitled to a federal habeas corpus review of their military commission convictions. More recently, the Court called a special session to hear the case of *McConnell v. Federal Election Commission* in September 2003. The case involved a major First Amendment challenge to the Bipartisan Campaign Reform Act, a federal law restricting soft money spending and other funding restrictions in political elections.

PROCESSES

How is a case brought to the U.S. Supreme Court?

The U.S. Supreme Court has discretionary jurisdiction over the vast majority of cases, at least since 1925, when Congress passed the Judiciary Act of 1925. This means that most cases originate in the lower courts and the U.S. Supreme Court does not have to review the lower court's decision unless it decides to grant certiorari, or review.

In more than 90 percent of the Court's cases, the party asking the Court to hear the case, the petitioner, petitions the court for review in a document called a petition for writ of certiorari. The opposing party, called the respondent, then responds in a document asking the Court not to accept the case for review. The Court then decides whether the case is "certworthy," or acceptable for review.

The briefs filed during the certiorari phase are sometimes called "the cert briefs." If the Court grants review, then each side files another brief. These are briefs on the merits, or "merit briefs."

The term *brief* is a bit of a misnomer. These legal documents are not short. Oftentimes, they are around 50 pages long, often much longer if you count pages in an appendix.

The Courtroom of the U.S. Supreme Court. The photo was taken in 2020, and the fourth chair from the right is draped in black to honor the late Justice Ruth Bader Ginsburg.

What determines if the U.S. Supreme Court will hear a case?

The Supreme Court has discretionary jurisdiction, which means that in the vast majority of cases, the Court has discretion whether or not it will hear a particular case. The Court only hears 80 out of 8,000 cases each term, so the chances for review in any particular case are extremely small.

However, the Court has provided "consideration" for cases that it might take in Rule 10 of its Supreme Court Rules.

Rule 10 provides:

Considerations governing review on writ of certiorari: Review on a writ of certiorari is not a matter of right, but of judicial discretion. A petition for a writ of certiorari will be granted only for compelling reasons. The following, although neither controlling nor fully measuring the Court's discretion, indicate the character of the reasons the Court considers:

(a) a United States court of appeals has entered a decision in conflict with the decision of another United States court of appeals on the same important matter; has decided an important federal question in a way that conflicts with a decision by a state court of last resort; or has so far departed from the accepted and usual course of judicial proceedings, or sanctioned such a departure by a lower court, as to call for an exercise of this Court's supervisory power;

(b) a state court of last resort has decided an important federal question in a way that conflicts with the decision of another state court of last resort or of a United States court of appeals;

(c) a state court or a United States court of appeals has decided an important question of federal law that has not been, but should be, settled by this Court, or has decided an important federal question in a way that conflicts with relevant decisions of this Court.

What is the importance of circuit splits?

Even experienced Court observers warn there is no way to predict with great accuracy when the U.S. Supreme Court will agree to hear a case. However, one of the best predictors is when a case presents an issue that divides the lower federal appeals courts. This is called a circuit split. Rule 10(a) of the Rules of the Supreme Court identifies as an important consideration when a federal appeals court decision conflicts with another federal appeals court decision.

A circuit split means that there is a different interpretation or ruling by different circuit courts of appeals. For example, let's say that on a key Fourth Amendment issue, the Sixth Circuit and the Ninth Circuit disagree. Because the Sixth Circuit and Ninth Circuit have ruled differently on this issue, there is a classic circuit split.

What are circuit assignments?

Sometimes, litigants will seek an immediate stay of a lower court ruling before a particular Supreme Court justice. The circuits are divided among the nine justices for them to consider these emergency applications. As of September 28, 2022, the Supreme Court's own website identifies the circuit assignments as follows:

Chief Justice John Roberts Jr. oversees the District of Columbia, the Fourth Circuit, and the Federal Circuit.

- District of Columbia Circuit—John G. Roberts Jr., Chief Justice

- First Circuit—Ketanji Brown Jackson, Associate Justice (Maine, Massachusetts, New Hampshire, Puerto Rico, Rhode Island)

- Second Circuit—Sonia Sotomayor, Associate Justice (Connecticut, New York, Vermont)

- Third Circuit—Samuel A. Alito Jr., Associate Justice (Delaware, New Jersey, Pennsylvania, Virgin Islands)

- Fourth Circuit—John G. Roberts Jr., Chief Justice (Maryland, North Carolina, South Carolina, West Virginia, Virginia)

- Fifth Circuit—Samuel A. Alito Jr., Associate Justice (Louisiana, Mississippi, Texas)

- Sixth Circuit—Brett M. Kavanaugh, Associate Justice (Kentucky, Michigan, Ohio, Tennessee)

- Seventh Circuit—Amy Coney Barrett, Associate Justice (Illinois, Indiana, Wisconsin)

- Eighth Circuit—Brett M. Kavanaugh, Associate Justice (Arkansas, Iowa, Minnesota, Missouri, Nebraska, North Dakota, South Dakota)

- Ninth Circuit—Elena Kagan, Associate Justice (Alaska, Arizona, California, Guam, Hawaii, Idaho, Oregon, Montana, Nevada, Northern Mariana Islands, Washington)

- Tenth Circuit—Neil M. Gorsuch, Associate Justice (Colorado, Kansas, New Mexico, Oklahoma, Utah, Wyoming)

- Eleventh Circuit—Clarence Thomas, Associate Justice (Alabama, Florida, Georgia)

- Federal Circuit—John G. Roberts Jr., Chief Justice

What is the discuss list?

The discuss list refers to a group of cases that the justices, primarily the chief justice, determine are cases worthy of discussion in the Court's focus at conference meetings. If a case makes the discuss list, it has a far better chance of being accepted for review.

On September 27, 2001, in a lecture at the University of Guanajuato in Mexico, Chief Justice William Rehnquist (1924–2005) spoke about the Court's discuss list, stating: "Shortly before each conference, I send out a list of the petitions to be decided during that conference that I want to discuss. Each of the other Justices may ask to have additional cases put on the discuss list. If at any particular conference there are 100 petitions to be decided, there may be anywhere from 15 to 30 that are on the discuss list. The petitions for certiorari that are not discussed are denied without any recorded vote."

What is the rule of four?

The rule of four refers to a Supreme Court practice that the Court will hear a case if four justices agree the case is certworthy, or worthy of being reviewed. The practice has been in existence since at least 1924.

DID YOU KNOW!?

Where do the justices decide whether to accept a case for review?

The justices decide which cases they will decide in their weekly meetings in conference. These meetings take place in the Conference Room in the Supreme Court building. Only the nine justices attend these conference meetings; law clerks and other personnel are not allowed to attend. If someone knocks on the door, the most junior justice must answer the door.

The chief justice normally begins the meetings by bringing up the cases on the "discuss list." The chief justice then speaks about particular cases and whether he or she believes the case should be reviewed. The customary practice is that each of the justices speaks in order of seniority. Each justice briefly states his position on the case and which way she or he is leaning in terms of voting.

When the Court decides to hear a case, what happens next?

The Court informs the clerk of the Court, who must then schedule oral argument. Under Rule 25, the petitioner then must draft a written document called a brief within 45 days of the Court's order that it has accepted the case. The respondent then has 30 days from the date of the petitioner's filing to file its response brief. The petitioner may then file a reply brief as long as it is filed more than one week before oral argument.

What is oral argument?

Oral argument is the process by which attorneys come before the U.S. Supreme Court and present their case. The attorneys face questioning about the case from the individual justices. Rule 28 provides that generally, each side is given 30 minutes for argument. The petitioner presents first, and then the respondent follows. The petitioner can reserve some time for rebuttal after the respondent's argument. Oral argument is important because it offers the advocates the only time with which to interact with the justices and persuade them to their points of view.

The justices vary in how much they question the attorney-advocates. Justice Antonin Scalia (1936–2016) was known for being quite vocal at oral argument, firing many questions at the attorneys. On the current Court, Justice Sonia Sotomayor (1954–) also is a very active questioner. On the other hand, Justice Clarence Thomas (1948–) is normally quite reticent at oral argument. In most cases, he does not ask a single question.

Justice Sonia Sotomayor is known for being a very active questioner during oral arguments before the Supreme Court.

What does Rule 28 say about oral argument?

Rule 28 provides: "Oral Argument should emphasize and clarify the written arguments in the briefs on the merits. Counsel should assume that all Justices have read the briefs before oral argument. Oral argument read from a prepared text is not favored.

"Unless the Court directs otherwise, each side is allowed one-half hour for argument. Counsel is not required to use all the allotted time.

"Regardless of the number of counsel participating in oral argument, counsel making the opening argument shall present the case fairly and completely and not reserve points of substance for rebuttal."

What types of attorneys argue cases before the U.S. Supreme Court?

Most lawyers never argue a case before the U.S. Supreme Court. Some attorneys practice regularly before the U.S. Supreme Court as members of the Supreme Court Bar. The great Daniel Webster (1782–1852), a U.S. congressman and attorney from Massachusetts, argued nearly 250 cases before the U.S. Supreme Court. He was involved in many landmark decisions, such as *Dartmouth College v. Woodward* (1819), *Gibbons v. Ogden* (1824), and *Charles River Bridge v. Warren Bridge* (1837). John William Davis (1873–1955), a U.S. congressman from West Virginia, solicitor general, and Democratic nominee for president in 1924, argued 140 cases before the U.S. Supreme Court, including *Youngstown Sheet and Tube Co. v. Sawyer* (1952) and *Brown v. Board of Education* (1954).

In more modern times, Tom Goldstein (1970–) of Goldstein & Howe argued 45 cases before the U.S. Supreme Court by the time he was in his early 30s. His practice consists nearly entirely of U.S. Supreme Court cases.

Those who serve as solicitor general, a position appointed by the president to argue for the United States, naturally argue many more cases than even those members of the Supreme Court Bar who argue regular cases.

When does the Court hear oral arguments?

The Court generally hears oral arguments two weeks of every month from October through April. During the weeks of oral argument, the Court hears cases from 10:00 A.M. to 12:00 P.M. Eastern Standard Time on Monday, Tuesday, and Wednesday.

After oral argument, when does the Court decide the case?

The Court meets in conference to discuss their initial votes in the case. The Court discusses the cases argued on Monday in its Wednesday afternoon conference meeting. For the cases argued on Tuesday and Wednesday, the Court discusses them in its Friday conference meeting.

The chief justice opens the discussions, outlining the applicable law and facts and their views of the case. This practice extends to all the justices in order of seniority. The justices also discuss how they plan to decide the case. The chief justice announces the vote. If the chief justice is in the majority, they assign who will write the majority opinion for the Court. If the chief justice is in the minority, the most senior justice in the majority makes the opinion assignments.

There is no specific timetable for when the Court will issue its opinions, though in nearly all cases, the Court will issue a decision by the end of June. In a few cases, however, the Court will not issue an opinion and ask for reargument. For example, the Roberts Court ordered reargument in 2006 in the case of *Garcetti v. Ceballos*, a highly watched case involving the free-speech rights of public employees.

Has the oral argument rule always provided for 30 minutes to each side?

No, the oral argument has not always been 30 minutes. In fact, oral arguments used to take several days in some cases. Many of the justices chafed under the process of hearing lawyers give speeches hour upon hour. In 1849, the Court adopted Rule 53, which set the time limit for each attorney at two hours. If attorneys wished to argue longer than two hours, they had to petition for special permission. In 1925, the Court limited the argument time to one hour on each side. The Court said this change was "due to the crowded calendar of the Court." In 1970, the Court changed its rules again, limiting each side to the present-day requirement of 30 minutes each.

What are the different types of opinions?

There are several different types of opinions, including majority, plurality, concurring, and dissenting opinions. There are also so-called per curiam opinions.

- A *majority opinion* is one that must have a majority of the Court sign on to it, namely five of nine justices. This opinion is the ruling of the Court. It stands as precedent for future cases. If all justices vote with the majority, the opinion is said to be a unanimous opinion.

- A *plurality opinion* is the main opinion of the Court but one that fails to command a majority of the justices. For instance, a case may have four justices agreeing with one opinion, two justices who file concurring opinions but not joining the other four, and three justices in dissent. In this 4–2–3 split, there is no majority opinion. However, the opinion of four, the plurality opinion, is the one that stands as the ruling of the Court.

- A *concurring opinion* is an opinion that agrees with the result but not the reasoning of the majority or main opinion of the Court. A justice who writes a concurring opinion may want to emphasize particular points of law or simply indicate that the main opinion reached the right result by taking the wrong path.

- A *dissenting opinion* is an opinion that disagrees with the result of the majority opinion.

- A *per curiam* opinion is an opinion rendered by the Court, or a majority of the Court, collectively instead of by a single justice.

If the majority opinion becomes the law of the land, are concurring and dissenting opinions important?

Yes, concurring and even dissenting opinions can be important. Sometimes, the law will develop such that a concurring opinion will actually become the guidepost for future decisions in the area. A classic example was Justice John Marshall Harlan II's (1899–1971) concurring opinion in the Fourth Amendment case *Katz v. United States* (1967). While Justice Potter Stewart (1915–1985) wrote the Court's majority opinion, Harlan's concurring opinion created the "reasonable expectation of privacy" test that has become the opinion relied on by the majority of lower courts.

Similarly, dissenting opinions can be important, particularly if the U.S. Supreme Court overrules itself in a particular area of the law. A classic example of a dissenting opinion that became the law of the land was Justice Hugo Black's (1886–1971) dissenting opinion in the Sixth Amendment right to counsel case of *Betts v. Brady* (1942). The majority in *Betts* ruled that state courts did not have to provide an attorney to all indigent defendants charged with felonies in non–death penalty cases. However, the Court overruled that decision 21 years later in *Gideon v. Wainwright* (1963) and, in a remarkable irony, Justice Black had the honor of writing the unanimous opinion for the Court, taking the same position that he took in dissent in *Betts*.

What are amicus briefs?

Amicus, or friend of the court, briefs are briefs filed by interested non-parties who wish to emphasize particular aspects of a case and stress its importance to the Court. Amicus briefs are a regular staple of U.S. Supreme Court practice, particularly in important, high-profile decisions. For example, approximately 90 amicus briefs were filed before the Court in the affirmative action in education cases of *Grutter v. Bollinger* and *Gratz v. Bollinger*.

But even that pales in comparison to the recent abortion decision, *Dobbs v. Jackson Women's Health Organization* (2022), as there were more than 140 amicus briefs filed in that decision.

DID YOU KNOW!?

What rule speaks of amicus briefs?

Rule 37 of the Supreme Court Rules addresses amicus briefs. It states that "an amicus curiae brief that brings to the attention of the Court relevant matter not already brought to its attention by the parties may be of considerable help to the Court. An amicus curiae brief that does not serve this purpose burdens the Court, and its filing is not favored. An amicus curiae brief may be filed only by an attorney admitted to practice before this Court as provided in Rule 5."

Sometimes, the justices seem to consider certain amicus briefs as very significant and persuasive. For example, Chief Justice William Rehnquist (1924–2005) cited the amicus brief of the Association of American Editorial Cartoonists written by attorney Roslyn Mazer (1949–) in his unanimous opinion for the Court in the celebrated First Amendment decision in *Hustler Magazine v. Falwell* (1988).

PERSONNEL

What is the reporter of the Supreme Court?

The reporter of decisions is the individual responsible for compiling the U.S. Supreme Court decisions into the *United States Reports*, the official compilation of U.S. Supreme Court opinions. There have been 16 reporters in the history of the Court. They include:

Alexander J. Dallas (1759–1817) was the first to serve as U.S. Supreme Court reporter. He went on to be secretary of the treasury from 1814 to 1816 and secretary of war in 1815.

Reporter	Years Worked
Alexander J. Dallas	1790–1800
William Cranch	1801–1815
Henry Wheaton	1816–1827
Richard Peters	1828–1842
Benjamin Howard	1843–1860
Jeremiah Black	1861–1862
John Wallace	1863–1874
William Otto	1875–1883
John Davis	1883–1902
Charles Butler	1902–1916
Ernest Knaebel	1916–1944
Walter Wyatt	1946–1963
Henry Putzel Jr.	1964–1979
Henry Curtis Lind	1979–1987
Frank D. Wagner	1987–2010
Christine Luchok Fallon	2011–2020
Rebecca Anne Womeldorf	2021–present

What is the background of the reporter?

The reporter is an attorney with an impressive background. For example, the current reporter, Rebecca Anne Womeldorf, graduated from law school summa cum laude and clerked for both Justices Lewis Powell Jr. (1907–1998) and Anthony Kennedy (1936–) on the U.S. Supreme Court. She worked for the litigation firm Hollingsworth LLP in Washington, D.C., for many years before serving as secretary and chief counsel to the Committee on Rules of Practice and Procedure of the Judicial Conference of the United States.

LAW CLERKS

What are law clerks?

Each U.S. Supreme Court hires several law clerks to assist in the screening of cases in the certiorari pool, writing of memoranda on legal issues, drafting of opinions, and other legal matters. Most of the justices hire four law clerks. Many of the law clerks are recent graduates of prestigious law schools such as Harvard or Yale. Many of the law clerks serve for a U.S. Supreme Court justice after having clerked for a federal circuit court of appeals judge. Most clerks work for a justice for one year, though some will work on two-year terms.

What Supreme Court justice started the practice of hiring a law clerk?

Justice Horace Gray (1828–1902) instituted the practice of law clerks in 1882 when he joined the Court. When he was a member of the Supreme Judicial Court of Massachusetts, Gray had started the practice there as well, hiring future Supreme Court justice Louis Brandeis (1856–1941). Gray paid for the clerk out of his own pocket. The clerks were selected by Justice Gray's half brother, Harvard Law professor John Chipman Gray (1839–1915). The practice became formalized when Congress passed a 1922 law that allowed each justice to hire one law clerk for a salary of $3,600.

Who is the clerk of the Court?

The clerk of the Court is the person who oversees the administration of the Court's docket and caseload. The position of clerk is established by federal law 28 U.S.C. § 671, which provides in part: "The Supreme Court may appoint and fix the compensation of a clerk and one or more deputy clerks. The clerk shall be subject to removal by the Court. Deputy clerks shall be subject to removal by the clerk with the approval of the Court or the Chief Justice of the United States."

There have been 19 clerks of the U.S. Supreme Court in its history, including:

Clerk	Years Served
John Tucker	1790–1791
Samuel Bayard	1791–1800
Elias B. Caldwell	1800–1825
William Griffith	1826–1827
William T. Carroll	1827–1863
D. W. Middleton	1863–1880
James H. McKenney	1880–1913
James Maher	1913–1921
William R. Stansbury	1921–1927
Charles Elmore Copley	1927–1952

Clerk	Years Served
Harold B. Willey	1952–1956
John T. Fey	1956–1958
James Browning	1958–1961
John F. Davis	1961–1970
E. Robert Seaver	1970–1972
Michael Rodak Jr.	1972–1981
Alexander Stevas	1981–1985
Joseph F. Spaniol Jr.	1985–1991
William K. Suter	1991–2013
Scott S. Harris	2013–present

The current clerk for the U.S. Supreme Court, Scott S. Harris, is a Yale graduate and previous legal counsel to the Court.

What is the background of the clerk of the U.S. Supreme Court?

The clerk of the U.S. Supreme Court is a well-respected attorney. The current clerk, Scott S. Harris (1965–), graduated from the University of Virginia School of Law and worked at the law firm Wiley Rein & Fielding in Washington, D.C., before becoming an assistant U.S. attorney general. In 2002, he became legal counsel to the U.S. Supreme Court and then assumed the title of clerk in 2013 upon the retirement of his predecessor, William K. Suter (1937–).

What Supreme Court law clerk was indicted in 1919?

Ashton Fox Embry (1883–1965), a law clerk to Justice Joseph McKenna (1843–1926), was indicted for providing secret, insider information about Court rulings to Wall Street traders. Embry had left his clerk position, ostensibly to work on his baking business. However, a few weeks later, the U.S. Department of Justice charged Embry with conspiring "to deprive the United States of its lawful right and duty of promulgating information in the way and at the time required by law and at departmental regulation."

However, the case against Embry never went to trial and eventually was dismissed in 1929.

DID YOU KNOW!?

What law clerk leaked the *Roe v. Wade* decision?

Larry Hammond (1946–2020), a law clerk to Justice Lewis Powell, leaked the *Roe v. Wade* ruling in 1973, or the basis of it, to an acquaintance of his from law school, who was a reporter for *Time* magazine. Chief Justice Warren Burger (1907–1995) forgave Hammond for his indiscretion, and he was allowed to stay for another term with Justice Powell.

What law clerk wrote a book about his experiences called *Closed Chambers*?

Edward Lazarus (1959–), who clerked for Justice Harry Blackmun (1908–1999) during the 1988–1989 term, later wrote a book entitled *Closed Chambers*. The book relied and relayed many internal Court discussions and to some represented a breach of secrecy that clerks are supposed to maintain. Lazarus has had a successful post-clerk career, including serving as the chief of staff at the Federal Communications Commission and as general counsel to Sonos.

What functions do law clerks serve?

Law clerks often serve as an initial screener of the thousands of cases that are appealed to the U.S. Supreme Court. They will often write memos explaining to the justices which cases are "cert-worthy," or worthy of their attention. Nearly all of the justices pool their clerks together in a "cert pool" to examine the thousands of petitions that come to the Court each year. Justice Lewis Powell proposed the idea of the cert pool in 1972 to save time and increase efficiency. Critics charge that it gives too much power to the law clerks. Seven of the nine current justices participate in the cert pool. The two exceptions are Justice Samuel Alito Jr. (1950–) and Justice Neil Gorsuch (1967–).

The law clerks also write research memoranda and draft opinions for the justices. The responsibility of law clerks obviously depends upon each particular justice. Some justices delegate more responsibility to the clerks for opinion drafting than others.

A former U.S. solicitor general under President George H. W. Bush and judge for the District of Columbia Circuit, Kenneth Starr was the independent counsel and author of the Starr Report that was used to impeach President Clinton.

Who are some of the more famous law clerks?

There have been many Supreme Court law clerks who have achieved great prominence in the legal profession. Here are just a few:

- *Kenneth Starr (1946–2022):* Former federal appeals court and independent counsel who investigated President Bill Clinton (1946–; leading to his impeachment); clerked for Chief Justice Warren Burger.

- *Richard Posner (1939–):* Longtime judge on the Seventh U.S. Circuit Court of Appeals and author of more than 40 books; clerked for Justice William Brennan (1906–1997). Justice Brennan once said that in his life, he met two geniuses: Justice William O. Douglas (1898–1980) and Richard Posner.

- *Robert O'Neil (1934–2018):* Former president of the University of Virginia and the founder of the Thomas Jefferson Center for the Protection of Free Expression; clerked for Justice William Brennan. He was a co-clerk with Richard Posner.

- *Alan Dershowitz (1938–):* Harvard Law professor and well-known author/legal commentator; clerked for Justice Arthur Goldberg (1908–1990).

- *Laura Ingraham (1963–)*: Fox television news commentator with her own show on the network called *The Ingraham Angle*; clerked for Justice Clarence Thomas (1948–).

What is the Supreme Court Fellows Program?

In 1973, Chief Justice Warren Burger established the Supreme Court Fellows Program to provide assistance to the Court, the Federal Judicial Center, the Administrative Office of the United States Courts, and the United States Sentencing Commission. The Fellows help with the Court's workload, write research memoranda, and do other work at the behest largely of the chief justice. Since the 2000–2001 term, the chief justice has selected four individuals to serve as Supreme Court Fellows. One goes with the Supreme Court, one with the Federal Judicial Center, one with the Administrative Office of the Courts, and one with the Sentencing Commission.

Who were among the inaugural Supreme Court Fellows class of 1974?

The inaugural Supreme Court Fellows class of 1973–1974 consisted of three individuals: Gordon Gee (1944–), who is now the president of the University of West Virginia; Russell Wheeler (1943–), a visiting fellow with the Brookings Institution who for many years directed the Federal Judicial Center in Washington, D.C.; and Howard R. Whitcomb (1939–), who for many years taught political science at Lehigh University in Pennsylvania.

What is the marshal of the U.S. Supreme Court?

The marshal of the U.S. Supreme Court is the person who oversees the security, maintenance, and operation of the Supreme Court Building. Federal law 28 U.S.C. §672 has provided for this position since 1867. There have been 11 head marshals of the Supreme Court, including:

Marshal	Years Served
Richard C. Parsons	1867–1872
John Nicolay	1872–1887
John M. Wright	1888–1915
Frank Key Green	1915–1938
Thomas E. Waggaman	1938–1952
T. Perry Lippitt	1952–1972
Frank M. Hepler	1972–1976
Alfred M. Wong	1976–1994
Dale E. Bosley	1994–2001
Pamela Talkin	2001–2020
Gail A. Curley	2021–present

Gail Curley, the current marshal of the Supreme Court, is the second woman to hold the position. She has a law degree from the University of Illinois and was an officer in the Army Signal Corps.

What is the Office of Legal Counsel?

The Office of Legal Counsel is an administrative unit under the control of the chief justice of the U.S. Supreme Court. It consists of two attorneys who help the Court in cases involving petitions for extraordinary writs and cases in which the Court's original jurisdiction is invoked.

What was the original oath that federal judges had to take?

Section 8 of the Judiciary Act of 1789 provides that Supreme Court and district judges had to take the following oath:

> I, [justice's name], do solemnly swear or affirm, that I will administer justice without respect to persons, and do equal right to the poor and to the rich, and that I will faithfully and impartially discharge and

perform all the duties incumbent on me as [type of judge] according to the best of my abilities and understanding, agreeable to the constitution and laws of the United States. So help me God.

The oath was amended in 1990 by replacing "according to the best of my abilities and understanding, agreeable to the Constitution" with the words "under the Constitution."

REFORMS

What president introduced an infamous court-packing plan in 1937?

President Franklin Delano Roosevelt (1882–1945), upset over the Supreme Court invalidating many key pieces of his New Deal legislative agenda, proposed a Judicial Reorganization Plan that would call for another justice to be added to the Supreme Court when a sitting member reached 70 years of age.

Roosevelt was primarily upset at the rulings of the so-called "Four Horsemen" of the Court, who were generally judicial conservatives who were resistant to the expansive nature of Roosevelt's New Deal agenda. Those "Four Horsemen" were Pierce Butler (1866–1939), George Sutherland (1862–1942), James Clark McReynolds (1862–1946), and Willis Van Devanter (1859–1941).

Roosevelt introduced his Judicial Reorganization Plan in one of his "Fireside Chats," where he spoke directly to the American public. Roosevelt stated in part:

I want to talk with you very simply about the need for present action in this crisis—the need to meet the unanswered challenge of one-third of a Nation ill-nourished, ill-clad, ill-housed.

Last Thursday I described the American form of Government as a three-horse team provided by the Constitution to the American people so that their field might be plowed. The three horses are, of course, the three branches of government—the Congress, the Executive and the Courts. Two of the horses are pulling in unison today; the third is not. Those who have intimated that the President of the United States is trying to drive that team, overlook the simple fact that the President, as Chief Executive, is himself one of the three horses.

It is the American people themselves who are in the driver's seat.

It is the American people themselves who want the furrow plowed.

It is the American people themselves who expect the third horse to pull in unison with the other two.

I hope that you have re-read the Constitution of the United States in these past few weeks. Like the Bible, it ought to be read again and again.

It is an easy document to understand when you remember that it was called into being because the Articles of Confederation under which the original thirteen States tried to operate after the Revolution showed the need of a National Government with power enough to handle national problems. In its Preamble, the Constitution states that it was intended to form a more perfect Union and promote the general welfare; and the powers given to the Congress to carry out those purposes can be best described by saying that they were all the powers needed to meet each and every problem which then had a national character and which could not be met by merely local action.

But the framers went further. Having in mind that in succeeding generations many other problems then undreamed of would become national problems, they gave to the Congress the ample broad powers "to levy taxes ... and provide for the common defense and general welfare of the United States."

That, my friends, is what I honestly believe to have been the clear and underlying purpose of the patriots who wrote a Federal Constitution to create a National Government with national power, intended as they said, "to form a more perfect union ... for ourselves and our posterity."

For nearly twenty years there was no conflict between the Congress and the Court. Then Congress passed a statute which, in 1803, the Court said violated an express provision of the Constitution. The Court claimed the power to declare it unconstitutional and did so declare it. But a little later the Court itself admitted that it was an extraordinary power to exercise and through Mr. Justice Washington laid down this limitation upon it: "It is but a decent respect due to the wisdom, the integrity and the patriotism of the legislative body, by which any law is passed, to presume in favor of its validity until its violation of the Constitution is proved beyond all reasonable doubt."

But since the rise of the modern movement for social and economic progress through legislation, the Court has more and more often and more and more boldly asserted a power to veto laws passed by the Congress and State Legislatures in complete disregard of this original limitation.

In the last four years the sound rule of giving statutes the benefit of all reasonable doubt has been cast aside. The Court has been acting not as a judicial body, but as a policy-making body.

When the Congress has sought to stabilize national agriculture, to improve the conditions of labor, to safeguard business against unfair competition, to protect our national resources, and in many other ways, to serve our clearly national needs, the majority of the Court has been assuming the power to pass on the wisdom of these Acts of the Congress—and to approve or disapprove the public policy written into these laws …

We have, therefore, reached the point as a Nation where we must take action to save the Constitution from the Court and the Court from itself. We must find a way to take an appeal from the Supreme Court to the Constitution itself. We want a Supreme Court which will do justice under the Constitution—not over it. In our Courts we want a government of laws and not of men.

I want—as all Americans want—an independent judiciary as proposed by the framers of the Constitution. That means a Supreme Court that will enforce the Constitution as written—that will refuse to amend the Constitution by the arbitrary exercise of judicial power—amendment by judicial say-so. It does not mean a judiciary so independent that it can deny the existence of facts universally recognized.

The Senate Judiciary Committee recommended against Roosevelt's court-packing plan, calling it "a needless, futile, and utterly dangerous abandonment of constitutional principle."

What various New Deal legislation did the Supreme Court invalidate?

Here is a listing of the New Deal legislation invalidated by the Supreme Court.

Legislation	Court Case
Agricultural Adjustment Act of 1933	*U.S. v. Butler* (1936)
Agricultural Adjustment Act of 1933 (later amendments)	*Rickert Rice Mills v. Fontenot* (1936)
Economy Act of 1933 (one clause)	*Lynch v. U.S.* (1934)
National Industrial Recovery Act	*A.L.A. Schechter Poultry Corp. v. U.S.* (1935)
Another part of the National Industrial Recovery Act	*Panama Refining Co. v. Ryan* (1935)
Home Owners Loan Act of 1933	*Hopkins Savings Assn. v. Cleary* (1935)
Railroad Retirement Act	*Railroad Retirement Board v. Alton Railroad Co.* (1935)
Bituminous Coal Conservation Act	*Carter v. Carter Coal Co.* (1936)
Frazier-Lemke Farm Bankruptcy Act of 1934	*Louisville Joint Stock Land Bank v. Radford* (1935)

Justice Owen Roberts served in the Court from 1930 to 1945 and is often remembered for heading the commission investigating the attacks on Pearl Harbor.

Which justice changed his vote from one minimum wage case to the other?

Justice Owen Roberts (1875–1955) switched his vote from striking down a minimum wage law in *Morehead v. New York ex. rel. Tipaldo* (1936) to upholding a similar Washington state law in *West Coast Hotel Co. v. Parrish* (1937). It was said that Roberts's change of mind was the "switch in time that saved nine," a reference to President Franklin D. Roosevelt's sharp criticism of the Court and proposal in 1937 to "pack" the Court with additional justices. In reality, Roberts had indicated his support for the minimum wage law in a Court conference in December 1936 before President Roosevelt's court-packing plan was announced.

Did Congress ever try to set the number of justices at nine permanently?

Yes, Senator John Marshall Butler (1897–1978), a Republican senator from Maryland, introduced a constitutional amendment in the 1950s to keep the Supreme Court membership at nine. Butler said that the purpose of the proposed amendment was to "forestall future attempts to undermine the integrity and independence of the Supreme Court." Butler's proposal cleared the Senate but did not pass the House.

In 2021, Mark Green (1964–), a U.S. Republican representative from Tennessee, introduced a House Joint Resolution that would set the number of justices at nine.

What president issued an executive order ordering a commission to study various reform proposals to the U.S. Supreme Court?

President Joseph Biden (1942–) signed Executive Order 14023, which created the Presidential Commission on the Supreme Court of the United States to study the Court and various reform proposals. The functions of the commission are listed in the order as follows:

Functions of Commission

(a) The Commission shall produce a report for the President that includes the following:

(i) An account of the contemporary commentary and debate about the role and operation of the

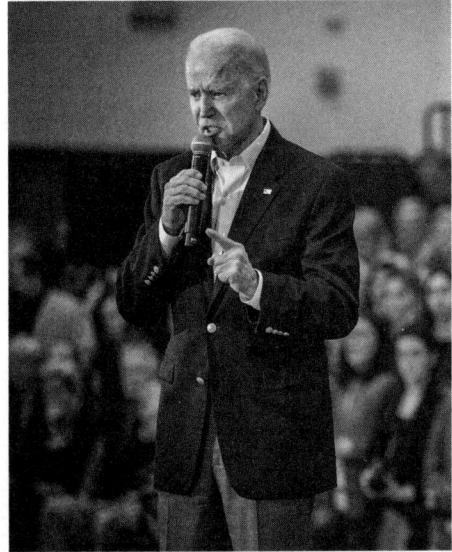

President Joe Biden created the Presidential Commission on the Supreme Court to analyze arguments and debates regarding reforming the nation's highest court.

Supreme Court in our constitutional system and about the functioning of the constitutional process by which the President nominates and, by and with the advice and consent of the Senate, appoints Justices to the Supreme Court;

(ii) The historical background of other periods in the Nation's history when the Supreme Court's role and the nominations and advice-and-consent process were subject to critical assessment and prompted proposals for reform; and

(iii) An analysis of the principal arguments in the contemporary public debate for and against Supreme Court reform, including an appraisal of the merits and legality of particular reform proposals.

(b) The Commission shall solicit public comment, including other expert views, to ensure that its work is informed by a broad spectrum of ideas.

(c) The Commission shall submit its report to the President within 180 days of the date of the Commission's first public meeting.

What were some of the reform proposals considered by this commission?

The Supreme Court commission studied proposals that it grouped into four categories of reforms: (1) size and composition of the Court; (2) the tenure of the justices; (3) the powers of the Court and its role in the constitutional system; and (4) transparency and the Court's internal processes.

What were the arguments for and against expanding the size of the Court?

The Commission in its draft report issued in December 2021 did not take a position on whether the Court's size and composition should be changed. Rather, it presented arguments both for and against expanding the number of justices. Proponents of such measures contend that the current U.S. Supreme Court has issued a series of rulings that undermine democracy and could serve to delegitimize the Court. Others contend that expanding the Court size could allow more diversity on the Court and give its members the opportunity to hear more cases.

"Expanded diversity could enrich the Court's decision making, and a Court that was drawn from a broader cross-section of society would be well received by the public," the report reads. "A larger Supreme Court might also be able to decide more cases and to spend more time on emergency applications—an element of the Court's work that has attracted considerable attention as is discussed in Chapter 5 of this Report."

The report also noted that most other courts around the world had more justices or judges on their high courts. Consider the following:

Country	Number of High Court Judges
Australia	7
Canada, United States	9
Chile	10
France, South Africa	11
Belgium, Ireland, Spain, United Kingdom	12
Austria, South Korea	14
Italy, Japan	15
Germany, Sweden	16
Denmark	18

However, opponents of changing the size of the Supreme Court emphasize that changing the size of the Court simply because many do not agree with certain rulings from the Court would threaten judicial independence.

"Critics of Court expansion worry that such efforts would pose considerable risk to our constitutional system, including by spurring parties able to take control of the White House and Congress at the same time to routinely add Justices to bring the Court more into line with their ideological stances or partisan political aims," the report reads. "Court packing, in the critics' view, would compromise the Court's long-term capacity to perform its essential role of policing the excesses of the other branches and protecting individual rights."

The current Supreme Court (as of 2024) consists of three justices considered to be liberal (Sonia Sotomayor seated at far left, Elena Kagan seated at far right, and Ketanji Brown Jackson standing at far right) and six conservative justices (seated left to right: Clarence Thomas, Chief Justice John G. Roberts Jr., and Samuel A. Alito; and standing left to right: Amy Coney Barrett, Neil M. Gorsuch, and Brett M. Kavanaugh).

A primary argument against Court expansion is that having nine Supreme Court justices has become something of a "constitutional norm" and that changing it would undermine the independence of the Court. Another argument is that there would be no stopping point to attempts to expand the Court: "Opponents of Court packing in this moment warn that it would also almost certainly generate a continuous cycle of future expansions. Expanding the Court would be on the agenda of every administration under unified government."

What other structural reforms did the Commission consider?

The Commission considered various proposals where Supreme Court justices would rotate on panels to decide cases, much like judges at the Court of Appeals normally hear cases with different panels. These rotation and panel systems may run into a constitutional hurdle, according to the Commission, which cited the language from Article III of the Constitution that "[t]he judicial Power of the United States, shall be vested in one supreme Court, and in such inferior Courts as the Congress may from time to time ordain and establish."

Another type of proposal was one that seeks to provide for some partisan or ideological balance to the Court. One proposal was that each president would get to appoint two members to the Court each term. A related proposal would be that the Court must consist of an equal, or closely equal, number of members from each of the two main political parties. This is what the Commission called a "balanced bench" proposal. However, the Commission noted that "it is far from clear that ideological balance is in and of itself a desirable goal. If there is no such balance in the political branches, requiring such balance on the Court could make the Court insufficiently reflective of or connected to electoral outcomes."

What proposals did the Commission consider regarding term limits?

The Court considered the proposal that justices serve one nonrenewable, 18-year term. The Commission noted that a group of scholars had proposed such a system and that similar proposals have been endorsed by think tanks along the ideological spectrum.

The Commission noted that the United States is an outlier in providing for life tenure for its high judges. "The United States is the only major constitutional democracy in the world that has neither a retirement age nor a fixed term limit for its high court Justices," the report reads. "Among the world's democracies, at least 27 have term limits for their constitutional courts. And those that do not have term limits, such as the Supreme Court of the United Kingdom, typically impose age limits."

At bottom, the argument for term limits devolves into the idea that justices wield too much power, as many serve more than 30 years on the Court. The report notes that "life tenure arguably arrogates too much power to single individuals."

However, the Commission also presented the arguments of those who are in favor of retaining life tenure for the justices. "In the main, the opponents argue that the current system of appointing and protecting the independence and neutrality of federal judges and Justices, through life tenure, has worked well for over 230 years," the report reads. "The independent federal judiciary, protected by lifetime tenure, is one of the most signal accomplishments of our constitutional system."

Ultimately, opponents of altering life tenure emphasize that the "federal system of life tenure is the gold standard for judicial independence."

Did any of the Commission members introduce separate statements?

Yes, two Commission members, former federal judges Thomas Griffith (1954–), and David Levi (1951–), submitted a joint statement in which they emphasize the importance of an independent federal judiciary. They wrote in part:

> In our view, most of the proposed reforms discussed in the Commission report—including "court packing" and term limits—are without substantial merit; they are not related to any defect or deficiency in the Court or its procedures and they threaten judicial independence. We must not permit

the Supreme Court to become collateral damage in the divisiveness that marks the current age.

Commissioner Adam White, senior fellow at the American Enterprise Institute, also issued a separate statement in which he decried proposals to pack the Court.

Court-packing is anathema to constitutional government. While Congress is empowered by the Constitution to add seats to the Court, the history of Court expansion is one of admirable self-restraint by Congress. Over the nation's first century, Congress largely set the Court's size by reference to the judiciary's genuine needs, particularly in terms of the justices' old circuit-riding duties in a fast-growing continental republic. Since 1869, the Court's size has remained stable, and for one and a half centuries the nine-justice bench has proved conducive to the justices' work of deliberation, decision, and explanation.

To pack the Court would impair the Court, not improve it: destabilizing it, further politicizing it, and complicating its basic work of hearing and deciding cases under the rule of law. And one needs a willing suspension of disbelief not to see that Court-packing would inaugurate an era of re-packing, destroying the Court's function and character as a court of law.

HISTORIC JUSTICES

Why is John Marshall considered the greatest chief justice in Court history by many historians and others?

In his 1996 biography of Chief Justice John Marshall (1755–1835), author Jean Edward Smith referred to Marshall as "the Definer of the Nation." Marshall's opinions gave the U.S. Supreme Court and the judicial branch the power and respect they deserved and placed the judicial branch on a closer level with Congress and the president. William Winslow Crosskey, in his essay on Marshall for the book *Mr. Justice* (edited by Allison Dunham and Philip B. Kurland), writes: "Some very distinguished and able men have been Chief Justice; but by universal consent, Marshall is recognized to stand pre-eminent—indeed,

Chief Justice John Marshall led the Supreme Court from 1801 to 1835. A Founding Father, he had previously served as secretary of state under President John Adams and as a congressman representing Virginia.

unrivaled—among them. The appellation, 'the Great Chief Justice,' is still, as it long has been, a completely unambiguous reference to John Marshall."

Marshall did this in many ways. He persuaded his colleagues to drop the practice of in sepiatim opinions, where each justice would speak and issue an individual opinion. Under Marshall, the Court often spoke in one unified voice—many times through the chief justice. He also established the principle of judicial review in *Marbury v. Madison* (1803), which gave the judiciary the power to review the constitutionality of legislative and executive acts. Supreme Court justice Sandra Day O'Connor (1930–2023) wrote in her book *The Majesty of the Law*: "It is no overstatement to claim that Chief Justice Marshall fulfilled the Constitution's promise of an independent federal judiciary."

Another factor contributing to Marshall's greatness was that he was the first chief justice to serve for a significant period of time. Marshall served on the Court for 34 years, while his predecessors—the nation's first three chief justices—combined for just over 11 years: John Jay (1745–1829) served just under six years, John Rutledge (1739–1800) served just under four months, and Oliver Ellsworth (1745–1807) served just under five years. Marshall also was on the Court during the formative years of the nation and the Court. Marshall also possessed great leadership abilities that enabled him to guide the Court during his long tenure.

Why is Oliver Wendell Holmes Jr. considered such a great justice?

Oliver Wendell Holmes Jr. (1841–1935) is considered perhaps the foremost legal thinker and developer of law (perhaps aside from Chief Justice Marshall) in Supreme Court history. He had a scholarly bent, knowledge of philosophy, and a mind that could absorb different kinds of information easily. For example, Judge Richard A. Posner (1939–) of the Seventh Circuit once called

Holmes "the most influential figure in the history of American law." Legal historian Richard MacGregor Burns writes of Holmes: "Holmes was a kind of Enlightenment philosopher, son of an eminent man of letters, acquainted with such literati as [Ralph Waldo] Emerson and [Henry Wadsworth] Longfellow, one of the few Americans who could converse on easy terms in London with John Stuart Mill and Prime Minister William Gladstone."

Why is Holmes considered so important for First Amendment jurisprudence?

Holmes is sometimes called "the Father of the First Amendment" because he wrote some of the seminal free-speech decisions back in 1919. Holmes created the so-called "clear and present danger" test to identify when political speech is protected and when it is not. In other words, the speech of a political dissident, such as a socialist or an anarchist, is protected under the First Amendment unless it creates a "clear and present" danger to the government or established order.

Initially, Holmes's articulation of the "clear and present" danger test was not very protective of free speech in *Schenck v. United States* (1919). In fact, Holmes applied that test quite broadly to cover the relatively harmless speech disseminated by Charles Schenck and Elizabeth Baer. His initial articulation of the clear and present danger test was this:

> The question in every case is whether the words used are used in such circumstances and are of such a nature as to create a clear and present danger that they will bring about the substantive evils that Congress has a right to prevent. It is a question of proximity and degree. When a nation is at war many things that might be said in time of peace are

An associate justice of the Supreme Court from 1902 to 1932, Oliver Wendell Holmes Jr. was an erudite judge known for his opinions of and influence on First Amendment rights.

such a hindrance to its effort that their utterance will not be endured so long as men fight and that no Court could regard them as protected by any constitutional right.

To Holmes, freedom of speech was not as protected during times of war as it was during times of peace. Thus, he affirmed the convictions of Schenck and Baer. There was much criticism of this opinion in scholarly circles.

However, Holmes came back with a dissenting opinion in the fall of 1919, *Abrams v. United States* (1919), that was very protective of freedom of speech. In fact, many refer to Justice Holmes's dissent as "the Great Dissent." In his dissenting opinion, Holmes introduced what is sometimes known as "the marketplace of ideas" metaphor. He wrote:

Persecution for the expression of opinions seems to me perfectly logical. If you have no doubt of your premises or your power and want a certain result with all your heart you naturally express your wishes in law and sweep away all opposition. To allow opposition by speech seems to indicate that you think the speech impotent, as when a man says that he has squared the circle, or that you do not care whole heartedly for the result, or that you doubt either your power or your premises. But when men have realized that time has upset many fighting faiths, they may come to believe even more than they believe the very foundations of their own conduct that the ultimate good desired is better reached by free trade in ideas—that the best test of truth is the power of the thought to get itself accepted in the competition of the market, and that truth is the only ground upon which their wishes safely can be carried out. That at any rate is the theory of our Constitution. It is an experiment, as all life is an experiment. Every year if not every day we have to wager our salvation upon some prophecy based upon imperfect knowledge. While that experiment is part of our system I think that we should be eternally vigilant against attempts to check the expression of opinions that we loathe and believe to be fraught with death, unless they so imminently threaten immediate interference with the lawful and pressing purposes of the law that an immediate check is required to save the country. I wholly disagree with the argument of the Government that the First Amendment left the common law as to seditious libel in force.

How did Louis Brandeis contribute to the development of the right to privacy as a lawyer?

Louis Brandeis (1856–1941) coauthored a seminal article in the *Harvard Law Review* with his law partner, Samuel Warren

(1852–1910), titled "The Right to Privacy." Brandeis and Warren argued that threats to privacy were endemic in society: "The press is overstepping in every direction the obvious bounds of propriety and decency. Gossip is no longer the resource of the idle and the vicious, but has become a trade, which is pursued with industry as well as effrontery."

Brandeis and Warren identified two grave threats to privacy: (1) new technology and (2) the conduct of the press. With regard to new technologies, they worried about instantaneous photographs and numerous mechanical devices that invade personal privacy. They also felt that the press was invading the private lives of persons.

They explained that "the common law secures to each individual the right of determining, ordinarily, to what extent his thoughts, sentiments, and emotions shall be communicated to others." However, the justices did explain that information was not private if it related to "public or general interest."

In what case did Brandeis write as a lawyer that became known as a "Brandeis brief"?

Brandeis wrote his first so-called "Brandeis brief" in *Muller v. Oregon* (1908), a case involving a challenge to an Oregon law limiting the number of hours women could work. Brandeis submitted a brief in support of the law that contained much social science, medical, and other materials rather than legal precedent. The brief was more than 100 pages long. It had an impact on the Court, which upheld the Oregon law.

An associate justice from 1916 to 1939, Louis Brandeis was the first Jewish justice to sit on the bench of the nation's highest court. He is also the namesake of Brandeis University in Waltham, Massachusetts.

In what famous dissent did Brandeis talk about the importance of privacy?

Justice Louis Brandeis issued the most comprehensive dissenting opinion in *Olmstead v. United States* (1928), though Justices Oliver Wendell Holmes Jr. (1841–1935), Pierce Butler (1866–1939), and Harlan Fiske Stone (1872–1946) also wrote dissenting opinions.

Brandeis recognized that individual privacy can be invaded in different ways through technological advancements. In a moment of prescience, he wrote: "Ways may someday be developed by which the government, without removing papers from secret drawers, can reproduce them in court, and by which it will be enabled to expose to a jury the most intimate occurrences of the home." He explained that invading privacy by listening to telephone conversations was as great, if not greater, than opening an individual's mail. He also questioned the government's culpability in sanctioning what he termed unlawful wiretapping. He warned that the government itself would become a lawbreaker.

He explained in potent language:

> The makers of our Constitution undertook to secure conditions favorable to the pursuit of happiness. They sought to protect Americans in their beliefs, their thoughts, their emotions and their sensations. They conferred, as against the government, the right to be let alone the most comprehensive of rights and the right most valued by civilized men. To protect that right, every unjustifiable intrusion by the government, whatever the means employed, must be deemed a violation of the Fourth Amendment.

In what famous concurring opinion did Brandeis lay out his theory of the First Amendment?

Brandeis wrote one of the most consequential opinions in a concurrence in *Whitney v. California* (1927), a case involving a First Amendment challenge to California's criminal syndicalism law. Such a law was used to target dissident political groups, including Communists and Socialists. Charlotte Anita Whitney (1867–1955) was convicted of violating the law for a speech she gave in Oakland, California, on behalf of the Communist Labor Party of California, which supported the International Workers of the World. The California law prohibited persons from organizing, assisting, and assembling persons together to advocate, teach, aid, and abet criminal syndicalism. Whitney was arrested during the height of the Red Scare, a time when government officials were concerned of a Communist uprising similar to the Bolshevik Revolution in Russia led by Vladimir Lenin (1870–1924).

The majority affirmed Whitney's conviction and upheld the statute, finding that it did not violate First Amendment freedoms. Writing for the majority, Justice Edward Sanford (1865–1930) concluded that the law is not "an unreasonable or arbitrary exercise of the police power of the State; unwarrantably infringing upon any right of free speech, assembly or association, or that those persons are protected from punishment by the due-process clause who abuse such rights by joining and furthering an organization thus menacing the peace and welfare of the State."

The decision is better known for the concurring opinion of Brandeis, which was joined by Justice Oliver Wendell Holmes. Brandeis's concurrence, which reads more like a dissent, became a blueprint for the justification of free speech. He wrote that even advocacy of illegal conduct could not justify restricting speech unless the speech incites immediate lawless action, a test that the U.S. Supreme Court would eventually adopt in the 1969 decision *Brandenburg v. Ohio*. However, Brandeis concurred with the majority because "there was other testimony which tended to establish the existence of a conspiracy, on the part of members of the International Workers of the World, to commit present serious crimes, and likewise to show that such a conspiracy would be furthered by the activity of the society of which Miss Whitney was a member."

In his opinion, Brandeis advocated for support of what has come to be known as the counter-speech doctrine—that when confronted by hostile or offensive speech, the response should be to counter it with positive speech rather than engage in outright censorship. Brandeis famously wrote: "If there be time to expose through discussion the falsehood and fallacies, to aver the evil by the processes of education, the remedy to be applied is more speech, not enforced silence."

Brandeis's concurrence was filled with other oft-cited passages that formed the basis of modern First Amendment jurisprudence. Here are a couple more gems from his pen:

> They believed that freedom to think as you will and to speak as you think are means indispensable to the discovery and spread of political truth; that

without free speech and assembly discussion would be futile; that with them, discussion affords ordinarily adequate protection against the dissemination of noxious doctrine; that the greatest menace to freedom is an inert people; that public discussion is a political duty; and that this should be a fundamental principle of the American government.

Fear of serious injury cannot alone justify suppression of free speech and assembly. Men feared witches and burnt women. It is the function of speech to free men from the bondage of irrational fears. To justify suppression of free speech there must be reasonable ground to fear that serious evil will result if free speech is practiced.

Why is Earl Warren considered among the greatest of U.S. Supreme Court justices?

Chief Justice Earl Warren led the court from 1953 to 1969. Previously serving as governor of California, his opinions were considered liberal, which was certainly appropriate during the social changes of the 1960s.

Chief Justice Earl Warren (1891–1974) is considered a great jurist because he was considered a great and persuasive leader of the Court. Henry Abraham writes:

> Earl Warren—who involved his clerks heavily in the production of his opinions—was not a great lawyer in the mold of a Taney or a Hughes; not a great legal scholar in the tradition of a Brandeis or Frankfurter; not a supreme stylist like a Cardozo or a Jackson; not a judicial philosopher like a Holmes or a Black; not a resourceful, efficient administrator like a Taft or a Warren Earl Burger, his successor. But he was the chief justice par excellence—second in institutional-leadership greatness to John Marshall himself in the eyes of most impartial students of the Court as well as the Warren Court's legion of critics. Like Marshall he understood and utilized the tools of pervasive and persuasive power leadership available to him; a genuine statesman, he knew how to bring men together, how to set a tone, and how to fashion a mood. He was a wise man and a warm, kind human being. He was his Court, the judicial activist Court: he viewed law as an instrument to get the right result.

Warren's Supreme Court colleague, William Brennan (1906–1997), said of the man he called "Super Chief": "He had everything. He was hard-working. He knew how to work with people. He was marvelous with people. He would take approaches that would often escape my eye. He was just extraordinary."

What were Earl Warren's positions before being a Supreme Court justice?

Earl Warren served in public office from 1919 until his resignation from the U.S. Supreme Court in 1969. From 1919 to 1920, he served as deputy city attorney for Oakland, California. From 1920 to 1925, he served as district attorney for Alameda County. From 1939 to 1943, he served as California attorney general. From 1943 to 1953, he served as governor of California. In 1948, Warren ran for vice president with Republican presidential candidate Thomas E. Dewey (1902–1971). In 1952, Warren sought the Republican nomination for president but later withdrew and supported General Dwight D. Eisenhower (1890–1969). Eisenhower returned the favor the next year by nominating Warren as chief justice.

Why is Justice Hugo Black considered such a significant justice?

Hugo La Fayette Black (1886–1971) was one of the most consequential justices ever to serve on the Court, where he enjoyed a nearly 34-year tenure. His impact was felt because he contributed opinions that changed and impacted many different areas of American law. While in his early political life he briefly joined the Ku Klux Klan in his native Alabama, he quickly renounced it and eventually became one of the greatest defenders of civil liberties in American legal history.

Irving Dilliard wrote of Justice Black's impact in his piece "The Individual and the Bill of Absolute Rights" in the book *Hugo Black and the Supreme Court: A Symposium* (1967): "But, Mr. Justice Black's unquestioned place in history stands on far more solid substance than three decades of Supreme Court service with almost as many colleagues in the span as years. His importance is secured in accomplishment, not in mere endurance. He has left his own clear impress on many vital aspects of our law and life, and has made significant contributions in still other areas."

Associate Justice Hugo Black was on the bench from 1937 to 1971. He was a staunch supporter of President Theodore Roosevelt and of his New Deal programs.

What was Justice Black's experience before being appointed to the U.S. Supreme Court?

Hugo Black engaged in the private practice of law in both Ashland and then Birmingham after earning a law degree from the University of Alabama. He also served as a police court judge in Birmingham for a time. His legal practice was interrupted when he went to serve his country in the U.S. Army during World War I, rising to the rank of captain. After returning home, he resumed the private practice of law until he ran for a seat in the U.S. Senate. He became a U.S. senator in 1926, where he served as a loyal supporter of President Franklin Delano Roosevelt's New Deal program. In 1937, Roosevelt picked Black to replace the retiring Justice Willis Van Devanter (1859–1941).

What case did Hugo Black argue before the U.S. Supreme Court as a lawyer?

Black argued the case of *Lewis v. Roberts* (1925) before the U.S. Supreme Court. Black represented Henry Lewis, an African American convict who was injured while working underground in a coal mine for Montevallo Coal Mining Company. Lewis and other inmates had been "leased" to the mining company. Lewis was seriously injured and had obtained a judgment against Montevallo. However, the company declared bankruptcy and claimed that it did not have to pay Lewis because the debt owed Lewis was not based on a contract.

The U.S. Supreme Court unanimously reversed the decision in *Lewis v. Roberts*, reasoning that a tort suit could not so easily be discharged in bankruptcy. Black had taken the case because he thought the treatment of Henry Lewis was a travesty of justice.

What was Justice Black's position on freedom of the press and the criticism of public officials?

Justice Black believed that the First Amendment free-press clause provided carte blanche to the press to criticize public officials free from defamation law. The U.S. Supreme Court provided significant—but certainly not absolute—protection to the press from defamation suits in *New York Times Co. v. Sullivan* (1964), reasoning that public officials could only recover for defamation claims if they could show that the press acted knowing the information it printed was false or acting in reckless disregard as to the truth or falsity of the statement.

This ruling did not go far enough for Justice Black, who wrote a separate concurring opinion. "We would, I think, more faithfully interpret the First Amendment by holding that at the very least it leaves the people and the press free to criticize officials and discuss public affairs with impunity." Black added that "an unconditional right to say what one pleases about public affairs is what I consider to be the minimum guarantee of the First Amendment."

In what famous decision did Justice Black get vindication 21 years later?

Justice Black wrote the Court's majority opinion in *Gideon v. Wainwright* (1963), ruling that the Sixth Amendment right to assistance of counsel also applied to state and local governments through the Due Process Clause of the Fourteenth Amendment. The decision meant that Clarence Earl Gideon (1910–1972), a Florida inmate convicted of theft for breaking into a poolroom, had his rights violated when a Florida state judge refused his request for an appointed lawyer.

The decision was sweet vindication for Justice Black, who had dissented on the exact same issue 21 years prior in *Betts v. Brady* (1942). In that decision, the Court ruled that Smith Betts, a Maryland farmhand convicted of robbery, did not have his rights violated when a Maryland judge refused to appoint him a lawyer. Maryland law at that time provided that indigent or poor defendants were entitled to an appointed lawyer only when they were charged with murder or rape.

Betts had argued that the Sixth Amendment right to assistance of counsel was part of the essential "liberty" protected by the Due Process Clause of the Fourteenth Amendment, which provides that no state shall deprive an individual of "life, liberty, or property without due process of law."

But the Supreme Court ruled against Betts. The majority reasoned that "in the great majority of the States, it has been the considered judgment of the people, their representatives, and their courts that appointment of counsel is not a fundamental right, essential to a fair trial. On the contrary, the matter has generally been deemed one of legislative policy."

Justice Black vigorously dissented in *Betts.* "Denial to the poor of the request for counsel in proceedings based on charges of serious crime has long been regarded as shocking to the 'universal sense of justice' throughout this country," he wrote.

Though Black was in the dissent in 1942, he was assigned the majority opinion in *Gideon v. Wainwright* and did not miss the opportunity to criticize and overrule *Betts v. Brady.* He emphasized the importance of having an attorney in memorable language:

> That government hires lawyers to prosecute and defendants who have the money hire lawyers to defend are the strongest indications of the widespread belief that lawyers in criminal courts are necessities, not luxuries. The right of one charged with crime to counsel may not be deemed fundamental and essential to fair trials in some countries, but it is in ours. From the very beginning, our state and national constitutions and laws have laid great emphasis on procedural and substantive safeguards designed to assure fair trials before impartial tribunals in which every defendant stands equal before the law. This noble ideal cannot be realized if the poor man charged with crime has to face his accusers without a lawyer to assist him.

Anthony Lewis, in his famous book on the *Gideon v. Wainwright* case entitled *Gideon's Trumpet*, writes that Justice Black told a friend shortly after the release of his decision in 1963: "When *Betts v. Brady* was decided, I never thought I'd live to see it overruled."

What was significant about the tenure of Justice William O. Douglas?

One of the most progressive justices to ever serve on the court, Associate Justice William O. Douglas still holds the record (almost 36 years, 7 months) as the longest-serving U.S. Supreme Court justice.

First of all, Justice William O. Douglas (1898–1980) holds the record for the longest tenure on the Court at more than 36 years, spanning from 1939 until 1975. Second, Douglas holds the record for the most opinions total and the most dissenting opinions. He was a progressive who had a very strong capacity for protecting freedom of expression values in his opinions. He probably was the most consistent and passionate defender of First Amendment freedoms in the history of the Court. There were countless times where he was the only person in dissent in favor of an individual while his colleagues favored the government. He also had a highly independent streak, as his nickname "Wild Bill" indicates. His personal life was different from other justices on the Court, as he had four marriages with progressively younger spouses.

What positions did Justice Douglas hold before ascending to the high court?

After graduating from Columbia Law School, Justice Douglas briefly worked in private practice at the New York law firm Cravath, de Gersdorff, Swaine and Wood. He then transitioned into academics, teaching first at Columbia and then at Yale Law School. President Franklin D. Roosevelt (1882–1945) then appointed him to the Securities and Exchange Commission in 1934. Five years later, Roosevelt tabbed him for the Supreme Court.

What was the "Black Fear of Silence"?

This was an article that Justice Douglas wrote in 1952 for the *New York Times Magazine*. In the piece, Douglas warned of an increasing orthodoxy of thought and fear of anything different. Douglas wrote this piece as the United States was gripped in an anti-Communism fervor that to many historians went overboard and threatened freedom of speech and conscience. Douglas warns in his article about an "ominous trend" toward orthodoxy and a fear for different ideas. Douglas advocated for wide protection of freedom of expression even for controversial or dissident ideas.

DID YOU KNOW!?

What famous decision regarding prosecutorial failure to turn over exculpatory evidence did Douglas write?

Douglas wrote the Court's opinion in *Brady v. Maryland* (1963), which generally stands for the principle that prosecutors must turn over exculpatory evidence to criminal defendants and their counsel. The case involved a death penalty prosecution of John Leo Brady, who along with Donald Boblit had committed armed robbery that led to the death of an older friend of Brady's named William Brooks. Brady and Boblit had planned to rob Brooks and steal his car for a bank robbery. However, Boblit shot and killed Brooks—something Brady did not want to happen. Brady was prosecuted for the death penalty and convicted. However, his counsel learned that prosecutors had failed to turn over evidence of Boblit's confession in which he had said that he (Boblit) was the shooter, not Brady.

Justice Douglas reasoned that the failure of the prosecution to turn over this evidence denied Brady his due-process rights and he was entitled to a new trial with regard to punishment. Douglas explained that "the suppression by the prosecution of evidence favorable to an accused on request violates due process where the evidence is material either to guilt or to punishment."

In part because of this ruling, Brady was spared the death penalty. Additionally, the state of Maryland and Brady's lawyers never agreed on when his new trial on punishment would start. In 1973, Brady's lawyers argued that his rights to a speedy trial were violated. Brady was paroled in 1974. He lived until the age of 76 and passed away in 2009. He never got in criminal trouble again.

In what dissent did Douglas warn about suppressing speech simply because the speakers were Communists?

Douglas dissented in *Dennis v. United States* (1951), a case in which the majority of the Court upheld convictions of a dozen members of the American Communist Party allegedly for plotting the overthrow of the United States and other seditious activities.

But in his dissenting opinion, Douglas said the evidence at the trial did not show evidence of sedition or terror. Instead, according to Douglas, the evidence showed that the defendants preached the tenets of Marxist–Leninist doctrine without resorting to sedition or terror.

He explained:

So far as the present record is concerned, what petitioners did was to organize people to teach and

Eugene Dennis (his real name was Francis Xavier Waldron) was head of the U.S. Communist Party and was persecuted during the McCarthy era. He was convicted in *Dennis v. United States* for speech posing a threat to overthrow the government, but Justice Douglas dissented.

themselves teach the Marxist-Leninist doctrine contained chiefly in four books: Stalin, *Foundations of Leninism* (1924); Marx and Engels, *Manifesto of the Communist Party* (1848); Lenin, *The State and Revolution* (1917); *History of the Communist Party of the Soviet Union* ([Bolsheviks]) (1939).

Those books are to Soviet Communism what *Mein Kampf* was to Nazism. If they are understood, the ugliness of Communism is revealed, its deceit and cunning are exposed, the nature of its activities becomes apparent, and the chances of its success less likely. That is not, of course, the reason why petitioners chose these books for their classrooms. They are fervent Communists to whom these volumes are gospel. They preached the creed with the hope that someday it would be acted upon.

The opinion of the Court does not outlaw these texts nor condemn them to the fire, as the Communists do literature offensive to their creed. But if the books themselves are not outlawed, if they can lawfully remain on library shelves, by what reasoning does their use in a classroom become a crime? It would not be a crime under the Act to introduce these books to a class, though that would be teaching what the creed of violent overthrow of the Government is. The Act, as construed, requires the element of intent—that those who teach the creed believe in it. The crime then depends not on what is taught but on who the teacher is. That is to make freedom of speech turn not on what is said, but on the intent with which it is said. Once we start down that road we enter territory dangerous to the liberties of every citizen.

In what opinion did Douglas explain that the purpose of speech was to invite dispute?

Douglas wrote these words in *Terminiello v. City of Chicago* (1949), a case involving the prosecution of Arthur Terminiello for giving a fiery speech in a Chicago auditorium. Terminiello, a Catholic priest, gave a speech at a meeting of the Christian Veterans group. He made some anti-Semitic comments as well as negative comments about President Franklin Delano Roosevelt and First Lady Eleanor Roosevelt (1884–1962).

Terminiello was arrested and charged with disorderly conduct. However, the U.S. Supreme Court reversed his conviction, with Justice Douglas writing the majority opinion. Douglas reasoned that a "function of free speech under our system of government is to invite dispute." He added that speech "may indeed best serve its high purpose when it induces a condition of unrest, creates dissatisfaction with conditions as they are, or even stirs people to anger."

In what decision did Douglas say obscenity law was a "hodge-podge"?

Douglas called obscenity law a "hodge-podge" in his dissenting opinion in *Miller v. California* (1973). The majority upheld the conviction of California-based pornographer Marvin Miller for mailing brochures advertising books of a sexual nature. The majority upheld his conviction and in the process created a new test for obscenity now known as the "Miller Test," which examines whether a work appeals predominately to a prurient (morbid or shameful) interest in sex, is patently offensive, and lacks serious literary, artistic, political, or scientific value.

Douglas wrote a dissenting opinion in which he criticized obscenity law. He also famously wrote that "Obscenity—which even we cannot define with precision—is a hodge-podge. To send men to jail for violating standards they cannot understand, construe, and apply is a monstrous thing to do in a Nation dedicated to fair trials and due process."

He added: "We deal with highly emotional, not rational, questions. To many the Song of Solomon is obscene. I do not think we, the judges, were ever given the constitutional power to make definitions of obscenity. If it is to be defined, let the people debate and decide by a constitutional amendment what they want to ban as obscene and what standards they want the legislatures and the courts to apply. Perhaps the people will decide that the path towards a mature, integrated society requires that all ideas competing for acceptance must have no censor. Perhaps they will decide otherwise. Whatever the choice, the courts will have some guidelines. Now we have none except our own predilections."

In what decision did Justice Douglas file a lone dissent against the practice of stop and frisk?

Justice Douglas filed a lone dissent in *Terry v. Ohio* (1968), a case in which the Court upheld the practice of "stop and frisk" if a police officer possesses reasonable suspicion that a person may be carrying a weapon. The case involved a veteran police detective named Martin McFadden, who observed three men involved in what he suspected was a potential stick-up job. McFadden went up to the men and frisked them. He found a weapon on defendant John Terry. Terry claimed that the police needed probable cause to frisk him for weapons. The majority of the Court disagreed with Terry and upheld the officer's conduct.

Justice Douglas filed a solitary dissent. He believed that to frisk a person required the police to have probable cause. He explained in powerful language:

> The infringement on personal liberty of any "seizure" of a person can only be "reasonable" under the Fourth Amendment if we require the police to possess "probable cause" before they seize him. Only that line draws a meaningful distinction between an officer's mere inkling and the presence of facts within the officer's personal knowledge which would convince a reasonable man that the person seized has committed, is committing, or is about to commit a particular crime. "In dealing with probable cause, … as the very name implies, we deal with probabilities. These are not technical; they are the factual and practical considerations of everyday life on which reasonable and prudent men, not legal technicians, act."

> To give the police greater power than a magistrate is to take a long step down the totalitarian path. Perhaps such a step is desirable to cope with modern forms of lawlessness. But if it is taken, it should be the deliberate choice of the people through a constitutional amendment. Until the Fourth Amendment, which is closely allied with the Fifth, is rewritten, the person and the effects of the individual are beyond the reach of all government agencies until there are reasonable grounds to believe (probable cause) that a criminal venture has been launched or is about to be launched.

> There have been powerful hydraulic pressures throughout our history that bear heavily on the Court to water down constitutional guarantees and give the police the upper hand. That hydraulic pressure has probably never been greater than it is today.

Yet if the individual is no longer to be sovereign, if the police can pick him up whenever they do not like the cut of his jib, if they can "seize" and "search" him in their discretion, we enter a new regime. The decision to enter it should be made only after a full debate by the people of this country.

Why is William J. Brennan Jr. considered such a great justice?

Justice William Brennan Jr. (1906–1997) is considered a great justice because he wrote so many influential opinions and shaped many different areas of the law. He was a driving force in his first 10 years or so on the Court, when he served as Chief Justice Earl Warren's (1891–1974) key ally. He served more than 33 years on the Court and was able to persuade colleagues not only because of his keen intellect but also because of his classy and personable nature.

William Brennan Jr. was a justice from 1956 to 1990. He was considered a progressive justice who favored abortion and gay rights and opposed the death penalty.

Justice Byron White (1917–2002) wrote of Brennan in a tribute published in the *Yale Law Journal*: "William J. Brennan will surely be remembered as among the greatest Justices who have ever sat on the Supreme Court. And well he should be." Justice Thurgood Marshall (1908–1993) wrote of Brennan in a tribute piece published in the *Harvard Law Review*: "To my mind, what so distinguished Justice Brennan was his faithfulness to a consistent legal vision of how the Constitution should be interpreted. That vision was based on an unwavering commitment to certain core principles, especially First Amendment freedoms and basic principles of civil rights and civil liberties."

What important contribution did Brennan make to state constitutional law?

It is no exaggeration to say that Justice William Brennan revitalized interest and passion for state constitutional law. Brennan became concerned with a series of rulings by the Supreme Court during the Burger Court era and realized that if the Supreme Court will not provide proper protection for individual rights, state high courts could provide such protection under their state constitutions.

The U.S. Constitution sets a floor on the protection of individual liberties but not a ceiling. This means that a state high court cannot provide less protection than the U.S. Supreme Court has done when it comes to interpreting the U.S. Bill of Rights, but a state high court can provide greater protection under its state bill of rights.

In a 1986 lecture published in the *New York Law Review* entitled "The Bill of Rights and the States: The Revival of State Constitutions as Guardians of Individual Rights," he wrote:

This rebirth of interest in state constitutional law should be greeted with equal enthusiasm by all those who support our federal system, liberals and conservatives alike. The development and protection of individual rights pursuant to state constitutions presents no threat to enforcement of national standards; state courts may not provide a level of protection less than that offered by the federal Constitution. Nor should these developments be greeted with dismay by conservatives; the state laboratories are once again open for business.

Why is Brennan considered such an important justice in freedom of expression jurisprudence?

Brennan authored numerous landmark opinions in the area of freedom of expression. For example, he wrote the Court's decision in *New York Times Co. v. Sullivan* (1964), which many regard as the most important free-speech opinion in American jurisprudence. Before *Sullivan*, state defamation laws were immune from First Amendment scrutiny. This left not enough protection for those who criticized government officials.

The *Sullivan* case involved an editorial advertisement published in the *New York Times* that criticized civil rights abuses occurring in Montgomery, Alabama. L. B. Sullivan (1921–1977), the police commissioner in Montgomery, sued for libel. An Alabama state jury awarded him $500,000 in damages. While there were some factually inaccurate statements, the U.S. Supreme Court reversed. Brennan explained that libel can claim no "talismanic immunity" from the First Amendment. He also explained that individuals must have the ability to criticize the government and government officials, writing that there is a "profound national commitment to the principle that debate on public issues should be uninhibited, robust, and wide-open, and that it may well include vehement, caustic, and sometimes unpleasantly sharp attacks on government and public officials."

Brennan also created a new standard for those suing public officials for defamation: that they must show by clear and convincing evidence that the plaintiff must show actual malice defined as knowing the information was false or acting in "reckless disregard" whether the statement was true or false.

Brennan added:

> What a State may not constitutionally bring about by means of a criminal statute is likewise beyond the reach of its civil law of libel. The fear of damage awards under a rule such as that invoked by the Alabama courts here may be markedly more inhibiting than the fear of prosecution under a criminal statute....

> A rule compelling the critic of official conduct to guarantee the truth of all his factual assertions—and to do so on pain of libel judgments virtually unlimited in amount—leads to a comparable "self-censorship." Allowance of the defense of truth, with the burden of proving it on the defendant, does not mean that only false speech will be deterred....

> The rule thus dampens the vigor and limits the variety of public debate. It is inconsistent with the First and Fourteenth Amendments. The constitutional guarantees require, we think, a federal rule that prohibits a public official from recovering damages for a defamatory falsehood relating to his official conduct unless he proves that the statement was made with "actual malice"—that is, with knowledge that it was false or with reckless disregard of whether it was false or not.

What other decisions did Brennan write that ensured his First Amendment legacy?

A few years later, he wrote an opinion that was very important for freedom of expression on college campuses. The decision in *Keyishian v. New York Board of Regents* (1967) involved a New York law that required public employees to sign an oath that they were not members of the Communist Party. The law was designed to rid college campuses of so-called "subversives." Brennan invalidated the provision, writing: "Our Nation is deeply committed to safeguarding academic freedom, which is of transcendent value to all of us, and not merely to the teachers concerned. That freedom is therefore a special concern of the First Amendment, which does not tolerate laws that cast a pall of orthodoxy over the classroom."

Brennan authored a powerful dissenting opinion in *Hazelwood School District v. Kuhlmeier* (1988), a case involving the censorship of a high school newspaper by the principal. The majority reasoned that the principal could engage in such censorship as long as he had a legitimate education reason. But Brennan in dissent wrote passionately: "Unthinking contempt for individual rights is intolerable for any state official. It is particularly insidious from one to whom the public entrusts the task of inculcating in its youth an appreciation for the cherished democratic liberties that our Constitution guarantees."

The following year, Brennan wrote the Court's opinion in the flag-burning case of *Texas v. Johnson* (1989). Gregory Lee Johnson (1956–) was charged with violating a Texas flag desecration law after burning an American flag outside of the Republican National Convention in Dallas, Texas. Brennan, however, explained that Johnson's act, however distasteful, was a form of political dissent. He famously explained: "If there is bedrock principle underlying the First Amendment, it is that the government may not prohibit the expression of an idea simply because society finds the idea itself offensive or disagreeable."

Political activist Gregory Lee Johnson became the focus of a Supreme Court case involving the First Amendment after he burned an American flag at the Republican National Convention in Dallas in 1984.

How did Brennan change his position with regard to obscenity?

Justice Brennan wrote the Court's seminal obscenity opinion in *Roth v. United States* (1957), reasoning that obscenity was not a form of protected speech and could be outlawed by federal and state authorities. Brennan reasoned that "obscenity is not within the area of constitutionally protected speech or press." He noted that for years, many states had passed laws outlawing obscene material. However, the difficult task was fashioning a test that judges could use to distinguish unprotected obscenity from sexual expression deserving of protection. In *Roth*, Brennan fashioned the following test: "whether to the average person, applying contemporary community standards, the dominant theme of the material taken as a whole appeals to the prurient interest."

However, 16 years later, in a dissenting opinion in *Paris Adult Theatre I v. Slaton* (1973), Brennan changed positions and ruled that obscenity laws were too vague and subjective and posed too great a threat to freedom of expression. "As a result of our failure to define standards with predictable application to any given piece of material, there is no probability of regularity in obscenity decisions in state and lower federal courts," he wrote. "I would hold, therefore, that at least in the absence of distribution to juveniles or obtrusive exposure to unconsenting adults, the First and Fourteenth Amendments prohibit the State and Federal Governments from attempting wholly to suppress sexually oriented materials on the basis of their allegedly 'obscene' contents."

Why is Justice Thurgood Marshall considered so great?

Thurgood Marshall (1908–1993) is considered great because of his historic significance in working as a civil rights advocate and for being the most consistent defender of individual rights on the Supreme Court during his 24-year tenure on the high court. Juan Williams wrote in 1990 that Marshall was "the most important black man of this century." Others have called him the most important lawyer of the twentieth century. Professor Drew Days wrote of Marshall: "He has been a supreme conscience. In the law he remains our supreme conscience."

His longtime colleague and confidant on the Court, Justice William Brennan, said of Justice Marshall: "Thurgood is one of our century's legal giants. Before he joined the judiciary, he was probably the most important legal advocate in America and the central figure in our nation's struggle to eliminate institutional racism."

What was Marshall's record as a Supreme Court litigator before he became a judge?

Before he became a judge, Thurgood Marshall was the leading civil rights lawyer in the United States. In that capacity as "Mr. Civil Rights," he argued many civil rights cases before the U.S. Supreme Court, including *Brown v. Board of Education*. He also argued many cases before the Supreme Court when he served as U.S. solicitor general. In his career, he argued 32 cases before the U.S. Supreme Court, winning 29 of them.

Who were Marshall's mentors in law?

Marshall's mentors were Charles Hamilton Houston (1895–1950) and William Hastie (1904–1976). Houston was the assistant dean of Howard Law School when Marshall was a student there. Houston took Marshall under his wing and later hired him to work for the NAACP in 1936 as special assistant counsel. Houston urged Marshall and his classmates that they must not only be lawyers but also social engineers for justice.

DID YOU KNOW!?

What was Marshall's first name at birth?

Marshall was born in 1908 as Thoroughgood Marshall in Baltimore, Maryland. He changed the name to Thurgood in the second grade.

Hastie, who was Houston's second cousin, was an instructor at Harvard Law School. He also had a significant impact on Marshall's development as a law student. Hastie later became the first African American to serve as a federal appeals court judge.

Where was Marshall denied admission to law school because of his race?

The University of Maryland denied Marshall admission to law school because of his race. That is why Marshall attended

Where was Marshall nearly lynched?

Marshall nearly faced death in Columbia, Tennessee, on November 28, 1946. Marshall had come down to Columbia after the so-called "Columbia Race Riots," when numerous African American men were tried in criminal court for a shootout with whites who had forcibly invaded the African American section of town.

Local law enforcement had grabbed Marshall from the vehicle that he drove with Nashville-based African American lawyer Z. Alexander Looby (1899–1972) and Chattanooga-based white attorney Maurice Weaver (1912–1983), who had helped defend the African Americans charged after the Columbia Race Riots. After the police grabbed Marshall, they took him down to the Duck River near a big tree. Fortunately, Looby and Weaver followed, and the police drove Marshall back to Columbia, where they tried to charge him with drunk driving—a false charge. A local magistrate let Marshall go.

Howard Law School. In a nice twist of justice, Marshall later represented with Houston a man named Donald Gaines Murray (1914–1986), who also was denied admission to Maryland's law school because of the color of his skin. Houston successfully argued the case of *Murray v. Pearson* before the Maryland Court of Appeals (Maryland's highest state court).

In his biography of Marshall, *A Defiant Life*, Howard Ball relates Marshall's comments about this case: "I filed it the first year I left law school to get even with the bastards ... to get even with the whole segregated system."

Why is William Rehnquist considered an important and significant justice in American history?

William Rehnquist (1924–2005) served as both associate justice and chief justice during his 33 years of service on the high court. He was a forceful advocate for the positions and issues he cared deeply about, such as federalism, but he also was known as an eminently fair and effective administrator of the Court. He was efficient in serving as chief justice and was very fair in the assignment power—the power of the chief justice to pick the author of an opinion when the chief justice is in the majority.

Upon his death, President George W. Bush (1946–) stated: "He was extremely well respected for his powerful intellect. He was respected for his deep commitment to the rule of law and his profound devotion to duty. He provided superb leadership for the federal court system, improving the delivery of justice to the American people and earning the admiration of his colleagues throughout the judiciary."

Even some of his ideological opponents praised him upon his death. For example, Senator Edward Kennedy (1932–2009)—who voted against Rehnquist's confirmation—said of the late

Chief Justice William Rehnquist led the Court from 1986 to 2005. A conservative, he tended to favor the importance of state rights over the federal government and was not afraid to make a judgment against the latter if he felt it overstepped its constitutional powers.

chief justice: "Chief Justice Rehnquist served this country with the greatest distinction, and I respected his leadership of the federal judiciary and his strong commitment to the integrity and independence of the courts."

Why was his confirmation as chief justice so contentious?

Much of the opposition to Rehnquist involved the same accusations made against him during his initial confirmation hearings in 1971—that he had participated in a Republican Party voter suppression operation while he was an attorney in Arizona, that he was not truthful about a memorandum he had authored about *Plessy v. Ferguson* when he was a law clerk in 1952, and that his views were too far to the right on issues of civil rights. Some also criticized him for refusing to recuse himself from the case of *Laird v. Tatum*, a case challenging the military's surveillance system, which had included his testimony prior to him being named to the Court.

But Rehnquist ultimately prevailed by a vote of 67–33. He earned a "well-qualified" mark from the American Bar Association. Democratic senator Howard Heflin (1921–2005) also came to support Rehnquist, stating:

> I know that there are those who question Justice Rehnquist's sensitivity to civil rights of minorities and women. I do not agree with every opinion of Justice Rehnquist. In fact, I find myself in disagreement with many. But I do not believe those opinions are so extreme as to be unreasonable. Every stream has a right bank and a left bank. There is no question that Justice Rehnquist's views are always close to the right boundary of the stream, but they are nonetheless within the mainstream of modern judicial thought.

President Ronald Reagan (1911–2004) praised the ultimate confirmation vote, stating: "This vote in the full Senate is a bipartisan rejection of the political posturing that marred the confirmation hearings. It is clear to all now that the extraordinary controversy surrounding the hearings had little to do with Justice Rehnquist's record or character—both are unassailable and unimpeachable. The attacks come from those whose ideology runs contrary to his profound and unshakable belief in the proper constitutional role of the judiciary in this country."

Why is Ruth Bader Ginsburg considered such a historic Supreme Court jurist?

Justice Ruth Bader Ginsburg (1933–2020), like Thurgood Marshall before her, was a famous lawyer far before she ever became a judge. Though she stood barely five feet tall, she was a giant in American jurisprudence. Known as "the Thurgood

Justice Ruth Bader Ginsburg served on the Court from 1993 to 2020. She was the second woman and the first Jewish woman to become a Supreme Court justice.

Marshall for gender equality," she litigated many cases before the Supreme Court on gender issues.

She served 13 years on the U.S. Court of Appeals for the District of Columbia and then 27 years on the U.S. Supreme Court. During this time, she became quite well known for her commitment, attention to detail, and, in her later years, her powerful dissenting opinions.

On her death, Chief Justice John Roberts (1955–) said of his colleague: "Our Nation has lost a jurist of historic stature. We at the Supreme Court have lost a cherished colleague. Today we mourn, but with confidence that future generations will remember Ruth Bader Ginsburg as we knew her—a tireless and resolute champion of justice." Another colleague, Justice Elena Kagan (1960–), was equally effusive in her praise: "To me, as to countless others, Ruth Bader Ginsburg was a hero. As an attorney, she led the fight to grant women equal rights under the law. As a judge, she did justice every day—working to ensure that this country's legal system lives up to its ideals and extends its rights and protections to those once excluded. And in both roles, she held to—indeed, exceeded—the highest standards of legal craft. Her work was as careful as it was creative, as disciplined as it was visionary. It will endure for as long as Americans retain their commitment to law."

The Bill of Rights

What is the Bill of Rights?

The Bill of Rights consists of the first ten amendments to the U.S. Constitution, ratified on December 15, 1791. It largely protects individual freedoms from invasion by the federal government. Through a process known as "incorporation," the Supreme Court has found that the vast majority of the freedoms found in the Bill of Rights now also limit state and local government officials.

Why did the Framers not add a Bill of Rights at the Constitutional Convention?

Good question. The Framers did not add a bill of rights in part because some members at the Convention felt that there was no need for a bill of rights. Some of these individuals pointed out that the Constitution itself was a bill of rights, as it protected individuals from bills of attainders, ex post facto laws, and the requirement that one must take religious oaths to hold office. Other members of the Convention were simply more focused on such issues as the powers of the three branches of government, the thorny issue of representation in the houses of Congress, and the ugly specter of slavery. After all, the Constitutional Convention almost ended in failure.

Delegate Charles Pinckney (1757–1824) of South Carolina made the first motion for freedoms now contained in the Bill of Rights. On August 20, he proposed that three clauses be added to the Constitution. These clauses concerned the liberty of the press, the quartering of troops in private homes, and a standing army. In those days, newspapers were the dominant mode of communication. Today, with flagging newspaper sales and the ubiquity of the Internet, many may not appreciate just how much influence newspapers had. Thus, freedom of the press was important. The second freedom Pinckney advocated for was prohibiting the quartering of troops in private homes. This concern ultimately led to the Third Amendment. The third freedom concerned a standing army. Some delegates did not want the country to have an army during times of piece.

Pinckney was not alone in calling for a bill of rights. On September 12, George Mason (1725–1792), the author of the Virginia Declaration of Rights, said he "wished the plan had been prefaced with a bill of rights and would second a motion if made for the purpose." Elbridge Gerry (1744–1814) made the motion, and Mason seconded it. The delegates voted down the motion unanimously. Gerry, who later served as James Madison's (1751–1836) second vice president, refused to sign the Constitution because it failed to have a bill of rights. He specifically emphasized protecting the right of conscience and a free press.

Other delegates argued that a bill of rights would not provide any greater liberty. For example, Roger Sherman (1721–1793) of Connecticut famously said: "No bill of rights ever yet bound the supreme power longer than the honeymoon of a new married couple, unless the ruler were interested in preserving the right." Finally, as historian Catherine Drinker Bowen writes in her book *The Miracle at Philadelphia*: "The framers looked upon the Constitution as a bill of rights in itself; all its provisions were for a free people and a people responsible."

A few delegates opposed the Bill of Rights because they thought it might lead to the abolition of slavery. General Charles Cotesworth Pinckney (1746–1825), a delegate from South Carolina (not to be confused with Charles Pinckney), bluntly stated his objection to a bill of rights: "Bill of rights generally begin with declaring that all men are by nature born free. Now, we should make that declaration with a very bad grace, when a large part of our property consists in men who are actually born slaves." Reading between the lines, General Pinckney meant that a bill of rights and its emphasis on individual freedom would provide support against slavery.

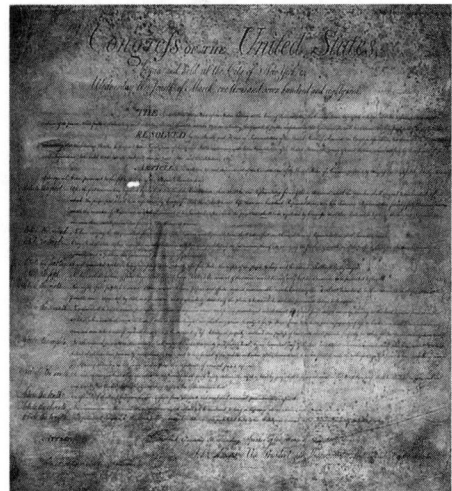

After considerable debate, the Bill of Rights was ratified in 1791. It limits certain federal powers in favor of rights for the states and citizens.

How did the Bill of Rights come to be added?

The battle over whether to ratify (or formally approve) the new Constitution by the states was an intense struggle. Many so-called Anti-Federalists criticized the new Constitution because it did not contain a bill of rights. They seized upon the lack of a bill of rights as a prime weapon in the ratification battles. Historian Robert Rutland writes: "The Federalists, failing to realize the importance of a bill of rights, miscalculated public opinion and found themselves on the defensive almost from the outset of the ratification struggle."

James Madison, a congressional representative from Virginia and a key member of the Philadelphia Convention, came to view the Bill of Rights as necessary to secure popular support for the new Constitution. Madison, who had worked so hard in Philadelphia, did not want the Constitution altered or changed. He recognized that the lack of a bill of rights was a trouble point. Though Madison had originally not wanted a bill of rights, he recognized that the Anti-Federalists were gaining popular support for their pro–bill of rights position.

Madison originally subscribed to the view of his fellow *Federalist Papers* author Alexander Hamilton (1755–1804) that the Constitution itself was a bill of rights. There is some support for this view, as the Constitution prohibits ex post facto laws—laws that increase punishment after the act was committed. It also prohibits so-called bills of attainder, laws targeting specific individuals. Madison also disparaged a bill of rights as a "paper barrier" that would not offer any real protection to the people and may even expand the power of the government.

But Madison became a convert on the need for a bill of rights to get the Constitution approved. However, his mentor and fellow Virginian convinced him that a bill of rights was necessary—that was Thomas Jefferson (1743–1826), the so-called "Sage of Monticello."

The two engaged in a correspondence across the Atlantic Ocean because Jefferson was serving his country as minister to France. Thus, while Madison took a leading role at the Philadelphia Convention, Jefferson could only wait to hear from overseas.

Jefferson persuaded Madison that the inclusion of a bill of rights was necessary to secure popular support for the new Constitution. Jefferson emphasized that the Constitution begins with the words "We the People" and there must be popular support for this new document. After all, the Framers were asking a lot of the people to accept a strong, new central government. Madison wrote to Jefferson in October 1788 that "my own opinion has always been in favor of a bill of rights." However, Madison also wrote in his letter that he believed a bill of rights would be a mere "parchment barrier" that could not protect citizens from an oppressive majority.

Jefferson convinced Madison that the Bill of Rights was necessary. On June 8, 1789, Madison talked about the Bill of Rights as "the great rights of Mankind." He warned his colleagues in Congress that the Bill of Rights should be added "to satisfy the public mind that their liberties will be perpetual."

THE FIRST AMENDMENT

What is the First Amendment and the freedoms it protects?

"Congress shall make no law respecting an establishing of religion or prohibiting the free exercise thereof; or abridging the freedom of speech, or of the press, or the right of the people to peaceably assembly and petition the government for a redress of grievances," reads the First Amendment.

The First Amendment consists of the first 45 words of the Bill of Rights and consists of five freedoms: religion, speech, press, assembly, and petition. Additionally, the U.S. Supreme Court also

Without the benefit of the First Amendment, Americans could very easily lose their religious freedoms and might even see a national religion established that would deny many people the right to practice their faith.

ruled in *NAACP v. Alabama* (1958) that the First Amendment protects the related freedom of association.

The First Amendment serves as our blueprint for personal freedom. It ensures that we live in an open society. Without the First Amendment, religious minorities could be persecuted or the government could establish a single national religion. The press could not criticize government, and citizens could not mobilize for social change. This would mean we would lose our individual freedom.

What are the religious liberty clauses in the First Amendment?

The first two clauses of the First Amendment—"respecting an establishment of religion or prohibiting the free exercise thereof"—are the religion clauses. The first is the Establishment Clause. The second is the Free Exercise Clause. Together, these clauses require that the government act in a neutral manner when it comes to religion.

The Establishment Clause provides that church and state remain separate to a certain degree. In a letter to the Danbury

Baptists in 1802, President Thomas Jefferson used the phrase a "wall of separation between church and state." The U.S. Supreme Court later used Jefferson's "wall of separation" metaphor to describe the meaning of the Establishment Clause and rule that state-mandated prayer in public schools violated the Establishment Clause.

The second religion clause of the First Amendment is the Free Exercise Clause. It protects a person's right to practice religion freely or to practice no religion at all. The First Amendment protects both the religiously devout and the fiercely atheistic.

There is absolute protection for freedom of belief under the Free Exercise Clause. A person can believe in God, Buddha, Allah, or the Flying Spaghetti Monster. In fact, courts are not supposed to determine free-exercise cases based on whether a religious practice is orthodox or a commonly practiced religion.

However, there is no absolute protection for religious-based conduct that may conflict with a neutral and generally applicable law that applies across the board. In fact, the level of free exercise protection has diminished somewhat over the years because of a difference in approach from the U.S. Supreme Court.

Why is freedom of speech considered so important?

Freedom of speech is considered so important because it is so intimately connected to the freedom of thought. The First Amendment and its protection of free speech is what Justice Benjamin Cardozo (1870–1938) once called "the matrix, the indispensable condition, of nearly every other freedom." Without freedom of speech, individuals could not criticize the government, speak out against abuses, achieve individual self-fulfillment, or participate in the process of democratic self-government.

DID YOU KNOW!?

What early federal law presented the country with arguably its first major debate over the meaning of free speech?

The Sedition Act of 1798, a law used by the Federalist Party to silence many Democratic-Republican newspaper editors, was the federal law that presented the country with a major debate on the meaning of freedom of expression. The administration of Federalist president John Adams (1735–1826) and a Federalist-dominated Congress passed the law.

The law was a draconian assault on free speech, providing in part that it was unlawful to "write, print, utter, or publish, … any false, scandalous and malicious writing or writings against the government of the United States, or either house of the Congress of the United States, or the President of the United States, with intent to defame the said government."

The law essentially criminalized harsh political criticism, treating it as defaming the government. The Sedition Act of 1798 turned the First Amendment on its head by criminalizing political speech—the type of speech that inspired the drafting of the provision in the first place. Sadly, many of the Framers did not see a problem in silencing their political opposition. Even members of the U.S. Supreme Court were actively involved in this process because of the unusual dual role that these jurists served in the early days of the country riding circuit. Justice Samuel Chase (1741–1811) later faced impeachment proceedings for this poor conduct during the Sedition Act trial of James Callender (1758–1803).

Ultimately, the country survived the Sedition Act ordeal when Thomas Jefferson became president, as he pardoned all those who had been convicted under it.

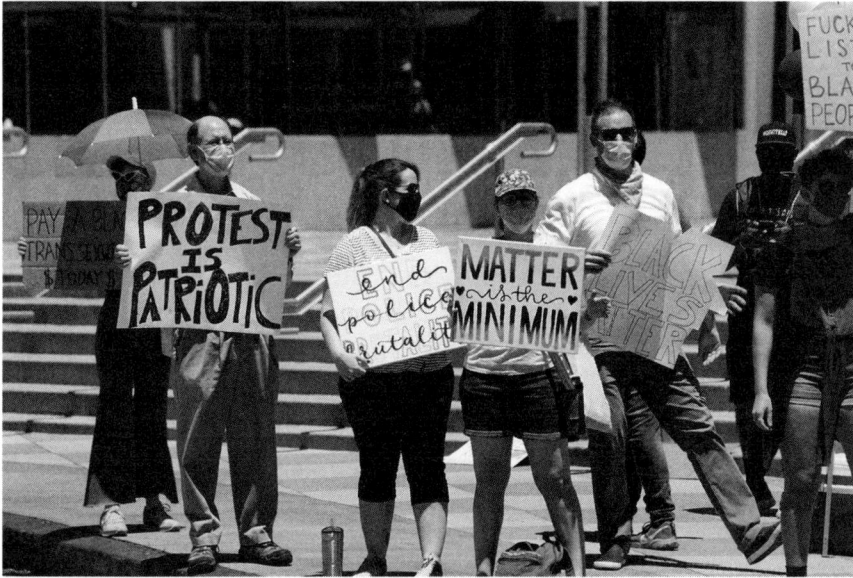

The Sedition Acts of 1798 and 1918 were basically gross attempts by the federal government to silence political opposition. Fortunately, the U.S. Supreme Court struck these laws down as unconstitutional; if it hadn't, such protests as the BLM movement would have led to jail time for any participants.

How did First Amendment law develop during World War I?

First Amendment free-speech law developed during the time of World War I. Historian and law professor Paul Murphy explained this well in his *World War I and the Origin of Civil Liberties in the United States*. The United States often suppressed the speech of political dissidents like anarchists and socialists.

In an act perilously similar to the Sedition Act of 1798, Congress passed the Espionage Act of 1917 and an amendment to it called the Sedition Act of 1918. These laws were used to prosecute political opponents. The Espionage Act criminalized attempting to cause insubordination to the war effort, willfully attempting to cause insurrection, and obstructing the recruiting or enlistment of potential volunteers.

The Sedition Act of 1918 was a more direct assault on free speech. It provided:

Uttering, printing, writing, or publishing any disloyal, profane, scurrilous, or abusive language intended to cause contempt, scorn … as regards the form of government of the United States or Constitution, or the flag or the uniform of the Army or Navy … urging any curtailment of the war with intent to hinder its prosecution; advocating, teaching, defending, or acts supporting or favoring the cause of any country at war with the United States, or opposing the cause of the United States.

Literally, thousands of people were prosecuted under these laws. Even labor organizer and frequent presidential hopeful Eugene Debs (1755–1826) was imprisoned for violating the Espionage Act for criticizing the draft. Debs had famously stated in a speech that "you need to know that you are fit for something better than slavery and common fodder."

What was the "clear and present danger" test?

The "clear and present danger" test was a test developed by U.S. Supreme Court justice Oliver Wendell Holmes Jr. (1841–1935) to determine when speech was protected and when it was not protected. He explained in his opinion in *Schenck v. United States* (1919):

The question in every case is whether the words used are used in such circumstances and are of such a nature as to create a *clear and present danger* that they will bring about the substantive evils that Congress has a right to prevent. It is a question of proximity and degree. When a nation is at war many things that might be said in time of peace are such a hindrance to its effort that their utterance will not be endured so long as men fight, and that no Court could regard them as protected by any constitutional right.

Holmes became even more protective of free speech and political dissent in his dissenting opinion later in 1919 in *Abrams v. United States* (1919). Holmes wrote: "It is only the present danger of immediate evil or an intent to bring it about that warrants Congress in setting a limit to the expression of opinion where private rights are not concerned."

What is the marketplace of ideas?

This was a metaphor used once again by Justice Oliver Wendell Holmes Jr. in his great dissent in *Abrams v. United States* (1919) to express the idea that it is better to let political thought into the marketplace of ideas rather than have government censorship. Holmes famously explained: "But when men have realized that time has upset many fighting faiths, they may come to believe even more that they believe the very foundations of their

How did the Jehovah's Witnesses contribute to First Amendment jurisprudence?

In the 1930s and 1940s, the Supreme Court protected First Amendment principles largely in a group of cases filed by Jehovah's Witnesses, who often ran afoul of city officials for their insistence on distributing religious literature even in the face of prosecution and persecution. A notable example was an African American man named Rosco Jones, who was prosecuted in Opelika, Alabama, for selling religious literature without a license and nearly beaten to death in LaGrange, Georgia.

DID YOU KNOW!?

own conduct that the ultimate good desired is better reached by free trade in ideas—that the best test of truth is the power of the thought to get itself accepted in the competition of the market, and that truth is the only ground upon which their wishes safely can be carried out."

Why was the Civil Rights Movement important to freedom of speech?

The 1960s witnessed a period of flourishing for First Amendment freedoms, as the Warren Court reached its apex of power and decided a litany of free-expression cases that arose out of the Civil Rights Movement. In civil rights cases during the 1960s, the Supreme Court breathed First Amendment life into libel law, invalidated discriminatory permit denials for civil rights protestors, overturned breach-of-the-peace convictions for peaceful protests on state capital grounds, and invalidated a conviction for peaceful sit-ins at segregated lunch counters and libraries.

The Civil Rights March on Washington, D.C., on August 28, 1964, was one of a long series of protests that led to great changes in the laws of the land, thanks in part to a Supreme Court led by a progressive chief justice: Earl Warren.

Does the First Amendment protect the right of citizens to criticize government officials?

Yes, and in fact, this is probably the most fundamental of all free-speech principles. The essence of the First Amendment is the ability of individuals to criticize the government. The Supreme Court defended this principle most notably in *New York Times Co. v. Sullivan* (1964), ruling that an editorial advertisement published in the *New York Times* that spoke of rights abuses perpetrated by Southern officials in Montgomery, Alabama, did not subject the newspaper or principal creators of the ad to liability for defamation. L. B. Sullivan (1921–1977), the head of the police department, had sued the *Times* and four African American clergymen who created the ad for defamation, even though he was not specifically identified.

An all-white, state court jury in Alabama had awarded Sullivan $500,000 in damages, a verdict upheld by the Alabama Supreme Court. The *Times* appealed to the U.S. Supreme Court, and the fate of media entities to report on civil rights abuse hung in the balance.

Justice William Brennan Jr. (1906–1997) memorably wrote that "there is a profound national commitment that debate on public issues should be robust, uninhibited, and wide-open and may well include vehement, caustic and unpleasantly sharp attacks on public officials."

What is the importance of content discrimination to First Amendment law?

Content discrimination refers to the fact that government officials generally should not censor speech based on its content or message. The concern is that the government might engage in thought control, and freedom of thought is the beginning of freedom of speech.

Laws that restrict speech based on content are treated differently—as more suspect—than laws that do not. The key terms in First Amendment law are "content-based" and "content-neutral." A content-based law is one that discriminates against speech based on content. A content-neutral law is one that applies across the board to *all* forms of speech or is passed without reference to the content of the speech. Content-based laws receive greater scrutiny from reviewing courts because courts are more suspicious that the government is trying to dictate thought and speech. Courts evaluate these laws under the highest form of judicial review known as strict scrutiny. This means that the government must show that it has a compelling, or very strong, interest in the law and the law is very narrowly drawn. On the other hand, content-neutral laws are subject to a lower standard of review, called intermediate or heightened scrutiny. Here, the government must have an important or substantial governmental interest (instead of a compelling one) and the law must be narrowly drawn.

Does the First Amendment apply to more than verbal speech and the printed word?

Yes, the First Amendment applies to more than verbal speech and words in print. The reach of the First Amendment extends to a wide range of symbolic speech and so-called expressive conduct. For example, the Supreme Court ruled in *Stromberg v. California* (1931) that then-19-year-old Yetta Stromberg had a free-speech right to display a red flag at a Communist youth camp.

Decades later, the U.S. Supreme Court ruled in *Tinker v. Des Moines Independent Community School District* (1969) that Iowa public school students John Tinker (1950–) and his sister Mary

Now a free speech and youth rights activist, Mary Beth Tinker is shown here speaking at the E. W. Scripps School of Journalism at Ohio University in 2014.

Beth Tinker (1952–) had a First Amendment right to wear black peace armbands to protest U.S. involvement in the Vietnam War at their schools. The Court protected their symbolic speech, calling it "akin to pure speech."

More controversially, the First Amendment also protected the right of political protestor Gregory Lee Johnson (1956–), who burned an American flag as part of a protest against policies of the Reagan administration. Prosecuted for violating a Texas flag desecration law, the Court found that Johnson's act was a form of pure speech in *Texas v. Johnson* (1989).

Why are expressive conduct cases challenging from a First Amendment perspective?

The difficult task is determining when expressive conduct is "expressive" enough to merit First Amendment review. The Supreme Court has examined this in a variety of contexts. One of their efforts came from the unusual expression of a student named Harold Spence, who flew an upside-down flag outside his dormitory room to express his displeasure at the U.S. bombing of Cambodia. The Court created what has become known as "the Spence Test." First, there must be an intent to convey a particularized message and, second, that message must be reasonably understood by others. The test is not as protective of First Amendment rights as it should be. After all, not all messages are particularized—nor should they be. Furthermore, First Amendment freedoms should not necessarily depend on the understanding of third parties.

But, it remains true that—as Chief Justice William Rehnquist (1924–2005) once wrote—there are a lot of things out there with a "kernel of free expression," but they are not sufficiently expressive enough to merit protection. Some of the First Amendment claims can border on the bizarre. Take the case of the Indiana man who claimed he had a First Amendment right to grow the grass in his yard as high as he wanted to protest the overly authoritarian nature of city officials. Or the Minnesota man who claimed he had a First Amendment right to throw a pie in the face of a city councilman whose policies he detested.

Does the First Amendment often protect offensive and obnoxious speech?

Yes, it most certainly does. The flag burner, the hatemonger, and the funeral protestor all have benefited from the generosity of the First Amendment's broad coverage. Justice William Brennan expressed this sentiment quite succinctly in *Texas v. Johnson* (1989), writing, "If there is a bedrock principle underlying the First Amendment, it is that the government may not prohibit the expression of an idea simply because society finds it offensive or disagreeable."

The Court continued that principle with its ruling in *Snyder v. Phelps* (2011), protecting members of the Westboro Baptist Church from liability. Members of the church engaged in the most repugnant sorts of speech and engaged in protests near the funerals of slain military men. The group claimed that God was punishing the United States for its toleration of homosexuality.

Yet, the Supreme Court protected the right of church members to protest peacefully. Chief Justice John G. Roberts Jr. (1955–) famously wrote:

> Speech is powerful. It can stir people to action, move them to tears of both joy and sorrow, and—as it did here—inflict great pain. On the facts before us, we cannot react to that pain by punishing the speaker. As a Nation we have chosen a different course—to protect even hurtful speech on public issues to ensure that we do not stifle public debate. That choice requires that we shield Westboro from tort liability for its picketing in this case.

Does the First Amendment protect all forms of speech?

No, the First Amendment does not protect all forms of speech, even though the text of the First Amendment is absolute—"Congress shall make no law … abridging the freedom of speech." In the words of the late Justice Hugo Black (1886–1971)—in certain contexts at least—"no law" meant no law.

But the freedom of speech is not absolute. You don't have a First Amendment right to perjure yourself in court or extort money from another person. There are a host of other examples of unprotected categories of speech. Some of the more common are obscenity, incitement to imminent lawless action, true threats, obscenity, child pornography, and fighting words.

What are "fighting words"?

The U.S. Supreme Court famously defined fighting words as "words which by their very utterance inflict injury or cause an immediate breach of the peace." Fighting words apply to direct, face-to-face personal insults.

What is obscenity?

Obscenity refers to a narrow range of sexually explicit material that appeals to a morbid interest in sex, is patently offensive, and has no serious value. To be legally obscene, material first must appeal predominately to a prurient interest in sex. Prurient is defined as morbid or shameful. Second, the material must depict sexual material in a "patently offensive" way. Both of these prongs of the so-called Miller test (named after the Supreme Court decision in *Miller v. California* in 1973) are considered under community standards—which essentially means whatever a local jury decides. Third, the material must have no serious literary, artistic, political, or scientific value. This last prong prohibits an overly puritanical prosecutor and community from criminalizing sexual material that really ought to be considered protected speech.

How does the First Amendment protect freedom of assembly and petition?

The last two freedoms of the First Amendment ensure that citizens can assemble together and directly petition the government to call public attention to a certain cause. There has been less case law on these last two freedoms in the First Amendment, as they often are viewed as appendages or extensions to freedom of speech. After all, when persons assemble together to protest, they also are speaking or expressing their opposition. Similarly, a petition to the government is a form of speech.

Over the course of American history, striking workers, civil rights advocates, antiwar demonstrators, and Ku Klux Klan marchers have sought the protections of the First Amendment. They sought the right to freely assemble and petition the government for a redress of grievances. Sometimes, these efforts have galvanized public support or changed public perceptions. The freedom of assembly was essential to both the Civil Rights Movement of the 1950s and 1960s and the women's suffrage movement.

Perhaps the most eloquent example of this occurred in March 1961, when nearly 200 African American students met at Mt. Zion

The Ku Klux Klan, a white supremacist group, has argued for their First Amendment right to assemble, allowing them to do, for example, public marches.

Baptist Church and marched down to the state capital in Columbia, South Carolina. Among these protestors was future U.S. Congress leader James Clyburn (1940–).

Carrying placards reading "Down with Segregation" and similar messages, the students walked single and double file for approximately 45 minutes, attracting a crowd of 200 to 300 onlookers, when the police gave them 15 minutes to disperse. Instead of leaving, the students chanted patriotic and religious songs. At the end of the 15 minutes, police officers arrested the students. A magistrate court convicted 187 students, subjecting them to fines and jail time. The South Carolina Supreme Court affirmed the convictions.

However, the students appealed to the U.S. Supreme Court, which reversed the convictions. In the majority opinion for the Supreme Court, Justice Potter Stewart (1915–1985) wrote that the students' actions "reflect an exercise of these basic constitutional rights [to speech, assembly, and petition] in their most pristine and classic form." Stewart emphasized that the students acted peaceably and never threatened violence or harm. He concluded that the First and Fourteenth Amendments do not "permit a State to make criminal the peaceful expression of unpopular views."

In recent years, a massive outpouring of social justice protests have taken place across the country over the deaths of individuals like George Floyd (1973–2020) in interactions with police officers. The deaths of Floyd and others seared the collective conscience of many and led to an increase in social activism. Many of the protests have remained peaceful, but some have degenerated into violence. The First Amendment protects the right to assembly peacefully but does not protect against violence, looting, and other criminal conduct.

THE SECOND AMENDMENT

What does the Second Amendment say?

"A well-regulated militia, being necessary to the security of the free state, the right of the people to keep and bear arms shall not be infringed."

What is odd about the wording of the Second Amendment?

The Second Amendment has odd wording because it combines two clauses—one dealing with the militia and the other with the right to keep and bear arms. This has led to different

Should the Second Amendment be interpreted as applying solely to militias such as the Helena, Montana, militia shown here? What about gun ownership for hunting or protecting one's home from intruders?

interpretations of the amendment as to whether the Framers meant for civilians to own arms solely for the purpose of maintaining militias or whether that right should extend to all people for any reason because gun ownership rights should not be infringed upon in any way.

What used to be the primary interpretation of the Second Amendment?

The primary interpretation used to focus on the militia clause, that the Second Amendment dealt with a collective right of the states to have a militia. In other words, the thinking was that the Second Amendment protected the collective right of the people as a whole to have a militia. Under this interpretation, a person only has a right to keep and bear arms if used in militia service.

The U.S. Supreme Court seemingly adopted the collectivist interpretation of the Second Amendment in *Miller v. United States* (1939), ruling that Jack Miller and Frank Layton violated the National Firearms Act of 1934 by transporting a double-barrel shotgun across state lines from Arkansas to Oklahoma. The Supreme Court, per Justice James McReynolds (1862–1946), determined that there was no reasonable relationship between such a weapon and militia service and, thus, there was no Second Amendment defense to prosecution. Many interpreted the decision as reasoning that the Second Amendment protected militia service, not an individual right to carry weapons. The Ninth Circuit in *Silveira v. Lockyer* (2002) wrote that "[w]hat *Miller* does strongly imply, however, is that the Supreme Court rejects the traditional individual rights view."

When did the Supreme Court find that the Second Amendment protected an individual right to keep and bear arms?

The U.S. Supreme Court first held that the Second Amendment protected an individual right to keep and bear arms in *District of Columbia v. Heller* (2008). The District of Columbia had a stringent law on guns, prohibiting even operable firearms in individual homes. The challengers to the law included Dick Heller, who provided security at the Thurgood Marshall Judicial Center as a special police officer with the District of Columbia police force. Heller had to carry a gun at this job but could not have an operable firearm at his home, which was directly across from abandoned public housing. Originally, the first listed plaintiff was Shelly Parker, an African American woman who had challenged drug dealers in her neighborhood. The complaint in the case read: "As a consequence of trying to make her neighborhood a better place to live, Ms. Parker has been threatened by drug dealers."

Other plaintiffs included Tom Palmer, a gay man who previously had successfully defended himself from an assault with a handgun. He contended that as a gay man, he needed the weapon to deal with antigay violence. The other three plaintiffs were Gillian St. Lawrence, Tracey Ambeau, and George Lyon. All three wanted to have firearms in their home for self-defense purposes.

Common to all six plaintiffs was a genuine belief that they should have the ability to own a firearm to defend themselves. However, the District of Columbia filed a motion to dismiss the complaint, arguing that the Second Amendment simply did not protect an individual right to keep and bear arms. Instead, the District argued that the Second Amendment was written for fear that the federal government might disarm state militias.

Dick Heller (shown here at the 2018 Conservative Political Action Conference [CPAC] in National Harbor, Maryland) protested a Washington, D.C., law prohibiting individuals from having guns in the home because he lived in a dangerous neighborhood where he was threated by drug dealers.

Ultimately, the Court sided with Heller and found that the Second Amendment protected an individual right by a 5–4 vote. In his majority opinion, Justice Antonin Scalia (1936–2016) relied heavily on the fact that the Second Amendment mentions "the right of the people." Scalia noted that the Bill of Rights contains three other mentions of the right of the people—(1) the right of the people to peaceably assemble in the First Amendment; (2) the right of the people to be free from unreasonable searches and seizures in the Fourth Amendment; and (3) the Ninth Amendment, which uses similar language—"retained by the people." Scalia explained: "All three of these instances unambiguously refer to individual rights, not collective rights, or rights may be exercised only through participation in some corporate body."

In his conclusion, Scalia recognized that handgun violence presented a serious problem in society and said that the District of Columbia had other tools to address this. However, he continued: "But the enshrinement of constitutional rights necessarily takes certain policy choices off the table. These include the absolute prohibition of handguns held and used for self-defense in the home."

DID YOU KNOW!?

Did Justice Scalia claim that the Second Amendment was unlimited?

No, Justice Scalia emphasized that the Second Amendment was not unlimited in scope. Scalia wrote that "nothing in our opinion should be taken to cast doubt on long-standing prohibitions on the possession of firearms by felons and the mentally ill, or laws forbidding the carrying of firearms in sensitive places such as schools and government buildings, or laws imposing conditions and qualifications on the commercial sale of arms."

When did the Court incorporate or extend the right to keep and bear arms under the Second Amendment?

Two years after *Heller*, the U.S. Supreme Court incorporated the Second Amendment and held that it applied to limit state and local governments in *McDonald v. City of Chicago* (2010). The City of Chicago had a virtual flat ban on handgun possession. Otis McDonald, an anti-gang activist in his 70s, was one of several individuals who challenged the ban. McDonald said he needed a handgun for self-defense because several gang members had threatened him for his anti-gang activity.

In his majority opinion, Justice Samuel Alito Jr. (1950–) reasoned that the core concept of the Second Amendment—and why it is so vitally important in a free society—is that it enables individuals to engage in the self-defense of their homes. He reasoned that those who drafted and ratified the Bill of Rights considered the Second Amendment right to keep and bear arms to be seminally important. The fear of many of the Framers, according to Justice Alito, was that a standing army supported by the federal government would disarm the citizenry and subject them to the whims of the government.

How did the Supreme Court further extend the Second Amendment in a 2022 decision?

The Supreme Court ruled in *New York State Rifle and Pistol Association v. Bruen* (2022) that a New York law imposing limitations on the right to carry a handgun outside the home violated the Second Amendment. Instead, the Supreme Court reasoned that the individual Second Amendment right to keep and bear arms included the right to carry a handgun outside for self-defense purposes outside the home.

In his majority opinion, Justice Clarence Thomas (1948–) explained:

> In *Heller* and *McDonald*, we held that the Second and Fourteenth Amendments protect an individual right to keep and bear arms for self-defense. In doing so, we held unconstitutional two laws that prohibited the possession and use of handguns in the home. In the years since, the Courts of Appeals have coalesced around a "two-step" framework for analyzing Second Amendment challenges that combines history with means-end scrutiny. Today, we decline to adopt that two-part approach. In keeping with *Heller*, we hold that when the Second Amendment's plain text covers an individual's conduct, the Constitution presumptively protects that conduct. To justify its regulation, the government may not simply posit that the regulation promotes an important interest. Rather, the government must

demonstrate that the regulation is consistent with this Nation's historical tradition of firearm regulation. Only if a firearm regulation is consistent with this Nation's historical tradition may a court conclude that the individual's conduct falls outside the Second Amendment's "unqualified command.

THE THIRD AMENDMENT

What is the Third Amendment?

The Third Amendment provides: "No Soldier shall, in time of peace be quartered in any house, without the consent of the Owner, nor in time of war, but in a manner to be prescribed by law." This amendment was a reaction by the Founding Fathers from a law called the Quartering Act of 1764 that England imposed upon the colonies. This law required the colonists to quarter or house British troops if asked by British military authorities or the royal governor.

This law rankled the colonists greatly and was one of the many authoritarian laws that caused the colonists to revolt against England in the Revolutionary War.

FOURTH AMENDMENT

What does the Fourth Amendment say?

"The right of the people to be secure in their persons, houses, papers and effects, against unreasonable searches and seizures, shall not be violated, and no Warrants shall issue, but upon probable cause, supported by Oath or affirmation, and particularly describing the place to be searched, and the persons or things to be seized."

A group of homicide detectives prepare to serve a warrant at a Northridge, California, home. The Fourth Amendment ensures that residences are protected against unreasonable searches and seizures.

Why was this amendment included in the Bill of Rights?

The Founding Fathers, particularly James Madison (1751–1836), included this right because of the colonial experience with so-called writs of assistance and general warrants. These broad tools allowed British and royal authorities to search the homes, businesses, and other property of the colonists and was considered an egregious invasion of privacy. During the colonial period, British custom officials would obtain search warrants called writs of assistance. These writs allowed the officials to inspect all of a colonist's cargo to prevent smuggling of goods that were to be taxed. These writs of assistance allowed the officials to search and seize whatever property they desired without prior approval by a judge or magistrate.

Because of the colonial experience with writs of assistance and the related general warrants—warrants that were not particular but quite broad—several states included provisions in their state constitutions prohibiting unreasonable searches and seizures. Virginia's Declaration of Rights declared that "general warrants ... are grievous and oppressive, and ought not to be granted." Pennsylvania's Declaration of Rights contained a similar provision that provided people should be "free from search and seizure" if there was not a warrant drafted with "sufficient foundation" and particularly described what was to be searched. Delaware, Maryland, Massachusetts, and New Hampshire also adopted provisions in their state constitutions prohibiting writs of assistance and general warrants. These state constitutional provisions were key precursors to the Fourth Amendment.

When is a search or seizure reasonable or unreasonable?

That is an unbelievably difficult question. But the text of the Fourth Amendment provides one example of when a search is reasonable—when it is backed up by probable cause and signed by a neutral and detached magistrate and the search warrant particularly describes what shall be searched.

There is much to unpack here. Suffice it to say that some searches are unreasonable. For example, the police cannot search without some level of individualized suspicion that you have engaged in wrongdoing. We do not live in a police state. Likewise, public school officials generally cannot engage in strip searches of students. Such searches are deemed excessive in most circumstances.

What is probable cause?

Probable cause means more than just a hunch. The police must point to specified evidence showing that the person likely is carrying certain material. Probable cause means that the police have individualized suspicion that a person is carrying illegal contraband or harboring illegal material in their home. Probable cause essentially means that the police have a reasonable and probable belief that someone is carrying contraband or engaging in illegal activities. "In dealing with probable cause, however, as the very name implies, we deal with probabilities," the U.S. Supreme Court explained in *Brinegar v. United States* (1949). "These are not technical; they are the factual and practical considerations of everyday life on which reasonable and prudent men, not legal technicians, act."

The Court in *Brinegar* further explained that there is a difference between "mere suspicion" and "probable cause." Mere suspicion is not enough. The police must have some basis grounded in fact, not speculation, that someone is engaging in illegal activity.

Who must sign a warrant?

A warrant must be signed by a neutral and detached magistrate, someone who independently examines a warrant and determines whether the police really have probable cause to search a home, for example.

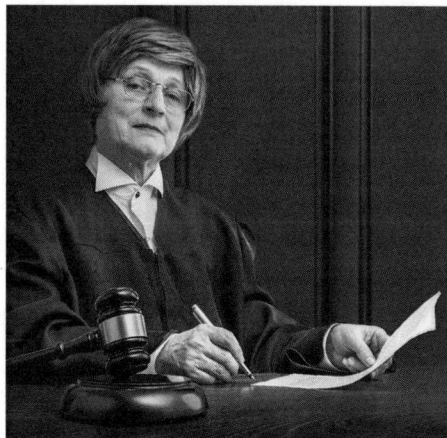

Warrants must be signed by a "neutral and detached" magistrate, meaning the magistrate must in no way be connected to law enforcement.

This requirement of a "neutral and detached" magistrate means that the magistrate must be independent, not a mere shill for the police. The term often used is a "rubber stamp." A magistrate who always approves of warrants, no matter what they say, is not neutral and detached; they are merely a rubber stamp for law enforcement.

The Supreme Court has explained that to be neutral and detached, a magistrate must be independent from law enforcement. A magistrate is not neutral and detached if they work in some capacity with law enforcement. "Whatever else neutrality and detachment might entail, it is clear that they require severance and disengagement from activities of law enforcement," the Supreme Court wrote in *Shadwick v. City of Tampa* (1972). The Supreme Court once invalidated a Georgia scheme that provided that justices of the peace would be paid for search warrants they authorized and not paid for search warrants they denied. Testimony revealed that a justice of the peace had issued some 10,000 warrants and never denied one. The Court reasoned in *Connally v. Georgia* (1977) that this scheme violated the key Fourth Amendment principle of having a "neutral and detached magistrate." The justices of the peace were not neutral and detached because they had a clear financial incentive under this Georgia law to approve, not deny, warrants.

What is the particularity requirement?

The particularity requirement is the last clause of the Fourth Amendment that reads, "particularly describing the place to be searched, and the persons or things to be seized." Under this requirement, the warrant also must explain what particular items or places are to be searched. Otherwise, the warrant authorizes a roving or fishing net type of search. The warrant must also state what material is being targeted in the search. The British would often use so-called "general warrants" when searching colonists' property. A general warrant allowed authorities to search all of a

Do the police always need a warrant to conduct a search?

No, the police do not always need a warrant. There are several exceptions to the Fourth Amendment's warrant requirement. Some of the more common exceptions are the automobile exception, plain view, exigent circumstances, stop and frisk, consent, school searches, border searches, and search incident to a lawful arrest.

person's property. The Fourth Amendment generally forbids the use of general warrants. It requires the police to state specifically what items they expect to find.

What is the automobile exception?

The automobile exception refers to the idea that the police do not need a warrant to search an automobile unlike, say, a home. The idea behind the automobile exception is that due to the inherent mobility of automobiles, there is not sufficient time for law enforcement officials to obtain a warrant to search the contents of an automobile. The Supreme Court created the automobile exception to the Fourth Amendment in *Carroll v. United States* (1925). The Court examined whether the police could stop a vehicle on the highway that officers reasonably believed was carrying illegal liquor. The Court upheld the warrantless stop and search of the vehicle because of what it identified as a "necessary difference" between searching "a store, dwelling house or other structure" and searching "a ship, motor boat, wagon or automobile." The difference, according to the Court, was that a "vehicle can be quickly moved out of the locality or jurisdiction in which the warrant must be sought."

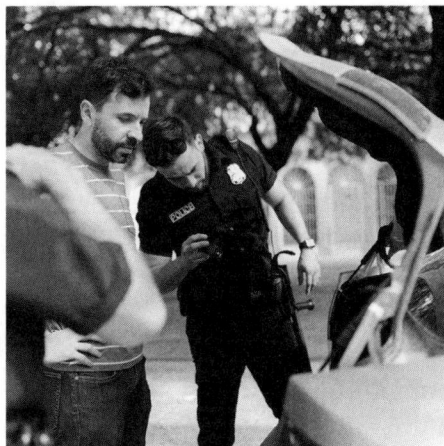

Unlike when the police want to search your home, law enforcement does not need to get a warrant to search your vehicle if they have a reasonable suspicion that there is something illegal inside.

However, the police still need to have some level of individualized suspicion to stop a vehicle. The police cannot just willy-nilly stop your automobile for no reason. They need to have reasonable suspicion—a level of individualized suspicion not quite as rigid as probable cause—rather than a general hunch. For example, most of the time, the police pull over vehicles because a person was speeding, violated a traffic ordinance, or has out-of-date vehicle registration plates.

When the police pull over your vehicle, the officer may then ask you to produce your license and registration. This is standard operating procedure. This does not give the police officer carte blanche to search your automobile. In other words, the police generally need probable cause to search your vehicle—this means that they have some clear indication or evidence that there is illegal contraband in your vehicle.

So, the police need a warrant to search my home?

Yes, in the vast majority of cases, the search of a home without a warrant violates the Fourth Amendment. This flows from the old English maxim, "A man's home is his castle." It is the first among equals in Fourth Amendment law, as Justice Antonin Scalia once wrote.

Here, a clear contrast exists between the treatment of the home and the car. Homes are not inherently mobile—unless perhaps we are talking about a mobile home. But most homes are fixed and cannot be moved. Thus, the police must obtain a warrant before searching a home. The Supreme Court declared in *Payton v. New York* (1979) that "[i]t is a basic principle of Fourth Amendment law that searches and seizures inside a home without a warrant are presumptively unconstitutional."

This enhanced protection of the home also extends to the area immediately outside the home called the "curtilage." The idea behind the special protections for the home and curtilage is that individuals have a clear and reasonable expectation of privacy in their homes and the area just outside their homes.

What is the plain view doctrine?

Under this doctrine, if the police are in a lawful vantage point—a place where they have a lawful right to be—and then inadvertently come across a piece of incriminating evidence, the police have not violated the Fourth Amendment.

For example, let's say that the police have a valid search warrant to search a home for certain illegal weapons. As the police are searching the home, they inadvertently see a large pile of cocaine sitting on a table. The police do not violate the Fourth Amendment just because they did not file a warrant to search for the cocaine because the cocaine clearly was in "plain view" of the officers and these officers were lawfully present in the home already due to a valid search warrant.

Contrast that with a police officer who suspects that a person is trafficking in illegal drugs in a home. The officer walks up to a window in the home, peers through the window, and sees the cocaine on the kitchen table. The officer then claims "plain view." This conduct violates the Fourth Amendment because the officer did not have a valid search warrant to search the home. The officer was not in a lawful vantage point when they saw the cocaine. Thus, the plain view doctrine is inapplicable.

What variant of the plain view doctrine applies with automobile stops?

The plain smell doctrine can sometimes justify the search of an automobile. If the police lawfully pull over your vehicle, come up to it, and then smell the presence of marijuana (in a jurisdiction where it is illegal to have it), then the police can search the car for the contraband.

What are exigent circumstances?

A glaring exception to the warrant requirement is when the police are confronted with emergency-type circumstances and need to act quickly—even enter a home without a warrant. Generally, entering a home without a warrant is a huge Fourth Amendment problem but not if there are so-called "exigent circumstances." Again, the rationale behind the exigent circumstances doctrine is that the police are confronted with emergency circumstances and do not have time to go get a warrant.

There are three major areas in which the exigent circumstances doctrine applies: (1) hot pursuit of a fleeing felon; (2) life-threatening or very dangerous circumstances; and (3) the imminent destruction of evidence. The hot-pursuit variant of

One example of an exigent circumstance that allows police to forego a search warrant is if the officers believe evidence is being destroyed.

exigent circumstances applies when the police are pursuing a person whom they have probable cause to believe committed a felony and the person enters a home for which the police have no valid search warrant. Because the police officers are in hot pursuit, they are deemed to be under exigent circumstances and can enter the home to capture the fleeing individual.

The most common application of exigent circumstances applies when the police are confronted with real-life threatening circumstances. For example, if the police reasonably believe that a homicide has been committed in the home, they may enter that home without a warrant under the exigent circumstances rationale. Or if there is real credible evidence that a person has harmed or is about to harm themself or others inside the home, the police likely have exigent circumstances to enter the home to prevent the harm.

The last exception refers to the immediate destruction of evidence. This can be a troubling application of the exigent circumstances rationale—and the Supreme Court has been quite loath to recognize this variant, but it has mentioned in dicta several times that this type of exigent circumstances can exist.

What is a stop and frisk?

A "stop and frisk" refers to the police practice of stopping an individual that they have reasonable suspicion is carrying contraband or a weapon and conduct a brief pat-down. This is sometimes called a "Terry stop" because the Court sanctioned the use of the practice in the case of *Terry v. Ohio* (1968). In this case, Martin McFadden (1901–1981), a more than 30-year veteran of the Cleveland police department, observed two men repeatedly walking back and forth past a jewelry store and peering through the store's window. The two men then met a third man and conversed with him on the street. McFadden approached the men, including defendant John Terry, frisked him, and found a weapon. Terry argued that the officer lacked any individualized suspicion to pat him down. The Supreme Court disagreed, reasoning that if a police officer reasonably believes that individuals pose a safety risk to the officer or to the general public, the officer may "conduct a carefully limited search of the outer clothing of such persons in an attempt to discover weapons which might be used to assault him."

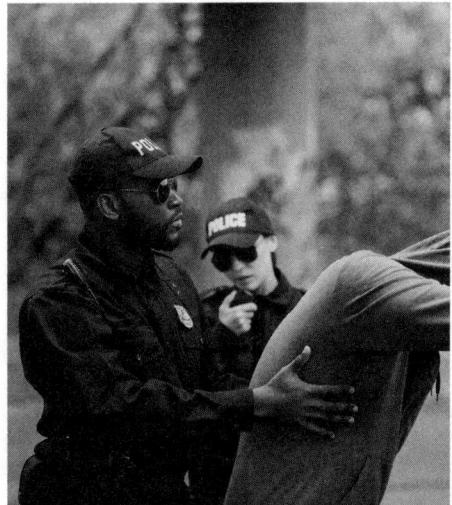

The Court has found that a police officer may stop and frisk someone who is in some way behaving in a suspicious manner.

The Court extended the reach of the *Terry* decision decades later in *Minnesota v. Dickerson* (1993) when the Court found guiltless a police officer who patted down a suspect and found illegal drugs. The Court held that when the officer conducted a lawful Terry stop and felt a lump in the defendant's jacket that appeared to be contraband, the officer did not violate the Fourth Amendment. Some refer to the Court's decision in *Dickerson* as an expansion of the plain view doctrine to the "plain feel" or "plain touch" doctrine.

What is a search incident to a lawful arrest?

Law enforcement officials do not need a warrant to conduct what is called a search incident to a lawful arrest. This means that when the police lawfully arrest a person, they may search that person and the nearby physical area within the person's wingspan. There are two primary rationales for this exception to the warrant requirement—to protect the safety of officers and to prevent the destruction of evidence. In fact, there is a pressing need to search a person who has been or is about to be arrested. The police need to make sure the person is not armed and dangerous and need to preserve evidence.

A key requirement for a lawful search incident to a lawful arrest is that the search must be contemporaneous with the arrest—that is, it must take place at about the same time as the arrest. This reduces the likelihood that any resulting search is pretextual or subject to abuse.

Do public school officials need a warrant before searching a public school student?

No; another exception to the warrant requirement is searches in the public schools. The idea is that school officials do not need probable cause and a warrant every time they have some individualized suspicion that a student is carrying contraband. In *New Jersey v. T. L. O.* (1985), the Supreme Court ruled that public school officials can conduct searches of students based upon a reasonableness standard rather than the traditional standard of probable cause. The case involved the search of a female student's purse by an assistant school principal, who suspected the student and another student of smoking in the school's bathroom. The assistant principal then searched the girl's purse and found evidence that she was trafficking in small amounts of marijuana.

What about strip searches in public schools?

The U.S. Supreme Court ruled that strip searches in public schools are normally too intrusive to withstand Fourth Amendment scrutiny. The Court explained in *Safford Unified School District v. Redding* (2009): "We do mean, though, to make it clear that the *T. L. O.* concern to limit a school search to reasonable scope requires the support of reasonable suspicion of danger or of resort to underwear for hiding evidence of wrongdoing before a search can reasonably make the quantum leap from outer clothes and backpacks to exposure of intimate parts. The meaning of such a search, and the degradation its subject may reasonably feel, place a search that intrusive in a category of its own, demanding its own specific suspicions."

DID YOU KNOW?

The Border Patrol is charged with preventing illegal border crossings or other illegal border activities such as drug dealing and the slave trade. It would be impractical to insist that they obtain a search warrant for such cases.

The student argued that the assistant principal violated the Fourth Amendment, but the Court disagreed, writing that "the constitutional rights of minors are not automatically coextensive" with that of adults. The Court also applauded the reasonableness standard as one that would give public school officials and administrators needed flexibility, writing that it will "spare teachers and school administrators the necessity of schooling themselves in the niceties of probable cause and permit them to regulate their conduct according to the dictates of reason and common sense."

Do government officials need a warrant for border searches?

No; yet another well-recognized exception to the warrant requirement is border searches. U.S. Customs officials may search persons at the border without individualized suspicion of wrongdoing. Such searches must take place at the international border or its basic equivalent. The idea is traced to the idea of

DID YOU KNOW!?

Do the police generally need a warrant before searching a cell phone?

Yes; the Court ruled in *Riley v. California* (2014) that generally, police need a warrant. The Court emphasized the ubiquity of cell phones in modern life, writing that they "are now such a pervasive and insistent part of daily life that the proverbial visitor from Mars might conclude they were an important feature of human anatomy." Chief Justice John Roberts (1955–) also emphasized how much private information people carry on their cell phones and noted that "cell phone" may be a misnomer—that they "could just as easily be called cameras, video players, rolodexes, calendars, tape recorders, libraries, diaries, albums, televisions, maps, or newspapers."

national sovereignty—that the United States and its officials have greater power to conduct searches to protect the integrity of its borders. There are some lower court cases, however, that have required customs officials to have a degree of individualized suspicion—reasonable suspicion—before conducting strip searches at the border.

What is a seizure?

A common definition of a seizure is that a person is seized when, in light of all the surrounding circumstances, they reasonably believe that they are not free to leave. For example, if a group of police officers come up to you, surround you, and one of them draws his weapon, you have been seized for purposes of the Fourth Amendment. If the police arrest you, you have been seized. If a police officer shoots you, you have been seized. If the police come up to your home and fire their weapons through your windows, you have been seized.

Much of Fourth Amendment jurisprudence concerns itself with whether a search warrant is valid or whether an exception to the warrant requirement applies in Fourth Amendment law. But the question of what constitutes a seizure is also very important. Certainly, there is a seizure when a government agent physically restrains a person and prohibits them from leaving. Thus, an arrest is a seizure for purposes of the Fourth Amendment.

What is the exclusionary rule?

The exclusionary rule provides that when the police violate the Fourth Amendment rights of an individual in obtaining evidence against that person, such evidence must be excluded or suppressed in the prosecution of the defendant.

Controversy surrounds the Fourth Amendment because sometimes, the police will violate the rights of a person who is carrying contraband, such as illegal drugs. A common example is when a police officer discovers drugs on a person—but only after an unreasonable search or seizure. The defendant's defense attorney then files a motion to suppress the evidence of the drugs as a result of an alleged unconstitutional search. The idea is that the resulting evidence from an improper search is fruit of a poisonous tree.

Our Constitution allows an illegally searched person to file a motion to suppress the evidence. This is called the exclusionary rule. Justice Benjamin Cardozo (1870–1938) expressed this concept when he said, "The criminal is free to go because the constable has blundered." The rationale behind the exclusionary rule is to require law enforcement officials to obey the law.

However, in *Mapp v. Ohio* (1961), the Supreme Court extended the exclusionary rule to state and local police because the justices found the concept so important. Justice Tom C. Clark (1899–1977) famously responded to Justice Cardozo's famous criticism of the exclusionary rule—"the criminal goes free because the constable has blundered"—with the memorable line: "The criminal goes free, if he must, but it is the law that sets him free. Nothing can destroy a government more quickly than its failure to observe its own laws, or worse, its disregard of the charter of its own existence."

What is the good faith exception to the exclusionary rule?

While the exclusionary rule remains a staple of Fourth Amendment jurisprudence, the Supreme Court has created a significant exception to the rule called the good faith exception. The idea behind the good faith exception is that the exclusionary rule should not apply when the police acted in objective good faith that they were acting pursuant to a valid search warrant that is later deemed invalid.

"In most such cases, there is no police illegality and thus nothing to deter," the Court wrote. "It is the magistrate's responsibility to determine whether the officer's allegations establish probable cause and, if so, to issue a warrant comporting in form with the requirements of the Fourth Amendment. In the ordinary case, an officer cannot be expected to question the magistrate's probable-cause determination or his judgment that the form of the warrant is technically sufficient."

The Court extended the good faith exception to the exclusionary rule in certain cases that involve mistakes by clerical employees.

THE FIFTH AMENDMENT

What is the Fifth Amendment?

The Fifth Amendment states: "No person shall be held to answer for a capital, or otherwise infamous crime, unless on a presentment or indictment of a grand jury, except in cases arising in the land or naval forces, or in the militia, when in actual service in time of war or public danger; nor shall any person be subject for the same offense to be twice put in jeopardy of life or limb; nor shall be compelled in any criminal case to be a witness against himself, nor be deprived of life, liberty, or property, without due process of law; nor shall private property be taken for public use, without just compensation."

What freedoms are found in the Fifth Amendment?

The Fifth Amendment, the longest in the Bill of Rights, contains several freedoms, including (1) the right to a grand jury; (2)

Having a trial judged by your peers in a jury is one of your rights under the Fifth Amendment.

the right to be free from double jeopardy; (3) privilege against self-incrimination; (4) due process; and (5) just compensation. Linda Monk writes in her book *The Words We Live By* that "the Fifth Amendment is a hodgepodge of provisions affecting both criminal law and civil law." The bulk of the amendment deals with freedoms for those charged with crimes, but the right to due process applies in the civil context too, as does the right to just compensation.

What is a grand jury?

A grand jury is a body of citizens, usually in groups of 16–23, who decide whether a prosecutor has presented enough evidence to obtain an indictment of an individual. Grand juries are designed to serve as a type of buffer between the prosecution and the defendant. Critics charge that grand juries—more often than not—do not serve this ideal buffering function and instead serve as a rubber stamp for the prosecution. There is a famous saying about grand juries that reflects this sentiment: "A grand jury will indict a ham sandwich."

Grand juries are distinct from trial juries—or petit juries—which usually consist of 12 people. Sometimes, prosecutors use the grand jury method of initiating criminal charges against individuals rather than filing an accusatory document—called an information—and proceeding with a preliminary hearing. The grand jury serves as a screening mechanism to determine whether the prosecutor has enough evidence to obtain what is known as a true bill. If the grand jury decides there is not enough evidence, it would issue what is called a no bill. Grand juries are used in federal court and in some states. Most states explain the operational workings and functions of the grand jury in their rules of criminal procedure.

What is double jeopardy?

The Double Jeopardy Clause serves as a constraint on both prosecutors and courts. It provides three constitutional protections: (1) no reprosecution for the same offense after a defendant has been acquitted; (2) no second prosecution for the same offense after a conviction; and (3) a limit on multiple punishments for the same offense.

The most common conception of double jeopardy concerns no second prosecution after a defendant has been acquitted. In the words of the U.S. Supreme Court, "an acquittal is afforded special weight." The idea is that a person should not be subject to the embarrassment, harassment, and stresses of a second prosecution after a jury or judge has rendered an acquittal or not guilty verdict. If this were not the case, then the government could keep subjecting a defendant to trial after trial until the prosecution obtained a favorable verdict.

A lesser-known conception of double jeopardy concerns a second prosecution after the defendant already has been convicted. That would amount to unnecessary and excessive punishments, as the defendant already has been punished.

The final conception of double jeopardy is the one that comes up the most often in litigation—multiple punishments for the same offense. How this plays out is that a prosecutor charges an individual under multiple statutes for the same offense. The prosecutor in effect is seeking cumulative punishments by charging violations under different laws. This may violate the Double Jeopardy Clause if the conduct arises out of the same offense.

What is the privilege against self-incrimination?

This privilege means that an individual has the right to not talk to the police. Instead, the person can remain silent and not incriminate themself. This right also means that a defendant does not have to testify at trial. Arguably, the most well-known freedom found in the Fifth Amendment is the privilege against self-incrimination. This means that the government cannot force a person to testify against themself in court. When somebody says, "I take the Fifth," it means they are taking their Fifth Amendment constitutional right not to incriminate themself.

The privilege applies even more frequently when the police arrest and place a person in custody. When a police officer arrests a suspect, the officer is supposed to read the suspect their rights. The officer warns the suspect: "You have the right to remain silent. Anything you say can and will be used against you."

Unfortunately, some law enforcement officers ignored this constitutional right and would beat confessions out of defendants. In *Miranda v. Arizona* (1966), the U.S. Supreme Court voided the conviction of a young Latino man in part because the police had not informed him of his right to remain silent.

What is due process?

Due process at its heart refers to fundamental fairness. Due process is one of the greatest rights Americans possess. One eminent legal historian has said the right of due process has "served as the basis for the constitutional protection of the rights of Americans."

Due process has often been divided into two basic categories: procedural due process and substantive due process. Procedural due process means that the government must guarantee a fair process before taking away an individual's life, liberty, or property. The basic elements to procedural due process are notice and the right to a fair hearing. This prevents the government from arbitrarily taking away someone's job or freedom.

Substantive due process means that laws must advance a legitimate, governmental objective. Normally, a law must be justified on a rational basis. It must be rationally related to a legitimate goal. Due process applies in both the criminal and civil law realms.

What is "just compensation"?

The last clause of the Fifth Amendment reads: "nor shall private property be taken for public use, without just compensation."

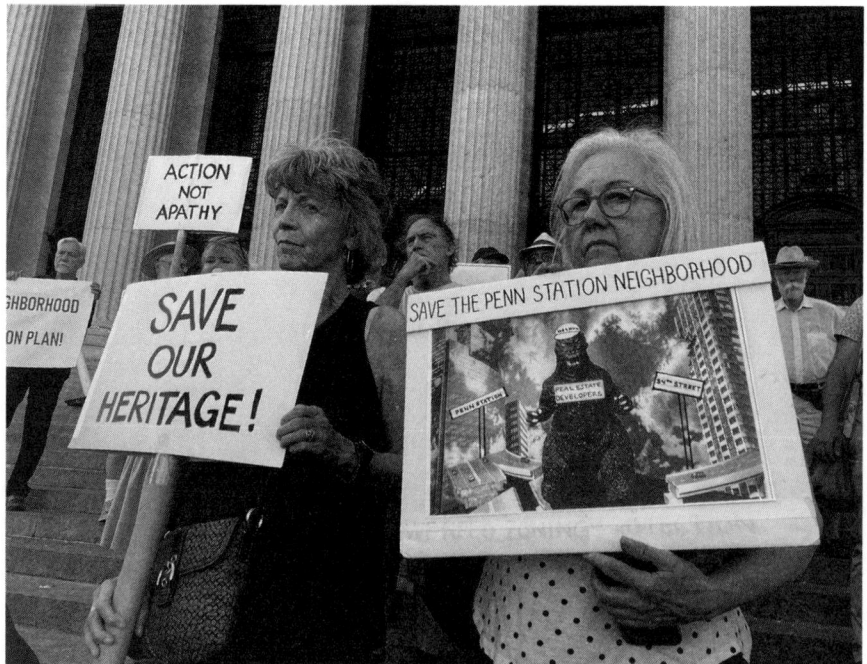

The concept of eminent domain can be controversial, such as in the case of homeowners in the Penn Station neighborhood of New York City, where the mayor has been working to force people out and build several skyscrapers by declaring the neighborhood "blighted."

This means that the government cannot simply take a citizen's land without paying for it.

The government does possess the power of eminent domain, or the right to take private property for public use. However, the Due Process Clause of the Fifth and Fourteenth Amendments requires that the government give "just compensation" before invoking this sovereign power.

There are two basic types of takings—possessory takings and regulatory takings. Possessory takings mean that the government—or another approved entity—takes over all or part of your land and you do not have the right to possess that land anymore. It is similar to voluntarily selling your property—once the deed changes hands, you would be trespassing if you went onto your property to use your land again.

Possessory takings can involve all of your land, which will require you to completely relocate yourself, your family, or even your business. In other situations, however, only a partial possessory taking will occur. Often, you can remain in your home or business—you just will not be able to use that part of your land.

There are also nonpossessory takings, as not all takings mean that someone has the right to move in and take over your land. A prime example of this is an easement, which gives a party a right to occupy and use part of your land. This can include installing and maintaining power lines or constructing a pipeline underground. The company can come onto your land in accordance with the easement while you remain on your land as well. Easements can often diminish property value and sometimes lead to litigation.

Regulatory takings occur when a governmental entity, such as a city or town, passes a law or regulation that limits your use of the law. A prime example of a regulatory taking could be a zoning ordinance that prohibits you from operating a building as a commercial property. Regulatory takings often involve changes to zoning and land use laws, and it can be difficult to prove that a taking truly occurred and that you deserve just compensation.

Many takings are relatively straightforward, as the government acknowledges that it is taking public property. The only issue in these situations is how much money, or "just compensation," the government will pay for taking your property.

THE SIXTH AMENDMENT

What is the Sixth Amendment?

"In all criminal prosecutions, the accused shall enjoy the right to a speedy and public trial, by an impartial jury of the state and district wherein the crime shall have been committed, which district shall have been previously ascertained by law, and to be informed of the nature and cause of the accusation; to be confronted with the witnesses against him; to have compulsory process for obtaining witnesses in his favor, and to have the assistance of counsel for his defense."

What is the right to a speedy trial?

The right to a speedy trial ensures that a criminal defendant will not sit in jail for too long before having a trial. As the old criminal justice saying goes, "justice delayed is justice denied." The Speedy Trial Clause seeks to ensure that criminal defendants don't languish in jail while the legal process moves along at a glacial pace. This clause prevents officials from keeping a defendant imprisoned for a lengthy period of time before a trial. If there was no provision for a "speedy" trial, an accused's defense could suffer. People's memories could wane, and so-called exculpatory evidence (evidence showing a defendant's innocence) could be lost.

The Supreme Court has identified several factors important to determining whether there was a violation of the right to a speedy trial. These factors are (1) length of the delay; (2) the reason for the delay; (3) whether the defendant asserted their speedy trial rights; and (4) prejudice to the defendant.

What does the Sixth Amendment mean by a "public trial"?

The Sixth Amendment right to a public trial ensures that defendants are not tried in secret, as was the case in, for instance, the Spanish Inquisition and the dreaded English Star Chamber. The Star Chamber was an English court dissolved by Parliament in 1641 that was known for its secretive judicial meetings and harsh sentences. It would convict and punish individuals without providing them with any protections comparable to those found in our Bill of Rights.

These practices are anathema to a free and open society. People facing criminal charges have the right to have their case heard in an open court of law. Justice Hugo Black (1886–1971) forcefully wrote in *In re Oliver* (1948) that "the guarantee [of a public trial] has always been recognized as a safeguard against any attempt to employ our courts as instruments of persecution."

What is an impartial jury?

An impartial jury must also judge every person charged with a crime. Sometimes, a judge will pick a jury from another county than the one in which the defendant allegedly committed the crime. In our legal system, this is called a change of venue. A judge will change venue if a defendant would be prejudiced (that is, adversely affected by prejudgment). This potential problem

Defendants are entitled to an impartial jury of their peers. Sometimes, when there is a high-profile case that has been heavily publicized, it can be a challenge to find jurors who have not already formed an opinion.

occurs when a high-profile criminal case receives a lot of pretrial publicity. Judges have a duty to ensure that a defendant will not be prejudged by the jury.

What does the Sixth Amendment say about "notice"?

The Sixth Amendment also provides that a defendant must have notice of the charges filed against them. Individuals need to know what charges they face so that they can prepare a defense to those charges. If defendants do not know the criminal charges they face, it is impossible to prepare a defense to those charges. It would run counter to the system of fairness that the Bill of Rights tries to provide for defendants to not have notice.

What is the Confrontation Clause?

The Confrontation Clause of the Sixth Amendment provides: "In all criminal prosecutions, the accused shall enjoy the right ... to be confronted with the witnesses against him." This clause ensures that a criminal defendant can cross-examine those who testify against him. U.S. Supreme Court justice Antonin Scalia (1936–2016) wrote: "The perception that confrontation is essential to fairness has persisted over the centuries because there is much truth to it.... It is always more difficult to tell a lie about a person 'to his face' than 'behind his back.'"

The U.S. Supreme Court has recognized that face-to-face confrontation ensures greater reliability by reducing the risk that an innocent person will be convicted. The Confrontation Clause ensures that a witness must face cross-examination—a process by which a witness must answer questions by an attorney from the other side. The Court has referred to cross-examination as the "greatest legal engine ever invented for the discovery of truth."

What is compulsory process?

The Sixth Amendment also provides that a criminal defendant can force witnesses to testify in the trial. Often, people do not want to get involved in a criminal trial. The Compulsory Witness Clause provides that a defendant can try to prove their case whether the witnesses want to get involved or not.

DID YOU KNOW!?

What is the assistance of counsel?

The last freedom in the Sixth Amendment is the assistance of counsel. This means that a criminal defendant has the right to an attorney even if they cannot afford one. The idea is that the protection of a defendant's constitutional rights is so important that the defendant is provided an attorney to help the defendant face the prosecutorial process. Justice Hugo Black famously wrote in *Gideon v. Wainwright* (1963) that attorneys in criminal cases are "necessities, not luxuries."

The Supreme Court explained that there is too much at stake in the criminal process—liberty and sometimes even life—to not have a trained legal advocate on the defendant's side.

The reality of the criminal court system in the United States is that the vast majority of criminal defendants cannot afford to hire a high-priced criminal defense attorney. This means that these defendants are represented by public defenders or by private attorneys who are appointed by the courts. Many U.S. criminal defense attorneys make at least part of their living off of appointed cases. Many jurisdictions have appointment lists from which judges will select attorneys for representation.

If you can't afford an attorney for your defense, one will be assigned to your case free of charge, thanks to the Sixth Amendment.

THE SEVENTH AMENDMENT

What does the Seventh Amendment say?

"In Suits at common law, where the value in controversy shall exceed twenty dollars, the right of trial by jury shall be preserved, and no fact tried by a jury, shall be otherwise reexamined in any Court of the United States, than according to the rules of the common law."

What is the basic right protected by the Seventh Amendment?

The Seventh Amendment essentially ensures that individuals have the right to a trial by jury in civil cases in federal court, not just criminal cases.

THE EIGHTH AMENDMENT

What does the Eighth Amendment say?

"Excessive bail shall not be required, nor excessive fines imposed, nor cruel and unusual punishment inflicted."

What is the problem with excessive bail?

Bail refers to money or security paid to the court in order to secure the temporary release of a defendant charged with a crime. The defendant—or the friend or family of the defendant—pays money to the court in the promise that they will reappear for the next court hearing in the case. Historically, bail did not require the delivery of money, but a person would serve as a surety and promise that the defendant would appear for later court dates.

A defendant can have a bail hearing at which they can argue that the setting of bail was too high—higher than what is normally imposed in similar cases. Thus, a defendant can file a motion to reduce bail.

Bail lessens or reduces the chances that innocent persons will be detained in jail. As Supreme Court justice Robert Jackson (1892–1954) wrote, "The spirit of the procedure [for bail] is to enable [defendants] to stay out of jail until a trial has found them guilty." Bail also reduces hardship on the defendant and the defendant's family members. It also gives a defendant the opportunity to get their affairs in order, hire a lawyer, and mount an effective defense. Bail also serves institutional purposes in that it can help to reduce the overcrowding of jails.

Not every criminal defendant is entitled to bail. If a crime is serious enough or the defendant is considered to be a flight risk, a judge does not have to provide bail. This means that the defendant will stay detained pending the outcome of the criminal process.

What are excessive fines?

The Eighth Amendment also prohibits excessive fines. This clause traces back to language in the venerable Magna Carta of 1215, which provided that:

> A freeman is not to be amerced for a small offence save in accordance with the manner of the offence, and for a major offence according to its magnitude, saving his sufficiency (*salvo contenemento suo*), and a merchant likewise, saving his merchandise, and any villain other than one of our own is to be amerced in the same way, saving his necessity (*salvo waynagio*) should he fall into our mercy, and none of the aforesaid amercements is to be imposed save by the oath of honest and law-worthy men of the neighbourhood. Earls and barons are not to be amerced save by their peers and only in accordance with the manner of their offence.

This difficult English language meant that any economic penalties needed to be proportional to the wrong committed and not so large as to prohibit a "free-man" from earning a living.

In more recent times, the focus of the Excessive Fines Clause has been on situations in which the government may imprison someone but apply forfeiture laws and take a person's money. Today, all 50 states have a constitutional provision in their state constitutions prohibiting excessive fines. As Justice Ruth Bader Ginsburg (1933–2020) wrote in *Timbs v. Indiana* (2019), "The protection against excessive fines has been a constant shield throughout American history." She explained that excessive fines can be used "to retaliate against or chill the speech of political enemies."

What is "cruel and unusual punishment"?

By far the most frequent source of Eighth Amendment concerns is what punishment is "cruel and unusual." The bulk of the most visible discussions involve whether the ultimate punishment—death—is cruel and unusual within the meaning of the Eighth Amendment. But the Cruel and Unusual Punishment Clause applies to any form of criminal punishment that is grossly disproportionate to the underlying conduct that led to the conviction. There is not a strict proportionality requirement in Eighth Amendment law. In order to rise to the level of a constitutional violation, the punishment must be grossly disproportionate.

A stark example of a grossly disproportionate punishment occurred in *Robinson v. California* (1962). The case concerned a Los Angeles city ordinance that criminalized being addicted to narcotics. The law did not require the charged person to be using narcotics illegally. It simply stated that narcotics addiction itself

What should be regarded as a cruel and unusual punishment? Certainly, death by hanging or by the electric chair are now considered cruel, but what about death by injection, as is done in some states now?

was a crime. The Supreme Court determined that this was akin to punishing a person for having a venereal disease or a mental illness.

Another example would be if a person jaywalks across a street and receives a 10-year prison sentence. That punishment is clearly excessive and grossly disproportionate to the underlying offense, which is more of an infraction than a serious crime. Another example occurred in the celebrated case of *Weems v. United States* (1910). The case involved the dishonest actions of Paul Weems, an official with the Coast Guard serving in the Philippines, then a colony of the United States. Weems committed fraud by falsifying a document to obtain cash. He received a sentence of 15 years' imprisonment. The Supreme Court reasoned that such a severe penalty for a relatively minor offense violated the Eighth Amendment.

How does a court determine if punishment is cruel or unusual?

The Court looks to see if the punishment is proportionate to the underlying offense. It also uses the concept known as "the evolving standards of decency." Under the evolving standards of decency test, the Court examines trends in state legislatures and essentially adopts a majoritarian view of punishment. For example, when the Supreme Court invalidated the death penalty in 2002, it found that there was an evolving standard of decency that surfaced with regard to the execution of defendants who were intellectually disabled. More and more states—and countries around the world—began to view it as fundamentally wrong to execute a person even for the awful crime of murder.

Some criticize the evolving standards of a decency test as a vehicle by which justices and judges can impose their own personal predilections into the Constitution. Perhaps the most consistent critic of the concept of evolving standards of decency was Justice Antonin Scalia, who referred to *Trop v. Dulles* in a most pejorative way, writing: "That case has caused more mischief to our jurisprudence, to our federal system, and to our society than any other that comes to mind." Scalia views the Court as ignoring the will of the people and the text of the Constitution when it comes to interpreting the Eighth Amendment, particularly with regard to capital punishment.

Is the death penalty cruel and unusual?

This is a most controversial question, as many people disagree over this contentious issue. Currently, the U.S. Supreme Court has ruled that the death penalty is not cruel and unusual, though it has ruled that the application of the death penalty to certain types of defendants—those who are intellectually disabled, insane, or those who commit murder when they are a juvenile—would be cruel and unusual.

In much modern death penalty litigation, the question is whether the specific practice of execution—most often lethal injection—is cruel and unusual.

THE NINTH AMENDMENT

What does the Ninth Amendment say?

"The enumeration in the Constitution, of certain rights, shall not be construed to deny or disparage others retained by the people."

What does the Ninth Amendment mean?

The Ninth Amendment means that just because rights are not enumerated, or listed, in the Bill of Rights does not mean that the people do not possess them. Thus, the Ninth Amendment is about unenumerated, or nonlisted, rights.

In *Griswold v. Connecticut* (1965), the Supreme Court struck down a Connecticut law that barred the use of contraceptives by married persons. The Court viewed this as violating the right to privacy. In his concurring opinion, Justice Arthur Goldberg (1908–1990) found this right to privacy protected by the Ninth Amendment. Goldberg explained that the clear purpose of the Ninth Amendment was to ensure that there are constitutional rights that are not explicitly listed in the Bill of Rights. He emphasized that the marriage relationship was one that demanded and required privacy.

Goldberg wrote that the Ninth Amendment "is surely relevant in showing the existence of other fundamental personal rights, now protected from state, as well as federal, infringement." He added that "the Ninth Amendment simply lends strong support to the view that the 'liberty' protected by the Fifth and Fourteenth Amendments from infringement by the Federal Government or the States is not restricted to rights specifically mentioned in the first eight amendments."

The Supreme Court also used the Ninth Amendment in an auxiliary manner in *Roe v. Wade* (1973), ruling that a woman's right to terminate her pregnancy was protected by the Constitution. Justice Harry Blackmun (1908–1999) explained: "This right of privacy, whether it be founded in the Fourteenth Amendment's concept of personal liberty and restrictions upon state action, as we feel it is, or, as the District Court determined, in the Ninth Amendment's reservation of rights to the people, is broad enough to encompass a woman's decision whether or not to terminate her pregnancy."

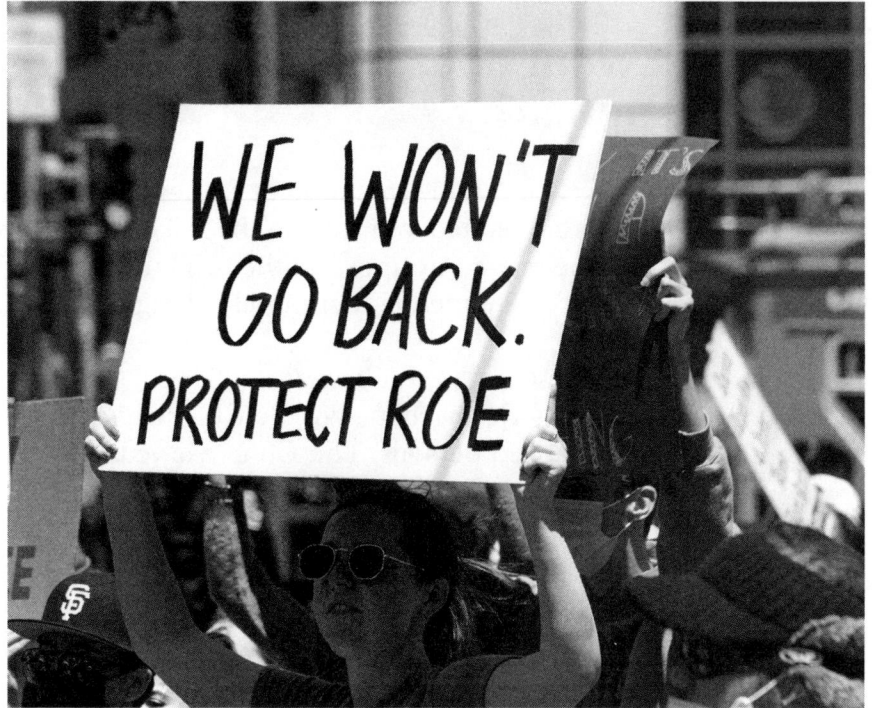

When the Supreme Court reversed the right to abortion in its 2022 decision in *Dobbs v. Jackson Women's Health Organization*, women protested around the country. Many felt the Court's decision was more political than constitutional.

THE TENTH AMENDMENT

What does the Tenth Amendment say?

"The powers not delegated to the United States by the Constitution, nor prohibited by it to the States, are reserved to the States respectively, or to the people."

What is the Tenth Amendment about?

The Tenth Amendment means that states retain a good deal of sovereign authority—that the state is in control of a lot of matters within its borders. This does not mean, however, that the federal government is powerless to act. The Constitution has on several occasions specifically taken authority for the federal government and divested that authority from the states. In certain matters, the federal government is sovereign, and states have to take a back seat.

The Tenth Amendment is the only part of the Bill of Rights that does not refer to individual rights. This amendment limits the power of the federal government with respect to state governments. The Tenth Amendment signifies the principle of federalism—the distribution of power between a central authority and its supporting units.

There have been times when the U.S. Supreme Court has used the Tenth Amendment as an independent constitutional bar and struck down federal laws that violated the Tenth Amendment. For example, in *New York v. United States* (1992), the Court struck down a federal law that compelled states "to provide for the disposal of the radioactive waste generated within their borders." Five years later in 1997, the U.S. Supreme Court again struck down a federal law in part on Tenth Amendment grounds. In *Printz v. United States*, the Court examined the so-called Brady Act, which required local law enforcement officials to conduct background checks on people wanting to buy handguns. The Court ruled 5–4 that the federal government could not force states to run a federal program. According to the majority, the "mandatory obligation" to run background checks "plainly runs afoul of that rule."

State and Local Governments

Do state governments have police powers?

Yes, state governments have general police powers to protect their citizens. Stated another way, state governments have the general authority to pass laws to protect the general public, health, safety, and welfare of their citizens within constitutional limits. This general authority is called the police power. The federal government, by contrast, does not possess this general police power.

Thus, for example, a state government—exercising its general police powers—could impose mandatory vaccinations. State and local governments have used these general powers to provide for mandatory vaccinations of public school children and emergency care workers in times of public emergency.

What does the U.S. Constitution say about state government?

The U.S. Constitution does not give a whole lot of space to state governments but it does provide that all states must uphold a "republican" form of government. The Tenth Amendment to the U.S. Constitution also says that all powers not granted to the federal government are reserved to the state governments and the people.

What document is the government document of each state?

Each state has its own state constitution, much like the federal government is created by the U.S. Constitution. State

Did some state constitutions predate the U.S. Constitution?

Yes, they did. A few states had constitutions before the creation of the U.S. Constitution. Recall that the first constitution that the country had was the Articles of Confederation. The Articles of Confederation tried to govern the states. These states all had constitutions of some sort.

Also, recall that it was James Madison (1751–1836), as a member of the U.S. House of Representatives, who called for the U.S. Constitution to be amended to include a bill of rights. When Madison selected the different proposed amendments composing this bill of rights, he looked to existing state governments.

constitutions vary quite a bit from each other, but each lays out the different branches or departments of government. But the state constitutions vary quite greatly in length. For example, the Alabama Constitution is one of the largest constitutions in the world.

When the Constitution was ratified in 1787, what state was the first to officially join the Union and ratify the Constitution?

Delaware became the first state to ratify the Constitution on December 7, 1787. This is why one of Delaware's nicknames is "the First State."

What was the order and date that the different states were admitted to the Union?

State	Date of Admission
Delaware	December 7, 1787
Pennsylvania	December 12, 1787
New Jersey	December 18, 1787
Georgia	January 2, 1788
Connecticut	January 9, 1788
Massachusetts	February 6, 1788
Maryland	April 28, 1788
South Carolina	May 23, 1788
New Hampshire	June 21, 1788
Virginia	June 25, 1788
New York	July 26, 1788
North Carolina	November 21, 1789

State	Date of Admission
Rhode Island	May 29, 1790
Vermont	March 4, 1791
Kentucky	June 1, 1792
Tennessee	June 1, 1796
Ohio	March 1, 1803
Louisiana	April 30, 1812
Indiana	December 11, 1816
Mississippi	December 10, 1817
Illinois	December 3, 1818
Alabama	December 14, 1819
Maine	March 15, 1820
Missouri	August 10, 1821
Arkansas	June 15, 1836
Michigan	January 26, 1837
Florida	March 3, 1845
Texas	December 29, 1845
Iowa	December 28, 1846
Wisconsin	May 29, 1848
California	September 9, 1850
Minnesota	May 11, 1858
Oregon	February 14, 1859
Kansas	January 29, 1861
West Virginia	June 20, 1863
Nevada	October 31, 1864
Nebraska	March 1, 1867
Colorado	August 1, 1876
North Dakota	November 2, 1889
South Dakota	November 2, 1889
Montana	November 8, 1889
Washington	November 11, 1889
Idaho	July 3, 1890
Wyoming	July 10, 1890
Utah	January 4, 1896
Oklahoma	November 16, 1907
New Mexico	January 6, 1912
Arizona	February 14, 1912
Alaska	January 3, 1959
Hawaii	August 21, 1959

What are the nicknames of the different states?

State	Nickname
Alabama	The Yellowhammer State
Alaska	The Last Frontier
Arkansas	The Natural State
Arizona	The Grand Canyon State
California	The Golden State
Colorado	The Centennial State
Connecticut	The Constitution State
Delaware	The First State
Florida	The Sunshine State
Georgia	The Peach State
Hawaii	The Aloha State
Idaho	The Gem State
Illinois	Land of Lincoln
Indiana	The Hoosier State
Iowa	The Hawkeye State
Kansas	The Sunflower State
Kentucky	The Bluegrass State
Louisiana	The Pelican State
Maine	The Pine Tree State
Maryland	The Old Line State
Massachusetts	The Bay State
Michigan	The Great Lakes State
Minnesota	Land of 10,000 Lakes
Mississippi	The Magnolia State
Missouri	The Show-Me State
Montana	Big Sky Country
Nebraska	The Cornhusker State
Nevada	The Silver State
New Hampshire	The Granite State
New Jersey	The Garden State

State	Nickname
New Mexico	The Land of Enchantment
New York	The Empire State
North Carolina	The Tarheel State
North Dakota	The Peace Garden State
Ohio	The Buckeye State
Oklahoma	Native America
Oregon	The Beaver State
Pennsylvania	The Keystone State
Rhode Island	The Ocean State
South Carolina	The Palmetto State
South Dakota	The Mount Rushmore State
Tennessee	The Volunteer State
Texas	The Lone Star State
Utah	The Beehive State
Vermont	The Green Mountain State
Virginia	Old Dominion
Washington	The Evergreen State
West Virginia	The Mountain State
Wisconsin	The Badger State
Wyoming	The Equality State

What do many state constitutions call their bill of rights?

Many state bill of rights are called declarations of rights. They contain many of the same provisions as found in the U.S. Bill of Rights, but they generally are longer and contain more individual rights reserved to the people in those respective states. These state declarations of rights usually are found at the beginning of the state constitutions rather than at the end.

What sort of additional protections are found in these state declarations of rights?

It varies pretty significantly from state to state. For example, Tennessee has a provision that prohibits government officials from treating those who have been arrested with "unnecessary rigor." Many states, such as California, have a provision that guarantees individuals a right to fish on public property. Others have provisions that allow for hunting on certain lands. Many state constitutions have a provision in their declaration of rights that prohibits the imprisonment of persons for debts. New York has a provision in its state bill of rights that protects the right of employees to workers' compensation benefits.

What state has the longest constitution by far?

The state of Alabama has the longest constitution by far among the states and one of the longest in the world. Alabama's

What two states have had the most constitutions in their history?

The state of Louisiana has had 11 different state constitutions, followed closely by Georgia with 10.

DID YOU KNOW!?

constitution spans more than 402,000 words. The second longest state constitution is Texas, which is at 92,000 words. Alabama's constitution is so long largely because it contains a host of amendments that apply to individual counties.

What is the importance of state capital cities?

State capital cities house the major parts of the state's governmental structures of each branch of government. The governor and legislature operate out of the capital city. Capital cities also often have much to offer citizens in the way of parks, gardens, museums, and other publicly funded entities. Much of a state's important business takes place in the capital city. In sum, the capital city hosts the seat of the state's government and for that reason alone is quite important.

Santa Fe, New Mexico, is the oldest capital city in the United States, having been founded way back in 1607. It wasn't the capital of a state then, of course. That happened in 1912, when New Mexico joined the Union.

What are the capital cities of each state?

State	Capital City
Alabama	Montgomery
Alaska	Juneau
Arizona	Phoenix
Arkansas	Little Rock
California	Sacramento
Colorado	Denver
Connecticut	Hartford
Delaware	Dover
Florida	Tallahassee
Georgia	Atlanta
Hawaii	Honolulu
Idaho	Boise
Illinois	Springfield
Indiana	Indianapolis
Iowa	Des Moines
Kansas	Topeka
Kentucky	Frankfort
Louisiana	Baton Rouge
Maine	Augusta
Maryland	Annapolis
Massachusetts	Boston
Michigan	Lansing
Minnesota	St. Paul
Mississippi	Jackson
Missouri	Jefferson City
Montana	Helena
Nebraska	Lincoln
Nevada	Carson City
New Hampshire	Concord
New Jersey	Trenton
New Mexico	Santa Fe
New York	Albany
North Carolina	Raleigh
North Dakota	Bismarck

State	Capital City
Ohio	Columbus
Oklahoma	Oklahoma City
Oregon	Salem
Pennsylvania	Harrisburg
Rhode Island	Providence
South Dakota	Pierre
Tennessee	Nashville
Texas	Austin
Utah	Salt Lake City
Vermont	Montpelier
Virginia	Richmond
Washington	Olympia
West Virginia	Charleston
Wisconsin	Madison
Wyoming	Cheyenne

Are capital cities the most populous cities in the states?

Sometimes they are, but sometimes they are not. New York City, for example, is the most populous city in the state of New York—and in the entire United States for that matter—but is not the state capital. On the other hand, Atlanta is the capital *and* the most populous city in Georgia. However, Sacramento—the capital of California—pales in population size to other Californian cities such as Los Angeles. Likewise, Frankfort is the state capital of Kentucky, but it is dwarfed in population by Louisville, the state's most populous city.

What is the smallest state capital?

The smallest state capital is Montpelier, the capital city of Vermont. It has a population of barely more than 8,000 people.

Charming Montpelier, Vermont, is the smallest state capital in terms of population. First settled in 1787, it became the state seat in 1805 and was incorporated as a city in 1895.

Contrast that with Phoenix—the capital of Arizona—which has a population of around 1.6 million people.

What type of governmental structure do state governments have?

All states have three branches of government, a model similar to the federal government as mandated by the U.S. Constitution. The states all have an executive branch, a legislative branch, and a judicial branch. These branches, however, can look quite different from the federal branches.

Who is the chief executive in state governmental structures?

All 50 states have a governor, who serves as the chief executive of the state. Governors are responsible for implementing the laws of their respective state and overseeing the operation of the executive branch of their respective state as well.

Each state also has a lieutenant governor, which is essentially the state equivalent of the vice president at the federal level. Nearly every state governor has a chief of staff, who handles much of the day-to-day coordination for the governors.

What are the typical powers of governors?

Governors outline legislative proposals or platforms that they send to the congresses of their states. Governors also have the power of signing or not signing legislation. Similar to the president of the United States, governors have the power to veto legislation that they disagree with. Governors also have broad appointment powers. They have the ability to nominate individuals to serve in their cabinet. In the vast majority of the states, the governors have the ability to nominate individuals to serve as judges. Governors also often appoint individuals to various boards and commissions though often delegate this task to some of their assistant officials.

Governors also possess the power of clemency, which generally refers to the ability of formally forgiving a person of a criminal offense. The range of clemency can extend from a full pardon to the commutation of a criminal sentence to a reprieve.

Governors, like the president of the United States, also have the ability to issue executive orders. Governors often utilize this power in times of emergency. Relatedly, governors often have various emergency powers in times of disasters and other public emergencies. Finally, governors also serve as the commander in chief of their state and often have control over the state's national guard.

How long are gubernatorial terms?

In 48 states, governors serve four-year terms similar to the president of the United States. Two states — New Hampshire and Vermont — have two-year terms for their governors.

Is there a minimum age requirement to be a governor?

Most states set a minimum age of 30 years of age to be governor. The lowest number qualification is 18 years of age — in California, Ohio, Rhode Island, Vermont, and Wisconsin.

Which state's governors make more than $200,000 in salary?

The governors of California, New York, and Pennsylvania all have salaries greater than $200,000 per year. The lowest

The highest-paid governor in the United States is New York's, making $250,000 annually. The latest governor there, taking office in 2021, is Kathy Hochul, a Democrat.

gubernatorial salary is Maine, whose governor makes $70,000 per year.

Can governors be impeached?

Yes, every state—except for Oregon—provides that governors can be impeached. In the vast majority of the states, the lower body of the legislature determines whether the government is impeached and then the higher body—called the Senate in nearly every state—conducts the impeachment trial.

Who are some of the most famous governors in American history?

There are almost too many to name, but a few stand out. For example, U.S. Supreme Court chief justice Earl Warren (1891–1974) served as the 30th governor of California from 1943 to 1953 before President Dwight D. Eisenhower (1890–1969) appointed him to serve as chief justice. Warren was an effective leader during a difficult period in American history. One negative mark against his record—for which he later regretted—was that he approved of the internment of 110,000 Japanese American citizens during the time of World War II.

George Wallace (1919–1998) served four terms as governor of Alabama—from 1963 to 1967, from 1971 to 1979, and from 1983 to 1987. He was well known early in his career for opposing integration, infamously standing at the front of the entrance to the University of Alabama. He later apologized for those views and actions. He ran for president of the United States but never won the Democratic Party nomination. He is the third longest-serving governor in U.S. history.

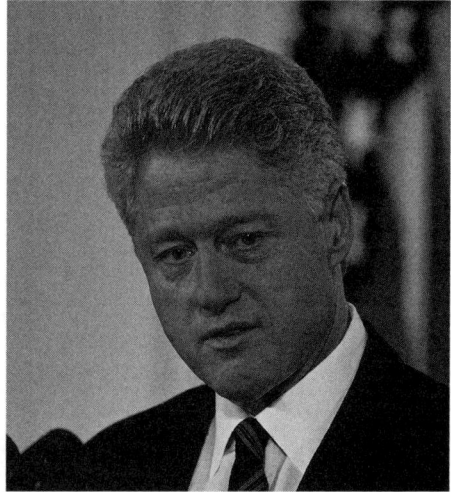

Among some of the famous recent governors in U.S. history is Bill Clinton, a Democrat who governed Arkansas before moving to the White House in 1992 for two terms.

Mario Cuomo (1932–2015) served three terms as governor of New York from 1983 to 1994. He was a very prominent member of the Democratic Party who even challenged President Ronald Reagan (1911–2004) with his address at the 1984 Democratic Party Convention. He was considered a frontrunner for the Democratic nomination for president in 1988 and 1992, but he declined to run.

Bill Clinton (1946–), the so-called "Boy Governor," was the governor of Arkansas from 1979 to 1981 and then from 1983 to 1991. He was 32 years old when he first served as governor. Clinton proved to be a very effective governor and surprised political pundits when he ran for and eventually captured the U.S. presidency during the 1992 election. He served two terms as president where he once again capably governed, though his tenure was marked by an impeachment arising from his sexual liaison with intern Monica Lewinsky (1973–).

What is the legislative branch of the state governments?

The legislative branch of the state governments consists of a bicameral legislature—two houses—with the exception of the state of Nebraska, which has a unicameral (one house) legislature. The names of the two houses vary from state to state. Some states use the terms Senate and House like the federal system, but others use terms like General Assembly, State Assembly, or House of Delegates.

For example, the state of Alabama's lower house is called the House of Representatives and the Senate, but the state of California uses the terms State Assembly and State Senate.

What are the basic powers of the state legislature?

Similar to the U.S. Congress, state legislatures are the chief lawmaking bodies in their states. They initiate and approve of legislation, they impeach state officials, and they initiate tax legislation in their states. They also approve of the states' budgets.

What is the structure of the state judiciary?

The structure of state judicial systems varies considerably across the United States. Many state court systems have a structure similar to the federal judiciary, which consists of a final appellate court, intermediate appellate courts, and trial courts. For example, the Alabama state judicial system consists of the

Alabama Supreme Court as the final appellate court, the Alabama Court of Civil Appeals and the Alabama Court of Criminal Appeals as the intermediate appellate courts, and circuit courts as the trial courts. Contrast that with the state of Washington, which has a supreme court as the final appellate court, the court of appeals as the intermediate appellate court, and the superior courts as the trial courts.

Are there other courts in the various states?

Yes, there are also many other courts of so-called limited jurisdiction in different states. For example, most states have separate probate courts to handle wills and estates, juvenile courts to hear matters involving minors, and general sessions or court of common plea courts to hear cases involving smaller dollar amounts.

What is the structure of each state's supreme court?

All state high courts in the United states have either five, seven, or nine justices. Six states have nine justices, 28 states have seven justices, and 16 states have five justices.

State	Court	Number of Justices
Alabama	Alabama Supreme Court	9 justices
Alaska	Alaska Supreme Court	5 justices
Arizona	Arizona Supreme Court	7 justices
Arkansas	Arkansas Supreme Court	7 justices
California	California Supreme Court	7 justices

State	Court	Number of Justices
Colorado	Colorado Supreme Court	7 justices
Connecticut	Connecticut Supreme Court	7 justices
Delaware	Delaware Supreme Court	5 justices
Florida	Florida Supreme Court	7 justices
Georgia	Georgia Supreme Court	9 justices
Hawaii	Hawaii Supreme Court	5 justices
Idaho	Idaho Supreme Court	5 justices
Illinois	Illinois Supreme Court	7 justices
Indiana	Indiana Supreme Court	5 justices
Iowa	Iowa Supreme Court	7 justices
Kansas	Kansas Supreme Court	7 justices
Kentucky	Kentucky Supreme Court	7 justices
Louisiana	Louisiana Supreme Court	7 justices
Maine	Maine Supreme Judicial Court	7 justices
Maryland	Maryland Supreme Court	7 justices
Massachusetts	Massachusetts Supreme Judicial Court	7 justices
Michigan	Michigan Supreme Court	7 justices
Minnesota	Minnesota Supreme Court	7 justices
Mississippi	Mississippi Supreme Court	9 justices
Missouri	Missouri Supreme Court	7 justices
Montana	Montana Supreme Court	7 justices
Nebraska	Nebraska Supreme Court	7 justices
Nevada	Nevada Supreme Court	7 justices
New Hampshire	New Hampshire Supreme Court	5 justices
New Jersey	New Jersey Supreme Court	7 justices
New Mexico	New Mexico Supreme Court	5 justices
New York	New York Court of Appeals	7 justices
North Carolina	Supreme Court of North Carolina	7 justices
North Dakota	North Dakota Supreme Court	5 justices
Ohio	Ohio Supreme Court	7 justices
Oklahoma	Oklahoma Supreme Court	9 justices
Oregon	Oregon Supreme Court	7 justices
Pennsylvania	Pennsylvania Supreme Court	7 justices
Rhode Island	Rhode Island Supreme Court	5 justices
South Carolina	South Carolina Supreme Court	5 justices
South Dakota	South Dakota Supreme Court	5 justices

State	Court	Number of Justices
Tennessee	Tennessee Supreme Court	5 justices
Texas	Texas Supreme Court	9 justices
Utah	Utah Supreme Court	5 justices
Vermont	Vermont Supreme Court	5 justices
Virginia	Supreme Court of Virginia	7 justices
Washington	Washington Supreme Court	9 justices
West Virginia	Supreme Court of Appeals of West Virginia	5 justices
Wisconsin	Wisconsin Supreme Court	7 justices
Wyoming	Wyoming Supreme Court	5 justices

DID YOU KNOW!?

What state has two courts of last resort?

Oklahoma has a unique state court structure in that it has two courts of last resort. The Oklahoma Supreme Court is the court of last resort for civil cases, but the Oklahoma Court of Criminal Appeals is the highest state court for criminal cases.

Do state high court justices have life terms?

Not generally, no. Most state high court justices serve for specific terms and then are subject to yes-no retention elections. For example, in the state of Tennessee, Tennessee Supreme Court justices serve eight-year terms. They then appear on the ballot, where the voters are asked whether they want to retain that justice.

It is a yes-no vote. If the voters retain the justice, then the justice serves another eight-year term.

The only pure exception to this is the state of Rhode Island. There, the state supreme court justices have life terms just like Article III federal judges. In two other states—Massachusetts and New Hampshire—the justices do not have term limits, but there is a mandatory retirement age of 70.

Are state high court judges elected or appointed?

It depends on the individual state. In some states, judges are appointed by the governor after the legislature approves of a certain number of candidates. However, in other states, the state high court judges are elected in contested races. For example, in the state of Vermont, the governor appoints the justices after a nominating commission identifies suitable candidates. But in the state of West Virginia, the supreme court justices are elected. In those states that have elections, there are states with partisan elections and states with nonpartisan elections. Partisan elections are those in which the judicial candidates align with a particular political party. However, in nonpartisan elections, the justices do not align with particular political parties.

Have any state supreme court justices later served on the U.S. Supreme Court?

Yes, Justice William Brennan Jr. (1906–1997) previously served as a judge on the New Jersey Supreme Court before President Dwight D. Eisenhower (1890–1969) nominated him to serve on the U.S. Supreme Court. John Jay (1745–1829) had previously

The most recent U.S. Supreme Court justice to have previously served on a state supreme court was David Souter, who was previously on the Louisiana Supreme Court.

served on the New York Supreme Court. Edward D. White Jr. (1845–1921) served one year on the Louisiana Supreme Court before being elevated to the U.S. Supreme Court. David Souter (1939–) previously served on the New Hampshire Supreme Court before being elevated to the U.S. Supreme Court.

Who is the top legal officer in each state?

The state attorney general is the leading legal officer in each state. The attorney general is responsible for overseeing litigation for a state. Attorneys general often argue cases in appellate courts representing the state. In many states, the attorney general office also issues opinions—called attorney general opinions—that provide guidance to state legislators on pending legislation or other important legal issues in the state.

Attorneys general also enforce federal and state environmental laws, propose legislation, and institute litigation on behalf of the states. For example, when many states sued tobacco companies in high-level litigation, it was the state attorneys general who spearheaded those lawsuits that led to million- and billion-dollar settlements.

How do state attorneys general obtain their positions?

In many states, the state attorneys general are elected. In other states, the governor appoints the attorney general. Two states have unique methods of selecting the state attorney general. In the state of Maine, the attorney general is appointed by the state legislature. In Tennessee, the state supreme court appoints the attorney general.

What sorts of activities do state and local governments participate in?

State and local governments engage in all sorts of work for the public. State governments broadly control affairs within a state's borders. This can include managing the economy, charging and collecting income taxes, and providing public benefits. For example, many people below a certain economic level may receive a

DID YOU KNOW!?

What former state attorney general later became president of the United States?

Martin Van Buren (1782–1862), the country's eighth president, served as New York's attorney general. He also served as a U.S. senator and New York governor before becoming U.S. secretary of state and then vice president in President Andrew Jackson's (1767–1845) administration. After Jackson left after two terms, Van Buren then ran and became president of the United States.

form of Medicaid, which provides health benefits for those in lower income brackets.

State and local governments have law enforcement agencies. Most cities and towns have local police departments that enforce the state and local laws and apprehend those who commit crimes. There usually is a state police force of some sort. For example, Tennessee has a force known as the Tennessee State Troopers. State and local government law enforcement officials do not generally enforce federal laws. Those are enforced or prosecuted by federal government officials.

State and local governments also provide educational resources for children. Children in the various states have free public schools. In fact, states have compulsory education laws that require children to attend school—whether it be public, private, or homeschooled. Most state governments have a department of education that oversees education and sets the curricular and other standards. But the day-to-day operations of schools takes place at the local levels.

State and local governments also provide public libraries. These are a great resource for those with limited means—and for any citizen. Access to ideas and information is important for any person, and public libraries still play a vital role in that even though more and more people rely on the Internet.

State and local government officials also oversee the parks—lands that are dedicated to public use.

Who funds public schooling in the United States?

State, local, and federal funding contributes to public schools in the United States, though the vast majority of the funding comes from state and local governments. For example, a 2019

Congressional Research Service report identifies that state governments fund 47 percent of the revenue, local governments fund about 44 percent of the revenue, and less than 9 percent is funded by the federal government. The report explains:

> All states (but not the District of Columbia) provide a share of the total revenues available for public elementary and secondary education. This state share varies widely, from approximately 25% in Illinois to almost 90% in Hawaii and Vermont. The programs through which state funds are provided to local educational agencies (LEAs) for public elementary and secondary education have traditionally been categorized into five types: (1) Foundation Programs, (2) Full State Funding Programs, (3) Flat Grants, (4) District Power Equalizing, and (5) Categorical Grants. Of these, Foundation Programs are most common, although many states use a combination of program types.

Who prosecutes state and local crimes?

State and local prosecutors handle the prosecution of state and local crimes. Most of the time, it is a city or county district attorney who oversees such criminal prosecutions. This district attorney is usually a manager or overseer of a cadre of assistant district attorneys, who are also lawyers and prosecutors. The prosecutor may be called a city prosecutor or a county attorney. There also is a state attorney general, who often handles more of the appellate work. For example, the local district attorney will handle the case at the trial court level. If the defendant is convicted, the defendant then has a right to appeal his conviction. At the appellate level, the state attorney general's office handles the case.

Who is the chief executive of most cities or towns in the United States?

The leader of most cities and towns in the United States is the mayor. A mayor is generally responsible for the well-being and welfare of the residents in their city or town. A rough analogy is the mayor is to city government as the governor is to state government.

Have any mayors become U.S. presidents?

Yes, three U.S. presidents previously served as mayors during their early political careers. They are Andrew Johnson (1808–1875), Grover Cleveland (1837–1908), and Calvin Coolidge (1872–1933). Johnson served as mayor of Greenville, Tennessee.

President Calvin Coolidge, who was in office from 1923 to 1929, was previously the mayor of Northampton, Massachusetts.

Cleveland served several terms as mayor of Buffalo, New York. Coolidge served as mayor of Northampton, Massachusetts.

Who are the leading law enforcement officials in cities?

The leading law enforcement official in most cities is the chief of police or police chief. Some police chiefs have the title of commissioner. The police chief or commissioner is responsible for managing the police departments. Some of the police chiefs in larger American cities are famous figures.

What future U.S. president was once the commissioner of the New York Police Department?

Theodore Roosevelt (1858–1919) served as the commissioner of the New York Police Department (NYPD) in the 1890s. He later served as both vice president and president of the United States.

DID YOU KNOW!?

Who is the only former U.S. president to previously serve as a sheriff?

Grover Cleveland previously served as sheriff of Erie County, New York. It was his first political office in a long and distinguished political career that also saw him serve as mayor of Buffalo, governor of New York, and president of the United States for two nonconsecutive terms.

Who are the leading law enforcement officials in counties?

Sheriffs are the leading law enforcement officials in local counties in the United States. The sheriff is the leading law enforcement official in what are generally called sheriff's departments or sheriff's offices. A primary responsibility of most sheriffs is to manage jails and prisons in the county. They also provide protection for local courthouses and county buildings. Still another duty of sheriffs is to enforce the county ordinances and to coordinate with city law enforcement officials.

Who was the first sheriff in what became known as the United States?

The first sheriff in North America in the land that later became the United States was Captain William Stone (c. 1603–c. 1660), who served as sheriff of the county of Accomack in the colony of Virginia in 1634. Stone later was appointed governor of Maryland by Lord Baltimore (1605–1675).

The Civil Rights Movement

BEGINNINGS

What impact did World War II have on civil rights?

World War II played a major impact on the burgeoning concept of civil rights for African Americans. Numerous African Americans joined the war effort, many to escape numbing poverty. While the armed forces were segregated, the war effort brought at least some mingling of the races. Many African Americans fought bravely in the war and earned the respect of many of their white colleagues. Some thoughtful Americans of all races also noticed the dissonance between the United States of America combating and opposing the racial hatred espoused by Nazi Germany and its fuhrer, Adolf Hitler (1889–1945) but then practicing discrimination and segregation at home. Furthermore, many African American soldiers noticed less discrimination in countries such as France and became less satisfied with the negative conditions in the United States. This provided an opportunity for many to question segregation more forcefully and persistently.

When did racial segregation end in the armed forces?

It ended on July 26, 1948, when President Harry Truman (1884–1972) signed Executive Order 9981, which stated: "It is hereby declared to be the policy of the President that there shall be equality of treatment and opportunity for all persons in the armed services without regard to race, color, religion, or national origin." The year before, civil rights leader A. Philip Randolph (1889–1979) helped form the Committee Against Jim Crow in Military Service.

President Harry Truman integrated the armed forces by signing Executive Order 9981 in 1948.

What Supreme Court decision inspired the Civil Rights Movement?

The U.S. Supreme Court's decision in *Brown v. Board of Education* (1954) invaliding segregated public education inspired the Civil Rights Movement. The Supreme Court ruled that segregation in public education violated the Equal Protection Clause of the Fourteenth Amendment. The decision inspired countless people who believed that the promise of civil rights and equality could be an actual reality. The decision in *Brown* led to a series of lawsuits, challenging segregation in nearly all aspects of public life.

What was the Montgomery Bus Boycott?

The Montgomery Bus Boycott was a seminal point in the American Civil Rights Movement that occurred in 1955 and 1956 to protest Montgomery's transit's system of segregation. Under the city's policy, black passengers had to sit in the back rows of the bus, while white passengers sat in the front. The policy was inspired after the arrest of an African American woman named Rosa Parks (1913–2005), who was arrested after she refused to give up her seat to a white passenger.

The African American community rallied to the cause and refused to use city buses. Many traveled together in carpools, rode in black-owned taxis, or walked to their jobs. Many suffered for their resistance. Parks lost her job as a seamstress as a result of her pivotal role in the protest.

In June 1956, a panel of three federal district judges ruled 2–1 the segregation system as unconstitutional in *Browder v. Gayle*. The majority reasoned the segregation policy violated both due-process and equal-protection rights. The majority concluded:

Along with 72 other people charged with organizing the bus boycott, Rosa Parks was taken in by police on February 22, 1956, for the defiant act of sitting toward the front of a bus.

"We hold that the statutes and ordinances requiring segregation of the white and colored races on the motor buses of a common carrier of passengers in the City of Montgomery and its police jurisdiction violate the due process and equal protection of the law clauses of the Fourteenth Amendment to the Constitution of the United States."

Who were some of the key leaders of the Montgomery Bus Boycott?

Some of the key leaders of the Montgomery Bus Boycott included E. D. Nixon (1899–1987), who had worked with Rosa Parks at the NAACP, Ralph Abernathy (1926–1990), minister at the First Baptist Church, and a young minister from Dexter Avenue Baptist Church named Martin Luther King Jr. (1929–1968).

King became president of the Montgomery Improvement Association and later the most visible leader of the Civil Rights Movement.

What was Dr. King's background before his involvement in the Civil Rights Movement?

Martin Luther King Jr. was born in 1929 in Atlanta, Georgia. He was named Michael King at birth but his father, the Reverend Martin Luther King Sr. (1899–1984), changed his first name to Martin. His father actually changed both their first names from "Michael" to "Martin" after a trip to Germany in 1934 and admiration for the great religious reformer Martin Luther (1483–1546). King was a precocious student who skipped two grades in high school and entered Morehouse College at the age of 15. He earned a degree in sociology and then attended Crozer Theological Seminary in Chester, Pennsylvania, where he graduated in 1951. He then earned his doctorate degree from Boston University. King followed in his father's footsteps and agreed to pastor the Dexter Avenue Baptist Church in the mid-1950s. It was from this position that Dr. King found himself in the middle of civil rights activities.

When did the U.S. Supreme Court earlier rule against segregated bus travel?

The U.S. Supreme Court invalidated a Virginia law mandating that races be separated on buses traveling through Virginia in *Morgan v. Virginia* (1946). The case began when 27-year-old Irene Morgan (1917–2007), an African American woman, refused to move from her seat and give it to a white patron. Authorities arrested her for violating the Virginia law.

The case proceeded all the way to the U.S. Supreme Court, where the high court determined that the law mandating separation of the races imposed too much of a burden on interstate commerce. Thus, the Court ruled that the Virginia law violated the Commerce Clause of the Constitution. "The interferences to interstate commerce which arise from state regulation of racial association on interstate vehicles has long been recognized," the Court explained. "Such regulation hampers freedom of choice in selecting accommodations."

Who were Irene Morgan's attorneys before the U.S. Supreme Court?

Irene Morgan's attorneys were William Hastie (1904–1976) and Thurgood Marshall (1908–1993)—two of the country's most successful and important civil rights attorneys. Hastie was the nation's first African American federal judge in 1937, when President Franklin D. Roosevelt (1882–1945) appointed him as a federal district court judge for the Virgin Islands. He later became dean of Howard University Law School. In 1946, President Harry Truman appointed Hastie to become the governor of the U.S. Virgin Islands. Then, in 1949, Truman appointed Hastie to become a judge on the U.S. Court of Appeals for the Third Circuit. He became the nation's first African American appellate judge. He served on the Third Circuit from 1949 until his death in 1976. Hastie, who graduated from Harvard Law School, argued the case for Irene Morgan before the U.S. Supreme Court.

Hastie's cocounsel was none other than Thurgood Marshall, who became the first African American to ever serve on the U.S. Supreme Court in 1967. Marshall became famous for his many years of litigating against segregation and racial discrimination with the National Association for the Advancement of Colored People (NAACP). He was one of the attorneys who argued against segregation in public education in the famous *Brown v. Board of Education* (1954) decision, where a unanimous Supreme Court ruled that segregated schools violated the Equal Protection Clause of the Fourteenth Amendment. President Lyndon B. Johnson (1908–1973) appointed Marshall in 1965 as the U.S. solicitor general, the first African American to hold that post. Two years later, he elevated Marshall to the U.S. Supreme Court.

Who were the Little Rock Nine?

The Little Rock Nine were the nine African American students who integrated Little Rock Central High School in 1957. Arkansas governor Orval Faubus (1910–1994) called out the Arkansas National Guard to prevent the students from entering the all-white school in September 1957. President Dwight D. Eisenhower (1890–1969) called on a segment of the U.S. Army and ordered the National Guard to obey Army troops, not the commands of the state governor. Eisenhower believed that no state should defy rulings of the U.S. Supreme Court and the federal government. "Under the leadership of demagogic extremists, disorderly mobs have deliberately prevented the carrying out of proper orders from a federal court."

The Little Rock Nine members were Ernest Green (1941–), Elizabeth Eckford (1941–), Jefferson Thomas (1942–2010), Terrence Roberts (1941–), Carlotta Walls LaNier (1942–), Minnijean Brown (1941–), Gloria Ray Karlmark (1942–), Thelma Mothershed (1940–), and Melba Pattillo Beals (1941–). President Bill Clinton (1946–), who was himself a former governor of Arkansas, presented the group with Congressional gold medals in 1999.

Little Rock Nine members: (back row, left to right) Terrence Roberts, Ernest Green, Melba Pattillo Beals, and Jefferson Thomas; (front row, left to right) Minnijean Brown, Elizabeth Eckford, Carlotta Walls, Thelma Mothershed, and Gloria Ray. At center is New York City's mayor, Robert Wagner.

What famous clash did President Eisenhower have with a governor over civil rights?

Dwight D. Eisenhower sent in federal troops to ensure that Arkansas governor Orval Faubus would not attempt to block nine African American students from attending the previously all-white Central High School in Little Rock, Arkansas. In the wake of the Supreme Court's desegregation decision in *Brown v. Board of Education* (1954), the city school board recognized its obligation to desegregate. However, Governor Faubus used the Arkansas National Guard to block the school to prevent the integration. He did this in defiance of a federal court order mandating integration.

Eisenhower met with Faubus personally and came away from the meeting thinking that Faubus understood he must not defy a federal court order. However, days later, Faubus defiantly refused to agree and said he would support segregation. Eisenhower then sent in federal troops to ensure that the "Little Rock Nine" could attend Central High. Federal troops from the 101st Airborne Division surrounded the school, controlled the crowd, and ensured integration. Eisenhower told his U.S. attorney general, Herbert Brownell Jr. (1904–1996), to use force if necessary to save lives and ensure integration.

Who was Daisy Bates?

Daisy Bates (1914–1999) was a civil rights activist and writer best known for her work in helping the Little Rock Nine. Bates was a leading member of the Arkansas NAACP and also publisher of the local black newspaper, the *Arkansas State Press*. She later wrote a memoir about the Little Rock Crisis, *The Long Shadow of Little Rock*. A 2012 documentary film calls her the "First Lady of Little Rock."

What was the Highlander Folk School?

The Highlander Folk School, now known as the Highlander Research and Education Center, played a key role in the Civil Rights Movement by providing key training in the principles of organization, activism, and other social justice causes to many

What was the anthem song of the Civil Rights Movement?

The spiritual "We Shall Overcome" was the anthem song of the Civil Rights Movement. Folk singer Pete Seeger (1919–2014) and others affiliated with the organization People's Songs produced the song in 1947. Many other popular artists sang the song, including Joan Baez (1941–), during the early 1960s. The music director at the Highlander Folk School, Zilphia Horton (1910–1956), is credited with creating the song with other musicians at the school in 1947. Many believe a basis for the song is Rev. Charles Tindley's (1851–1933) "I'll Overcome Someday."

DID YOU KNOW!?

members of the Student Nonviolent Coordinating Committee (SNCC). Civil rights leaders John Lewis (1940–2020), Ralph Abernathy, and Dr. Martin Luther King Jr. visited Highlander during the mid- to late 1950s for training. Founded in 1932, the school was located in Grundy County, Tennessee, near Monteagle. The school was closed in 1961 due to political pressure caused by opposition to the Civil Rights Movement. It later reopened in Knoxville as the Highlander Research and Education Center.

What was the nonviolence movement?

The Reverend Martin Luther King Jr. was committed to bringing about change by staging peaceful protests. He had carefully studied the works of Mahatma Gandhi (1869–1948) and was impressed by the Indian man's commitment against official authority. King led a campaign of nonviolence as part of the Civil Rights Movement. King rose to prominence as a leader during the Montgomery Bus Boycott in 1955, when he delivered a speech that embodied his Christian beliefs and set the tone for the nonviolence movement, saying, "We are not here advocating violence … The only weapon we have … is the weapon of protest." Throughout his life, King staunchly adhered to these beliefs— even after terrorists bombed his family's home. King's "arsenal" of democratic protest included boycotts, marches, the words of his stirring speeches (comprising an impressive body of oratory), and sit-ins.

With other African American ministers, King established the Southern Christian Leadership Conference (1957), which assumed a leadership role during the Civil Rights Movement.

The nonviolent protest of black Americans proved a powerful weapon against segregation and discrimination: A massive demonstration in Birmingham, Alabama, in 1963 helped sway public opinion and motivate lawmakers in Washington to act when news coverage of the event showed peaceful protesters being subdued by policemen using dogs and heavy fire hoses. In response to the outcry over the event in Birmingham, President John F. Kennedy (1917–1963) proposed civil rights legislation to Congress; the bill was passed in 1964. That same year, Martin Luther King Jr. received the Nobel Peace Prize for his nonviolent activism.

King's policy of peace was challenged two years later when the Student Nonviolent Coordinating Committee (SNCC), tired of the violent response with which peaceful protesters were often met, urged activists to adopt a more decisive and aggressive stance and began promoting the slogan "Black Power." The Civil Rights Movement, having made critical strides, became fragmented, as leaders, including the highly influential Malcolm X (1925–1965), differed over how to effect change.

King explained the essence of nonviolence in his "Letter from the Birmingham Jail": "Nonviolent direct action seeks to create such a crisis and establish such creative tension that a community that has constantly refused to negotiate is forced to confront the issue. It seeks to dramatize the issue that it can no longer be ignored."

ALABAMA

What were the civil rights activities of Dr. Martin Luther King Jr.?

Dr. King became the national symbol for civil rights and the preeminent leader of the Civil Rights Movement. He first entered prominence as a 26-year-old pastor of the Dexter Avenue Baptist Church during the Montgomery Bus Boycott. He later served as the president of the Southern Christian Leadership Conference (SCLC). He helped lead civil rights protests in St. Augustine, Florida; Selma, Alabama; Birmingham, Alabama; and Albany, Georgia.

Martin Luther King Jr., who led the Southern Christian Leadership Conference from 1957 until his death in 1968, was the most prominent leader of the Civil Rights Movement.

He entered national consciousness when he delivered his famous "I Have a Dream" speech at the March on Washington in August 1963. He won thc Nobel Peace Prize in 1964 for his nonviolent attempts to fight for racial equality. In his later years, Dr. King focused on poverty. He was assassinated in April 1968 in Memphis, Tennessee.

What lessons did Dr. King learn in Albany?

The Albany Movement represented a pivotal moment in the Civil Rights Movement. While the movement to desegregate public facilities and arouse public consciousness failed, it helped Dr. King learn how better to achieve his goals of arousing national consciousness. A determined opposition, led by cagey Albany chief of police Laurie Pritchett (1926–2000), managed to thwart many of Dr. King's efforts. Pritchett wisely instructed his officers to never use violence in dealing with civil rights demonstrators—a strategy that eluded his counterpart in Birmingham, Theophilus Eugene "Bull" Connor (1897–1973).

Pritchett, who had studied the nonviolent protest movement and its tactics, sometimes would pray with demonstrators and managed to avoid the condemnation of the outside world.

What was the "Letter from the Birmingham Jail"?

The "Letter from the Birmingham Jail" was an open letter written by Dr. Martin Luther King Jr. from a Birmingham jail to eight white ministers in Birmingham. King wrote the letter in response to a published letter by the eight white ministers called a "Call to Unity." The white ministers supported racial equality but disagreed with direct, nonviolent action. The ministers urged protestors not to engage in unlawful action but contended that protestors should use more patience and rely on court decisions to slowly move the country in a positive direction. They wrote: "We further strongly urge our own Negro community to withdraw support from these demonstrations, and to unite locally in working peacefully for a better Birmingham. When rights are consistently denied, a cause should be pressed in the courts and in negotiations among local leaders, and not in the streets. We appeal to both our white and Negro citizenry to observe the principles of law and order and common sense."

King disagreed with this more passive strategy. He said that civil rights activists must continue their push for a more just society. He famously wrote, "Injustice anywhere is an injustice everywhere." The white ministers in Birmingham had questioned the pace of the Civil Rights Movement and the breaking of laws as a form of protest. In his letter, Dr. King emphasized that there was a difference between just laws and unjust laws. "I would agree with St. Augustine that 'an unjust law is no law at all.'" He explained:

"I submit that an individual who breaks a law that conscience tells him is unjust, and willingly accepts the penalty by staying in jail to arouse the conscience of the community over its injustice, is in reality expressing the very highest respect for law."

Author Jonathan Rieder in his book *The Gospel of Freedom* (2013) writes that Dr. King's letter "provided nothing less than the moral and philosophical foundations" of the Civil Rights Movement.

To what religious leader did Dr. King compare himself in the Letter?

Dr. King compared himself to the apostle Paul in the New Testament. He wrote: "Just as the Apostle Paul left his little village of Tarsus and carried the gospel of Jesus Christ to practically every hamlet and city of the Graeco-Roman world, I too am compelled to carry the gospel of freedom beyond my particular hometown."

King explained that he was invited to come to Birmingham by Reverend Fred Shuttlesworth (1922–2011) of the Alabama Christian Movement for Human Rights. He also explained that "injustice anywhere is a threat to injustice everywhere" and that he was not an "outside agitator."

Who was Fred Shuttlesworth?

Fred Shuttlesworth (1922–2011) was a civil rights leader from Alabama during the Civil Rights Movement. He cofounded the Southern Christian Leadership Conference and also the Alabama Christian Movement for Human Rights. A minister of a Baptist church, Shuttlesworth challenged segregation in

Fred Shuttlesworth cofounded the Southern Christian Leadership Conference and was a key figure in the Birmingham campaign for civil rights.

Birmingham—often at great personal risk. Shuttlesworth's courage was legendary. Dr. King referred to him as "one of the nation's most courageous freedom fighters." Some even referred to him as the "Wild Man from Birmingham." He was nearly beaten to death by a white mob after he tried to enroll his children in a nearby all-white school. When a doctor treated him and amazingly found no concussion, he famously replied: "Doctor, the Lord knew I lived in a hard town, so he gave me a hard head."

His house and church were bombed. But Shuttlesworth survived and remained a fearless civil rights leader. He often directly challenged police commissioner "Bull" Connor and other civil rights leaders. He suffered chest injuries from the spray of fire hoses on Connor's orders. Shuttlesworth later moved to Cincinnati, where he pastored a church. He moved back to Birmingham in 2008 after suffering a stroke. In 2008, the Birmingham International Airport was renamed the Birmingham-Shuttlesworth International Airport.

Why was Birmingham called "Bombingham"?

The city of Birmingham, Alabama, was called "Bombingham" by some because of the sheer number of bombings in black neighborhoods in the city. There were at least 18 unsolved bombings in black neighborhoods in the city. Dr. Martin Luther King called Birmingham "the most thoroughly segregated big city in the United States." He added that "[t]here have been more unsolved bombings of Negro homes and churches in Birmingham than any city in this nation."

What was the most notorious bombing during the civil rights era?

The most notorious bombing in Birmingham, Alabama, and of the entire Civil Rights Movement was the 16th Street Baptist Church Bombing, an act of terrorism that occurred on September 15, 1963. The blast on Sunday morning killed four young black girls: Addie Mae Collins (1949–1963), Cynthia Wesley (1949–1963), Carole Robertson (1949–1963), and Denise McNair (1951–1963). More than 20 other people were injured in the blast.

The church had been a focal point for civil rights leaders in Birmingham. Leaders such as Martin Luther King Jr., Fred Shuttlesworth, and others used the church for meetings. Three members of the Ku Klux Klan were later tried and convicted decades later. They were Robert Chambliss (1904–1985), Thomas E. Blanton Jr. (1938–2020), and Bobby Frank Cherry (1930–2004).

What was the Children's Crusade?

The Children's Crusade was a key part of the Civil Rights Movement in Birmingham when thousands of black students participated in what civil rights leaders referred to as "D-Day." The students skipped school and marched in the streets to protest segregation and injustice. More than 600 students were arrested. Some of the students were even subjected to fire hoses by law enforcement officials, which turned public opinion more strongly in favor of the movement itself. Some, including President Kennedy and Malcolm X, condemned the use of children in this manner in the Civil Rights Movement. Many parents also were worried about their children being this directly involved in the movement. But Dr. King told the worried parents: "Don't worry about your children; they are going to be alright. Don't hold them back if they want to go to jail, for they are not only doing a job for themselves, but for all of America and for all of mankind."

The Crusade received front-page coverage by national media outlets and was effective in showing the brutality and unfairness of those enforcing segregation laws.

What was Bloody Sunday?

Bloody Sunday refers to the tragic events surrounding a civil rights march on March 7, 1965, from Selma, Alabama, to Montgomery, Alabama. The march was designed to draw attention to voting rights abuses and the killing of a young civil rights protestor in Marion, Alabama. State and local police used brutality and their billy clubs to repress and abuse the more than 600 civil rights protestors who marched across the Edmund Pettus Bridge, risking their personal safety. Civil rights leaders John Lewis and Hosea Williams (1926–2000) led the march. Bloody Sunday was televised across the world.

Whose death inspired the Selma march?

Jimmie Lee Jackson (1938–1965) was a 28-year-old protestor and deacon at a local church who was shot to death behind Zion Methodist Church in Marion, Alabama, by Alabama state trooper James Bonard Fowler (1933–2015). Jackson and others were marching to the Perry County jail to protest the imprisonment of civil rights worker James Orange (1942–2008). Jackson was unarmed. Fowler claimed that he acted in self-defense as Jackson made a move for Fowler's holster to grab his gun. A grand jury declined to indict Fowler in September 1965.

In May 2007, Fowler was indicted for the murder of Jackson. He pled guilty to manslaughter and was released from prison after serving only five months.

Who was John Lewis?

John Lewis (1940–2020) was a key participant and leader in the American Civil Rights Movement of the 1960s, participating

In addition to his work in the Civil Rights Movement of the 1960s, John Lewis was a U.S. congressman from Georgia from 1987 to 2020.

in marches, freedom rides, and other forms of nonviolent direct action. He served as chairman of the Student Nonviolent Coordinating Committee (SNCC) for many years and helped organize Freedom Summer in Mississippi. He organized sit-in protests in Nashville, Tennessee, where he was arrested. He was one of the original 13 freedom riders in 1961. He suffered a horrific beating in Alabama on "Bloody Sunday," a proposed civil rights march from Selma to Montgomery.

In the 1980s, he began a long and storied political career with an election to the Atlanta City Council. He was a member of the U.S. House of Representatives, representing Georgia's Fifth District from 1987 until his death in 2020.

What other House leader participated in civil rights demonstrations, including as a litigant before the U.S. Supreme Court?

James Clyburn (1940–) has served as a member of the U.S. House of Representatives for the state of South Carolina since 1993. He has been the House minority whip and the assistant House Democratic leader in his distinguished congressional career. In the early 1960s, Clyburn—then a student—participated in a peaceful protest at the state capital in Columbia, South Carolina. Clyburn and more than 180 other students displayed signs criticizing segregation. This led to their arrest and charges of violating the peace.

The case made its way to the U.S. Supreme Court. In *Edwards v. South Carolina* (1963), the U.S. Supreme Court reversed the convictions of the students, finding that the First Amendment protected the peaceful free-assembly and free-expression rights of the students.

Who was Malcolm X?

Malcolm X (1925–1965) was an influential civil rights leader known for his activism and advocacy on behalf of civil rights. Born Malcolm Little in Omaha, Nebraska, he went to prison for robbery at the age of 20. In prison, Little converted to Islam and joined the Nation of Islam. He later became a key follower of Elijah Muhammad (1897–1975), the leader of the Black Muslims. For a time, Malcolm X was Muhammad's most eloquent and powerful spokesman, but he began to have differences with his older mentor. Eventually, Malcolm X left the Nation of Islam in March 1964. He disavowed the Nation of Islam's hard-line stance on segregation and agreed to work with other civil rights leaders. This apparently displeased a segment of the Nation of Islam, as three members of the group assassinated Malcolm X in New York in February 1965. These three members were convicted, though they continued to maintain their innocence even decades later.

Malcolm X was a Muslim minister and civil rights leader who transitioned from the violent message of the Nation of Islam to a more peaceful perspective on obtaining racial justice as an aspect of human rights for all.

DID YOU KNOW!?

What does the letter X in Malcolm X's name stand for?

The influential but controversial African American leader, who was born Malcolm Little, was a staunch defendant of black rights. He took the surname X in 1952 upon his release from prison. He explained that the letter stood for the unknown African name of his ancestors. Malcolm X's family's name, Little, was given to his slave ancestors by their owner. By adopting X as his surname, it was at once a bitter reminder of his family's slavery and an affirmation of his (unknown) African roots.

What was CORE?

CORE is the acronym for the civil rights group Congress of Racial Equality. Founded in 1942 by James L. Farmer Jr. (1920–1999) and several others, it played a significant role in the American Civil Rights Movement. CORE focused on exposing the evils of segregation and discrimination through various acts of nonviolent direct action. CORE did not just engage in activism in the South. CORE attacked employment discrimination, voting rights abuses, and other modes of discrimination in society. Much of its activities occurred in the city of Chicago.

CORE also was active in Freedom Summer—a campaign of civil rights in Mississippi during the summer of 1964. CORE proposed the creation of Freedom Schools and trained young civil rights activists. Three members of CORE—James Chaney (1943–1964), Michael Schwerner (1939–1964), and Andrew Goodman (1943–1964)—were brutally murdered near Philadelphia, Mississippi, during that summer.

MISSISSIPPI

Who was Emmitt Till?

Emmett Till (1941–1955) was a black 14-year-old from Chicago who was brutally mutilated and killed in the Deep South in August 1955. The young man was visiting relatives in Mississippi when he allegedly whistled at a white female store clerk. Till was sharing a bed with his 12-year-old cousin when two white men came to get him on the morning of August 28; he was not seen alive again. His body was later found in a river, tied to a cotton-gin fan with barbed wire. An all-white jury acquitted the store clerk's husband, Roy Bryant (1931–1994), and half brother, J. W. Milam (1919–1980), of the crime.

The events stirred anger in the black community and among civil rights proponents in general, setting off the Civil Rights Movement.

For four decades, Till's grisly murder remained unresolved in the minds of many. Though no one was ever convicted of the crime and the two men who were tried for it had, by 2005, died, some of Till's family and friends, as well as investigators, believed others who participated in the lynching might still be alive. In a quest for clues, Till's body was disinterred in June 2005 to gather evidence. He was reburied in a quiet funeral. The Till family hoped the pending investigation would yield answers and justice.

What was Freedom Summer?

Freedom Summer, or the Mississippi Summer Project, was a project in the summer of 1964 to combat voting discrimination and campaign for voting rights in Mississippi, a state with stark civil rights abuses. Members of CORE and other civil rights groups set up Freedom Schools, Freedom House, and other havens to help those who faced discrimination and repression.

Who were the three civil rights workers murdered during Freedom Summer?

James Chaney, Michael Schwerner, and Andrew Goodman were three civil rights workers active in Freedom Summer who were murdered near Philadelphia, Mississippi. Chaney was an African American activist from Mississippi, while Schwerner and Goodman were from New York. The three had traveled to Philadelphia to investigate the burning of a black church that had been designated as a future Freedom School.

The three men were pulled over by Neshoba County deputy sheriff Cecil Price (1938–2001), who took them to the Neshoba County jail. They were later released. However, a group of Ku Klux Klan members stopped them and murdered them. Their bodies were later discovered by the Federal Bureau of Investigation.

Federal prosecutors charged 18 men, including Price, with conspiracy in violating the civil rights of the three civil rights workers. Seven men were convicted, including Price, while eight men were acquitted. Three others, including Edgar Ray Killen (1925–2018), had hung juries. Nobody served more than six years in prison.

Years later, Killen was convicted of manslaughter in the death of the three civil rights workers in June 2005, more than 40 years after the crime. He died in prison.

Who was Fannie Lou Hamer?

Fannie Lou Hamer (1917–1977) was an African American female voting rights activist during the American Civil Rights Movement. She helped organize the Mississippi-based Freedom Summer project for the Student Nonviolent Coordinating Committee. She attended the 1964 Democratic National Convention as a leader of the Mississippi Freedom Democratic Party, who had broken with the Lyndon Johnson-led Democratic Party because it considered the Democratic Party not protective enough of civil rights. Hamer was known for her plain-spoken language and bluntness about civil rights abuses.

Who was Medgar Evers?

Medgar Evers (1925–1963) was a civil rights leader and field secretary for the National Association for the Advancement of

Civil rights activists Fannie Lou Hamer and Medgar Evers.

Colored People (NAACP) in Mississippi. He became a martyr for the movement after his assassination in June 1963 by a white supremacist named Byron De La Beckwith (1920–2001). A veteran of World War II, Evers helped lead the fight for integration of the University of Mississippi by James Meredith (1933–). He also applied for admission to the University of Mississippi's law school, but his application was denied.

When was De La Beckwith finally convicted of murdering Evers?

Byron De La Beckwith was tried for murder twice in 1964. However, the all-male, all-white juries could not agree on a verdict. He moved to eastern Tennessee in relative obscurity. But 30 years later, De La Beckwith was tried again. In 1994, a jury of eight blacks and four whites found him guilty of first-degree murder, and he was sentenced to life in prison. He died in 2001.

What impact did James Meredith have on the Civil Rights Movement?

James Meredith (1933–) had an indelible impact on the Civil Rights Movement with his personal courage and resolve in the face of grave danger. In 1962, Meredith became the first African American to attend the University of Mississippi (Ole Miss). Riots occurred when Meredith attempted to enroll, but federal troops eventually quelled the disturbances. Meredith attended his first class on October 1, 1962, and graduated in 1963 with a degree in political science. After graduating from Ole Miss, Meredith spent a couple of years in Nigeria and wrote a memoir entitled *Three Years in Mississippi*.

When James Meredith became the first black student at the University of Mississippi in 1962, the result was the Ole Miss Riot that required 31,000 troops to quell.

Meredith returned to center stage in the Civil Rights Movement in June 1966 when he conducted his solo "March Against Fear." He designed the march to increase voting among African Americans after the passage of the Voting Rights Act of 1965. Meredith said that one of his goals was to "challenge that all pervasive fear that dominates the day to day life of the Negro in the United States, especially in the South, and particularly in Mississippi." He also said he wanted to "encourage the 450,000 unregistered Negroes in Mississippi to go to the polls and register." On the second day of his march, a sniper shot and wounded him. Various civil rights organizations continued Meredith's march from Memphis to Jackson. Meredith rejoined the march when it reached Jackson.

Meredith earned a law degree from Columbia University in 1968 and later entered politics. In his later years, Meredith ran for office as a Republican and even worked on the staff of ultra-conservative North Carolina Republican senator Jesse Helms (1921–2008).

Who won a Pulitzer Prize for his photograph of Meredith as he was shot?

Jack Randolph Thornell (1939–) won the 1967 Pulitzer Prize for photography for the photograph he took of James Meredith being shot on Highway 51, screaming in pain. The image earned greater respect for Meredith and his mission, the "March Against Fear."

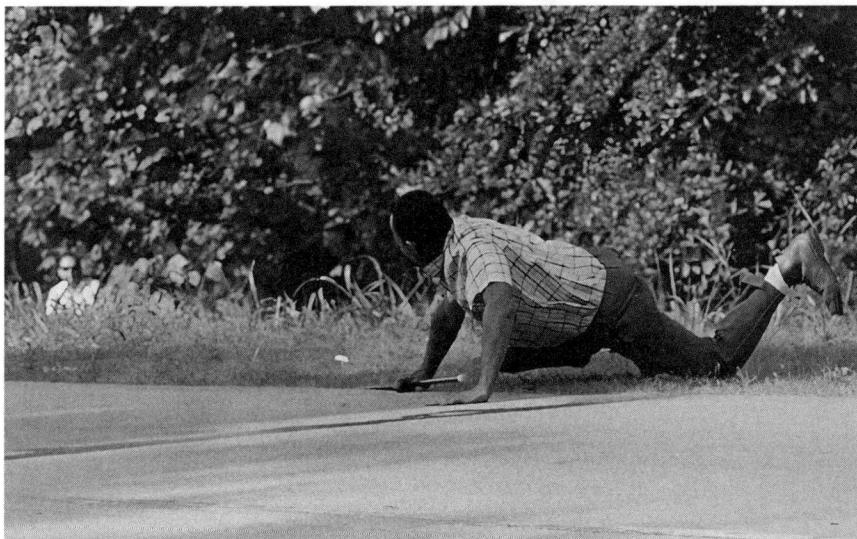

In this Pulitzer-winning photo, photographer Jack Randolph Thornell captured the moment when James Meredith was shot by a white sniper named Aubrey James Norvell.

In his book *Down to the Crossroads: Civil Rights, Black Power, and the Meredith March Against Fear* (2014), Aram Goudsouzian writes of Meredith: "James Meredith may fit no classic definition of a civil rights icon. His mind may be askew. Certainly, his extraordinary trials scarred him—on his scalp and neck, he still has hard, tiny lumps of embedded bird shot. Yet it took Meredith's singular audacity to integrate Ole Miss and start the March Against Fear. He remains his own man, following his own course, walking down a Mississippi road."

What was the White Citizens' Council?

The White Citizens' Council was a group of white citizens adamantly opposed to the desegregation of public schools and for the advancement of civil rights for African Americans. It was formed in either Greenwood or Indianola, Mississippi. Local chapters sprouted up all across the South. The group was not a violent white supremacist group like the Ku Klux Klan but instead preferred to use economic and political retaliation as weapons against civil rights activists.

What was the SNCC?

SNCC was the Student Nonviolent Coordinating Committee, a major player in the American Civil Rights Movement. Founded in 1960 at Shaw University, it played a significant role in the sit-ins, freedom rights, and other forms of nonviolent, direct action during the movement. The SNCC also played a major role in organizing and getting greater participation for the March on Washington.

What were sit-ins?

Sit-ins were a form of nonviolent, direct action in which a protestor occupies a particular place by sitting down and expressing their opposition to a policy or course of action. The most famous types of sit-ins occurred during the Civil Rights Movement in the 1950s and 1960s when young students and other activists challenged segregation policies. For example, many activists conducted sit-ins at lunch counters, restaurants, libraries, and other public facilities.

These forms of mass disobedience often led to violent responses from those who supported segregation. They were a very effective tool in showing the righteousness and dedication of the civil rights activists and the negativity of those opposed to such action.

What were some of the earliest sit-ins during the Civil Rights Movement?

There were some sit-in protests conducted during the late 1930s and the 1940s. But the first sit-ins as part of the Civil Rights Movement of the 1950s and 1960s occurred in Durham, North Carolina (1957); Oklahoma City, Oklahoma (1958); Greensboro, North Carolina (1960); and Nashville, Tennessee (1960).

What was the most famous sit-in of the Civil Rights Movement?

The sit-ins that had the widest impact were the sit-ins conducted in Greensboro, North Carolina. These actions attracted national and even international attention and dramatized the evils of segregation in stark terms for much of the rest of the country. In February 1960, four students at North Carolina A & T conducted a sit-in at the lunch counter of the Woolworth's store in Greensboro. The four students were Joseph McNeil (1942–), Franklin McCain (1941–2014), Ezell Blair Jr. (1941–), and David Richmond (1941–1990). The four were members of the NAACP's Youth Council.

Another influential set of sit-ins occurred in Nashville, Tennessee, between February and May 1960. These sit-ins took place in many downtown businesses, including Woolworth's and Walgreens. Some angry whites engaged in violence against the

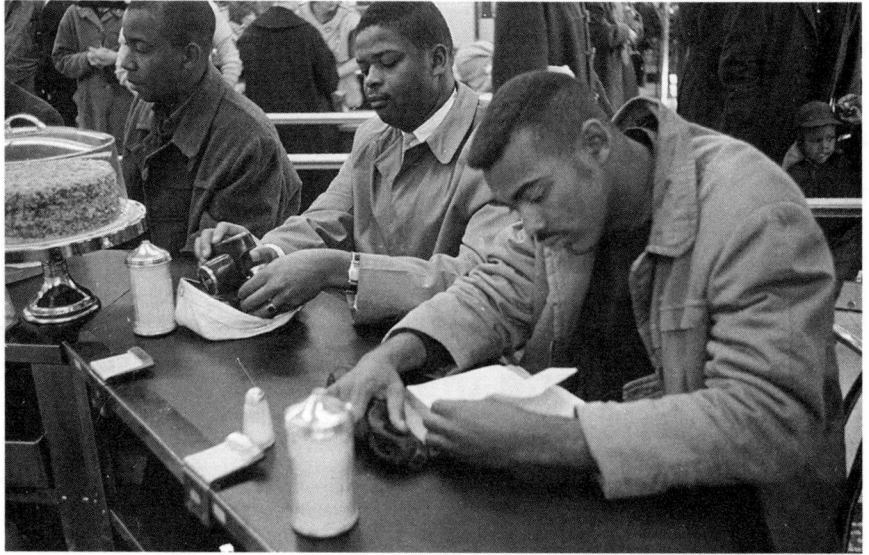

Possibly the most famous sit-in in history came in 1960, when four black students sat at a lunch counter at the segregated Woolworth's department store in Greensboro, North Carolina.

sit-in protestors, who were nearly all black college students. The Nashville sit-ins led to the desegregation of several downtown stores in May 1960.

Who is James Lawson?

James Lawson (1928–) is an American civil rights activist who was the leader of the Nashville sit-in movement. Lawson moved to Nashville to attend Vanderbilt Divinity School and participate in civil rights activism. He conducted nonviolence seminars for the Southern Christian Leadership Conference and served as a leader of CORE all across the South. In Nashville, he trained many of the future leaders of the Civil Rights Movement, including John Lewis (1940–2020) and Diane Nash (1938–). Nashville had the most sustained and successful sit-in movement. Vanderbilt University leaders expelled Lawson from Vanderbilt because of his involvement in the civil rights causes. The university formally apologized to Lawson in 2006.

Who were the Freedom Riders?

The Freedom Riders were a group of civil rights activists who rode interstate buses into states that practiced segregation. The activists were visibly challenging the policies of segregation on buses. They sought to draw larger public attention to the civil rights cause. The riders would have a black and a white sit-in together. They also would have several black riders ride in the first few rows of the bus. Both of these practices violated custom and tradition in some Southern states. The first Freedom Ride began in May 1961 from Washington, D.C.

Some of the Freedom Riders endured frightful beatings, particularly in Alabama. Ku Klux Klan members attacked Freedom Riders in Anniston, Birmingham, and later Montgomery.

What member of the U.S. attorney general's team was beaten protecting Freedom Riders?

John Seigenthaler Sr. (1927–2014) was a special assistant to U.S. attorney general Robert Kennedy (1925–1968), who was sent to Alabama to negotiate on behalf of the administration with Alabama governor John Patterson (1921–2021). Seigenthaler was beaten over the head with a lead pipe while trying to assist Freedom Rider Susan Wilbur from an angry white mob. Seigenthaler recovered and continued an outstanding career in journalism as the publisher of *The Tennessean* in Nashville, Tennessee. *The Tennessean* gave favorable coverage to the Civil Rights Movement. He later founded the First Amendment Center, a nonprofit organization dedicated to providing greater public awareness and appreciation of First Amendment values in society.

What was the March on Washington?

The March on Washington was a famous civil rights gathering and political rally of more than 250,000 people conducted in Washington, D.C., on August 28, 1963. The purpose of the march was to galvanize public support for the Civil Rights Movement and to bring greater public awareness to the cause of civil rights. The march is considered perhaps the most influential single event during the movement. Many consider it an important catalyst in the eventual passage of federal legislation designed to bring equal justice in the country.

Numerous civil rights leaders gave speeches, including NAACP president Roy Wilkins (1901–1981), Whitney Young Jr. (1921–1971) of the Urban League, John Lewis (1940–2020), A. Philip Randolph (1889–1979), and others. The highlight of the March was an inspiring speech by Dr. Martin Luther King Jr. (1929–1968) entitled "I Have a Dream." The speech is considered one of the greatest in history. King delivered in his majestic voice and captivated millions. The repetitive refrain of "I Have a Dream" remains embedded in the collective conscience of the nation. For example, King said: "I have a dream that my four little

The 1963 March on Washington boasted over a quarter of a million participants and featured Rev. Dr. Martin Luther King Jr.'s famous "I Have a Dream" speech.

children will one day live in a nation where they will not be judged by the color of their skin but by the content of their character."

Who was A. Philip Randolph?

Asa (A.) Philip Randolph (1889–1979) was a famous civil rights leader who led the first black labor union and planned the influential March on Washington that took place in August 1963. He organized the Brotherhood of Sleeping Car Porters, the first labor union composed predominately of blacks. Randolph was instrumental in convincing Presidents Franklin D. Roosevelt (1882–1945) and Harry Truman (1884–1972) to issue executive orders banning discrimination in the defense industries and the desegregation of the armed forces. In 1941, Randolph said that "a wave of bitter resentment, disillusionment and desperation was sweeping over the Negro masses."

Who was James Farmer?

James L. Farmer Jr. (1920–1999) was an African American civil rights leader best known as the leader of the Congress on Racial Equality (CORE). Farmer organized the 1961 Freedom Rides and participated in other civil rights activities during the Civil Rights Movement. He was considered one of the "Big Four" in the civil rights struggle along with Dr. Martin Luther King Jr., Whitney Young, and Roy Wilkins. President Bill Clinton (1946–) awarded Farmer a Presidential Medal of Freedom in 1998.

Who was Z. Alexander Looby?

Zephaniah Alexander Looby (1899–1972) was an African American attorney best known for defending civil rights activists in Nashville, Tennessee, on trumped-up charges of disorderly conduct for their roles in sit-ins and other forms of nonviolent direct action. Someone bombed his house shortly after he represented the Nashville students who participated in the sit-ins. In the 1940s, he defended several African Americans who were charged with crimes after race riots in Columbia, Tennessee. He filed the first lawsuit asking for the desegregation of public schools in Nashville, Tennessee.

What was the most famous speech given during the March on Washington?

The most famous speech delivered at the March on Washington was the "I Have a Dream" speech delivered by Dr. Martin Luther King Jr. It is considered one of the greatest speeches in world history. King famously aspired that his children be judged "not be the color of their skin, but by the content of their character." His refrains of "I Have a Dream" and "Let Freedom Ring" reverberated through much of the nation's collective conscience. Historian William Bennett in *America: The Last Best Hope* (vol. II) wrote of King's speech: "But Dr. King's speech changed things. It changes things still."

What did President John F. Kennedy do in the area of civil rights?

John F. Kennedy (1917–1963) called for Congress to pass major civil rights legislation. Tragically, he died before seeing that objective accomplished. Under President Lyndon B. Johnson (1908–1973), Congress passed the historic Civil Rights Act of 1964, which prohibited racial discrimination in public employment, public accommodations, and other aspects of society.

Kennedy sent in federal troops to protect civil rights protestors, including the Freedom Riders in the South. He established the President's Committee on Equal Employment Opportunity and issued an executive order that prohibited government contractors from discriminating on the basis of "race, creed, color, or national origin." He also used the public platform of the presidency to condemn segregation and racial discrimination.

What were the Watts riots?

The Watts riots occurred August 11–16, 1965, in the Watts section of Los Angeles. The six-day tragedy resulted in 34 deaths and more than 1,000 people injured. The uprising began after a young black man named Marquette Frye (1944–1986) was arrested by a white police officer. Allegedly, several officers used excessive force in arresting Frye. They also later arrested his mother and brother. Many individuals in the community protested what they perceived to be unfair treatment at the hands of law enforcement. This incident incited more large-scale protests that degenerated into the burning of businesses and looting. A 1965 report, "Violence in the City: An End or Beginning," identified poverty, lack of educational opportunities, and a precipitous relationship between blacks and the Los Angeles police department as part of the problem. The report recommended the creation of a City Human Rights Commission and called on society to help provide greater opportunities for blacks.

Unfortunately, other riots occurred in black neighborhoods in other cities in the summer of 1967, including Newark, Detroit, and Cleveland. Many of these riots were troubling and resulted in multiple deaths. For example, the Detroit riots led to more than 40 deaths. The U.S. Riot Commission Report, chaired by Illinois governor Otto Kerner (1908–1976), later found in 1968 that "almost invariably the incident that ignites disorder arises from police action." The commission warned that "[o]ur nation is moving toward two societies, one black, one white—separate and unequal."

The commission recommended that the government take an active role in trying to break up patterns of residential segregation.

How did Dr. King die?

Dr. King was assassinated while standing outside the second-floor balcony of the Lorraine Motel in Memphis, Tennessee, on April 4, 1968. The day before, Dr. King gave his last speech, entitled "I've Been to the Mountaintop." Almost prophetically, King declared in the speech that he was not afraid to die:

> Like anybody, I would like to live—a long life; longevity has its place. But I'm not concerned about that now. I just want to do God's will. And He's allowed me to go up to the mountain. And I've looked over. And I've seen the Promised Land. I may not get there with you. But I want you to know tonight, that we, as a people, will get to the Promised Land. So I'm happy, tonight. I'm not worried about anything. I'm not fearing any man. *Mine eyes have seen the glory of the coming of the Lord.*

Dr. King was shot while standing on the second-floor walkway outside his room at the Lorraine Motel in Memphis, Tennessee. In 1991, the hotel became the National Civil Rights Museum.

James Earl Ray (1928–1998), a career criminal, was arrested and charged with assassinating Dr. King. Ray confessed and pled guilty to avoid the death penalty. However, he later recanted his confession and for the rest of his life maintained his innocence. Some believe he may not have been involved in the killing of Dr. King or that at least there were many others involved in the assassination of the leading civil rights leader.

What was Black Power?

The Black Power Movement was a political movement that focused on black pride and a more aggressive stance toward a racist white establishment. The movement is generally traced to 1966, when some leaders of the Student Nonviolent Coordinating Committee (SNCC), tired of the violent response with which peaceful protesters were often met, urged activists to adopt a more decisive and aggressive stance and began promoting the slogan "Black Power." A key leader of this movement was Stokely

Members of the Black Panthers are shown here demonstrating in 1967. Their approach to black pride was militaristic, threatening, and doomed to failure.

Carmichael (1941–1998), who began using the slogan "Black Power" in speeches. For example, he said: "It is a call for black people in this country to unite, to recognize their heritage, to build a sense of community. It is a call for black people to define their own goals, to lead their own organizations."

What was the Black Panther Party?

The Black Panther Party was a political organization known for its advocacy of radical socialism and black nationalistic pride. The Panthers rejected the nonviolent teachings of Dr. Martin Luther King Jr. and adopted a more confrontational stance toward white America. They particularly preached against police brutality and urged confrontation at times with white police officers. The leaders of the Black Panther Party included Huey Newton (1942–1989) and Bobby Seale (1936–). Newton and Seale cofounded the party in 1966, calling it the Black Panther Party for Self-Defense.

What were some of the great pieces of federal legislation that arose because of the Civil Rights Movement?

Some of the most important federal laws enacted as a result of the Civil Rights Movement included the Civil Rights Act of 1964, the Voting Rights Act of 1965, and the Fair Housing Act of 1968. The Civil Rights Act of 1964 remains the most important federal law prohibiting discrimination in employment, education, and public accommodation. It prohibits discrimination in employment based on race, color, religion, sex, or national origin. This law remains the premier federal antidiscrimination law. The Voting Rights Act of 1965 prohibited the use of discriminatory means, such as the use of literary tests, to prohibit people from voting. Some states had used literary tests and other similar devices to try to prohibit, or at least limit, voting by African Americans. The Fair Housing Act of 1968 prohibits refusing to rent or sell property to someone based on their race, ethnicity, gender, marital status, or physical disability.

Who were the Chicago Eight?

The Chicago Eight were a group of defendants charged with inciting rioting at the 1968 Democratic National Convention in Chicago, Illinois. The defendants were Abbie Hoffman (1936–1989), Jerry Rubin (1938–1994), David Dellinger (1915–2004), Tom Hayden (1939–2016), Rennie Davis (1940–2021), John Froines (1939–2022), Lee Weiner (1939–), and Bobby Seale (1936–). The eight were prosecuted in the federal courtroom on charges of conspiracy and inciting a riot. The presiding judge was federal district court judge Julius Hoffman (1895–1983), who showed evident bias against the defendants. He ordered Seale bound and gagged in the courtroom for his repeated outbursts and eventually had his case severed from the other seven defendants. For this reason, the seven are often known as the Chicago Seven.

A jury acquitted the defendants of conspiracy charges but found five of the defendants (all except Froines and Weiner) guilty of inciting a riot. They were sentenced to five years in prison. However, a federal appeals court reversed the convictions, in part because of the evident bias of Judge Hoffman. The U.S. Department of Justice opted not to seek a second trial against the defendants.

SUPREME COURT AND THE LAW

What happened in *Brown v. Board of Education*?

In *Brown v. Board of Education* (1954), the U.S. Supreme Court unanimously ruled 9–0 that segregated public schools are "inherently unequal" and violated the Equal Protection Clause of the Fourteenth Amendment. The case before the U.S. Supreme Court was a consolidation of cases from four different states—Kansas, South Carolina, Virginia, and Delaware. The case listed first was the case from Kansas, *Brown v. Board of Education.*

Oliver Brown (1918–1961)—an African American man from Topeka, Kansas—filed suit because his daughter, Linda Brown (1943–2018), had to walk a mile to go to an all-black school instead of a mere seven blocks to attend an all-white school. Linda was in the third grade at the time of the lawsuit's events. The other cases were *Briggs v. Elliott* in South Carolina, *Davis v. County School Board of Prince Edward County* in Virginia, and *Gebhart v. Belton* in Delaware. The challenging plaintiffs lost in the lower federal courts in Kansas, South Carolina, and Virginia. The plaintiffs actually prevailed in a Delaware state trial court. All four cases were combined before the U.S. Supreme Court and became collectively known as *Brown v. Board of Education.*

The Court overruled its 1896 decision in *Plessy v. Ferguson,* which had upheld a Louisiana law mandating for separate races on railroads. The justification in *Plessy* was the "separate but equal" doctrine, which provided states could require separate facilities for separate races as long as the facilities were roughly equivalent. This was a fiction, however, as states usually provided inferior facilities to African Americans.

Chief Justice Earl Warren (1891–1974) wrote the opinion for a unanimous Court. He attacked the separate but equal doctrine, saying that it had no place in public education. He explained that separating the races generated feelings of inferiority on the part of young black children: "To separate them from others of similar age and qualifications solely because of their race generates a feeling of inferiority as to their status in the community that may affect their hearts and minds in a way unlikely ever to be undone."

"We conclude that in the field of public education the doctrine of 'separate but equal' has no place," Warren wrote. "Separate educational facilities are inherently unequal." The *Brown* decision is considered perhaps the most important of all decisions in American constitutional law history.

Why did the Court place the *Brown* case before the cases from the other states?

Juan Williams explains in his book *Eyes on the Prize* that "it was no accident that *Brown* was chosen to head the list." He quotes Justice Tom C. Clark (1899–1977), who explained that the Court wanted the nation to view the case as more than a Southern problem. Since Kansas was a Midwestern state, *Brown* made for an attractive choice.

Why did *Brown* not lead to an immediate integration of the schools?

The Court's decision in 1954 in *Brown v. Board of Education* did not lead to immediate integration of the schools in part because of a subsequent decision by the Court in 1956—often called *Brown II*. The Court knew there was massive public opposition to segregation, particularly in the South. The Court in *Brown II* indicated that public schools should be integrated "with all deliberate speed." Many school districts and state leaders focused more on the adjective "deliberate" than the noun "speed." For this reason, many school districts in the South were not integrated until the 1970s.

DID YOU KNOW!?

What decisions involving the freedom of association also arose out of the Civil Rights Movement?

In two decisions, the U.S. Supreme Court protected the right of the National Association for the Advancement of Colored People (NAACP) to freely associate without governmental interference. In *NAACP v. Alabama* (1958), the Court ruled that the state of Alabama could not compel the NAACP to release its membership list. The Court wrote that "privacy in group association may in many circumstances be indispensable to preservation of freedom of association, particularly where a group espouses dissident beliefs."

In *NAACP v. Button* (1963), the Court struck down a Virginia law that prohibited organizations from seeking out people to file lawsuits. The state had attempted to use the law to prohibit the NAACP from finding persons to be plaintiffs in racial discrimination suits. The Court wrote that the NAACP's litigation tactics were "modes of expression and association protected by the First Amendment." The *Button* case ensured the survival of public interest law firms, which often seek clients to advance certain causes through litigation.

In what famous decision did the Court protect press freedoms in the Civil Rights Movement?

The Supreme Court ruled in *New York Times Co. v. Sullivan* (1964) that L. B. Sullivan (1921–1977), a commissioner with authority over the police department in Montgomery, Alabama, must prove that the *New York Times* acted with "actual malice" before he could recover damages in his defamation action against the newspaper. The decision increased press freedoms and determined that libel laws must meet a certain constitutional baseline to comport with the First Amendment.

The case involved a March 1960 editorial advertisement published in the *New York Times* entitled "Heed Their Rising Voices." The ad referred to violations of civil rights in the South. The ad contained some factual inaccuracies. For example, the ad said that police in Montgomery had padlocked a dining hall at Alabama State College, which was not true. The ad also said that Dr. Martin Luther King Jr. had been arrested seven times when he had been arrested only four times.

Sullivan had sued the *Times* for defamation. An all-white jury in Alabama state court had awarded him $500,000 in damages. On appeal, the newspaper contended that the verdict and Alabama libel law chilled free speech on important public issues.

The Court agreed with the newspaper, noting that a central purpose of the First Amendment was to give citizens the right to freely criticize government officials. The Court considered the case "against the background of a profound national commitment that debate on public issues should be uninhibited, robust, and wide-open and that it may well include vehement, caustic and sometimes unpleasantly sharp attacks on government and public officials." The Court also reasoned that sometimes the press would veer away from reporting on important matters if it could be punished for every mistake: "That erroneous statement is inevitable in free debate, and that it must be protected if the freedoms of expression are to have the breathing space that they need to survive."

The decision was incredibly important to the Civil Rights Movement because the Court's decision allowed the press to report on civil rights abuses without fear of being sued for every error. In his concurring opinion, Justice Hugo Black (1886–1971) noted that there were 11 libel suits against the *New York Times* and five libel suits against CBS for reporting on similar civil rights abuses. Black wrote: "Moreover, this technique for harassing and punishing a free press—now that it has been shown to be possible—is by no means limited to cases with racial overtones; it can be used in other fields where public feelings may make local as well as out-of-state newspapers easy prey for libel verdict seekers."

In his book *Make No Law: The Sullivan Case and the First Amendment* (1991), Anthony Lewis wrote: "By the time the Supreme Court decided the *Sullivan* case, Southern officials had brought nearly $300 million in libel actions against the press."

What civil rights activist successfully challenged a state legislature that sought to expel him for his critical speech?

Julian Bond (1940–2015), a longtime official with the National Association for the Advancement of Colored People (NAACP), successfully challenged the Georgia state legislature, which sought to exclude him from the state congress because of his critical comments of U.S. involvement in Vietnam. In June

Julian Bond was an accomplished activist. He helped found the Student Nonviolent Coordinating Committee and cofounded the Southern Poverty Law Center in Montgomery, Alabama. Later, he was a Georgia state representative and senator, history professor at the University of Virginia, and, from 1998 to 2010, chair of the NAACP.

1965, Bond was elected to the Georgia House of Representatives. However, Bond's congressional colleagues voted 184–12 to exclude him taking his seat. They opposed Bond because of statements such as: "I think it is sort of hypocritical for us to maintain that we are fighting for liberty in other places and we are not guaranteeing liberty to citizens inside the continental United States."

Bond's case reached the U.S. Supreme Court, which ruled in his favor. "The manifest function of the First Amendment in a representative government requires that legislators be given the widest latitude to express their views on issue of policy," Chief Justice Earl Warren (1891–1974) wrote in *Bond v. Floyd* (1966). "Just as erroneous statements must be protected to give freedom of expression the breathing space it needs to survive, so statements criticizing public policy and the implementation of it must be similarly protected."

What Supreme Court decisions involved freedom of assembly or petition during the Civil Rights Movement?

The Supreme Court decided many cases that protected the First Amendment rights of those participating in the Civil Rights Movement. The First Amendment provided the constitutional tool by which aggrieved individuals were able to assemble together to protest injustices and petition the government to change such unjust laws. These decisions included:

- *Garner v. Louisiana* (1961): The U.S. Supreme Court reversed the breach-of-the-peace convictions of several African American students who had engaged in "sit-ins" at restaurants that would serve only white customers.

- *Edwards v. South Carolina* (1963): The U.S. Supreme Court reversed the breach-of-the-peace convictions of 187 African American students who marched on the South Carolina statehouse in Columbia to protest segregation. The students were arrested even though they only sang religious and patriotic songs. The Court wrote that "the Fourteenth Amendment does not permit a state to make criminal the peaceful expression of unpopular views."

- *Shuttlesworth v. City of Birmingham* (1965): The U.S. Supreme Court reversed the conviction of civil rights activist Fred Shuttlesworth (1922–2011), who did nothing more than stand on a public sidewalk with several other individuals outside a department store in Birmingham.

- *Cox v. Louisiana* (1965): The U.S. Supreme Court reversed the conviction of a civil rights protester who was punished for leading a group of 2,000 persons who picketed across the street from a courthouse to protest the illegal arrest of 23 students.

- *Adderley v. Florida* (1966): The U.S. Supreme Court upheld the trespass convictions of 32 college students who demonstrated outside a county jail to protest the arrest of some of their classmates.

- *Shuttlesworth v. City of Birmingham* (1969): The U.S. Supreme Court reversed another conviction of Shuttlesworth for the violation of a Birmingham law that made it a crime to participate in a parade or march on city streets without first obtaining a permit.

- *Gregory v. City of Chicago* (1969): The U.S. Supreme Court reversed the disorderly conduct conviction of activist/comedian Dick Gregory (1932–2017), who led a procession down city streets while advocating for school desegregation.

Citizens' Rights and Responsibilities

What types of rights do citizens possess?

Citizens possess a variety of rights, some of which noncitizens do not possess, at least to the same degree. These rights include personal rights, political rights, and economic rights. Personal rights include the right to travel, the right to privacy, the right to live where one chooses, the right to freedom of expression, the right to freedom of religion, and the right to associate with whomever we want.

Political rights include the right to due process of law and fair procedures; the right to equal protection of the law; the right to examine the conduct of public officials; the right to express ourselves for political purposes; the freedom to serve on a jury; the freedom to run for public office; the freedom to vote in full, fair, and free elections; and the right to political association.

Economic rights include the freedom to buy and sell property, to choose one's work or vocation, to enter into contracts, to establish and operate a business, and to join professional associations or labor unions.

Noncitizens enjoy many of these same rights, but some of these rights are restricted to citizens.

What does it mean to be a good citizen?

To be a good citizen means that a person respects the rights of other persons and does not infringe on those rights. It also means that a person adheres to the laws and regulations of the federal government, the state government, and local law. It also means being tolerant and empathetic to other persons and not discriminating on the basis of race, religion, sex, creed, national origin, disability, or any other reason.

A good citizen also stays informed on the pressing issues of the day, staying up to date on the important issues to one's community, state, country, and the world. Furthermore, a good citizen is active in the community, providing a good example for younger persons and children. A good citizen takes responsibilities for one's actions and owns up to making mistakes.

What is civic virtue?

Civic virtue means that a citizen respects the rights of others and embraces the obligation of being a good citizen, often placing the common welfare over individual interests. Civic virtue means that the good citizen acts in the common good over selfish desires. Civic virtue also means that the citizen votes, stays informed of pressing political and social issues, and acts in a way that does not discriminate against others.

What Founding Fathers–era concept is related to good civic virtue?

The Founding Fathers spoke of the concept of the common good, which means that a citizen acts more in the interests of the community, the state, and other people in general rather than selfishly pursue only personal interests and goals. The idea is that each citizen sacrifices something in order to contribute to the common good—the collective, positive advancement of society.

What have some of our most famous presidents said about good citizenship?

Thomas Jefferson (1743–1826), the nation's third president, once said: "A nation, as a society, forms a moral person, and every member of it is personally responsible for his society."

Andrew Jackson (1767–1845), the nation's seventh president, once said: "Every good citizen makes his country's honor his own, and cherishes it not only as precious but as sacred. He is willing to risk his life in its defense and its conscious that he gains protection while he gives it."

Abraham Lincoln (1809–1865), the nation's sixteenth president, who led the country through the bloody U.S. Civil War, famously said: "Let us at all times remember that all American citizens are brothers of a common country, and should dwell together in bonds of fraternal feeling."

President John F. Kennedy famously implored citizens to "ask not what your country can do for you but what you can do for your country."

President Theodore Roosevelt (1858–1919) said of this good citizenship: "The first requisite of a good citizen in this republic of ours is that he shall be able and willing to pull his own weight."

And perhaps, most famously, President John F. Kennedy (1917–1963), said in his inaugural address in 1961: "My fellow Americans, ask not what your country can do for you, but what you can do for your country."

What part of the Constitution limits how a state discriminates against citizens of other states?

The Constitution generally prohibits many forms of discrimination by a state against citizens of other states through what is called the privileges and immunities clause of Article IV of the Constitution. The Constitution also limits the ways in which states can discriminate against out-of-staters by recognizing a constitutional right to travel and the free flow of interstate commerce.

However, a state can impose or give benefits to its own citizens. If a person moves to a new state, that person must after a short period of time be allowed to have the same rights as others who live in that state.

What are some leading civic responsibilities?

Some leading civic responsibilities include staying informed on public issues that impact your community; voting in local, state, and federal elections; obeying the laws of the land; participating in a civic group or groups; paying one's taxes; respecting the rights of others; serving on a jury trial if called to serve; and perhaps to serve in the armed forces.

What are other responsibilities that citizens have?

Citizens often have a host of personal responsibilities, too. These include supporting one's family, paying child support if under a court order, taking care of oneself, considering the rights of other people, behaving in a lawful and civil manner, and accepting the consequences of one's actions.

Citizens also have the responsibility to defend the United States from all enemies, both foreign and domestic. This doesn't mean that citizens must join the military; there are other nonmilitary ways that a citizen can support the United States in a time of need or crisis.

As a citizen, do I have freedom of religion in the United States?

Absolutely. Citizens and noncitizens alike possess the freedom of religion under the First Amendment of the U.S. Constitution. The government cannot force citizens to decide what religion to believe in or whether to believe in any religion at all. In fact, the First Amendment's religious liberty clauses protect both the religiously devout and the fiercely atheistic alike. In fact, one reason why many people seek asylum or refuge in the United States is this strong protection of religious freedom.

Does the United States protect freedom of nonreligion as well as freedom of religion?

Yes, the Free Exercise Clause of the First Amendment protects the fiercely atheistic as well as the religiously devout. In fact, the Free Exercise Clause protects all types of religious and nonreligious beliefs. In other words, a person is entitled to absolute

The Constitution protects Americans' right to practice any religion, and it also protects your right to *not* have a religion or be pressured to have a religion. This is one reason the separation of church and state is important.

protection of freedom of belief under the Free Exercise Clause of the First Amendment. However, individuals do not have absolute protection for religiously inspired conduct that might violate a generally applicable health, safety, or welfare law.

What are the two different religious liberty clauses in the First Amendment?

The two religious liberty clauses in the First Amendment are the Establishment Clause and the Free Exercise Clause. The first clause is the Establishment Clause. The second is the Free Exercise Clause. Together, these clauses require that the government act in a neutral manner when it comes to religion.

The Establishment Clause provides that church and state remain separate to a certain degree. The Free Exercise Clause protects a person's right to practice religion freely or to practice no religion at all. There is absolute protection for freedom of belief under the Free Exercise Clause. A person can believe in God, Buddha, Allah, or the Flying Spaghetti Monster.

What about the military?

The United States does not currently have a military draft. However, if you are male and between the ages of 18 and 25, then you must register with the Selective Service. This applies to male citizens and male immigrants. This act of registering with the Selective Service tells the U.S. Armed Forces that you technically are available to serve in the military if needed. You can register at a U.S. post office, or you can register at the Selective Service's website at http://www.sss.gov.

SERVING ON A JURY

What legal duties generally may only citizens perform?

Only U.S. citizens can serve on federal juries. Furthermore, in the vast majority of states, only U.S. citizens can serve on juries as well. Serving on a jury duty is perhaps the most important civic duty that a person can perform. Serving on a jury gives an individual the opportunity to see how justice is dispensed up close and personal. Juries are the triers of facts and ultimately decide the cases over which they preside. For example, a jury in a criminal case ultimately decides whether a criminal defendant is guilty or not guilty of the charged offenses. A jury in a personal injury suit decides whether the defendant is liable to the plaintiff and usually decides the amount of damages, if any, that a plaintiff is entitled to receive as compensation for the injuries they suffered.

What are the general requirements to serve on a jury?

The general requirements to serve on a jury are that you are a U.S. citizen; you are 18 years of age or older; you have the ability to read, speak, and understand the English language; and you are a resident of the county to which you have been summoned to serve as a prospective juror. Another requirement in some states is that you not have a pending lawsuit in the county for which you have been called to serve.

DID YOU KNOW!?

What individuals are exempt from jury duty?

Most states provide that the governor of their state is exempt from jury duty. Also, active members of the armed forces are exempt from jury duty. In some states, those who are 80 years of age or older are excused from jury duty.

Can a person be excused from jury duty for hardships?

Yes, in many instances, a judge will allow a person to be excused from jury duty if they have a valid hardship reason. Such reasons may include that the person is a caregiver to family members, has serious health concerns, or has a vacation during that period that already has been paid for.

What is the foreperson of the jury?

The foreperson of the jury is considered the leader or spokesperson for the jury. This person, elected by the members of the jury before deliberations, is the person who often reads the jury's verdict in front of the judge and the courtroom audience.

What is voir dire?

Voir dire refers to the process of selecting a jury. Generally, when a person is called for jury duty, they report to a room full of other called individuals. Then, a group of about 30 or 40 individuals are called together and head to a courtroom that has a pending trial. It is here that the individual courtrooms seat the jury, or what is called the petit, or trial, jury.

Most juries consist of 12 persons. During voir dire, attorneys from each side ask a series of questions designed to see if certain individuals would make jurors suitable for their side.

Each side asks questions and then can remove a certain number of individuals from the jury through what are called peremptory challenges. A peremptory challenge is the removal of a juror for any reason. The attorney has a belief or a hunch that that individual would not make a good juror for their side.

Peremptory challenges are to be distinguished from so-called for-cause challenges. A for-cause challenge means that a juror is too biased or partial to be able to serve on a jury. For example, let's say that there is a criminal trial and a prospective juror admits during voir dire that they do not trust the testimony of police officers, that they think many police officers do not tell the truth. That person could be subject to a for-cause challenge.

Each side has an unlimited number of for-cause challenges but only a set number of peremptory challenges. For-cause challenges are relatively rare, as most of the time, prospective jurors do not evince obvious bias. But every side will use their peremptory challenges to ensure that they have the best jury possible.

Are there any limits on peremptory challenges?

Yes, the U.S. Supreme Court has ruled that attorneys may not engage in the racially discriminatory exercise of peremptory challenges. The Court explained this in *Batson v. Kentucky* (1986), writing that such racial discrimination in the exercise of peremptory challenges violates the Equal Protection Clause of the Fourteenth Amendment. "The harm from discriminatory jury selection extends beyond that inflicted on the defendant and the excluded juror to touch the entire community," wrote Justice Lewis Powell Jr. (1907–1998) in his majority opinion. "Selection procedures that purposefully exclude black persons from juries undermine public confidence in the fairness of our system of justice."

The Court in *Batson* ruled that prosecutors violated the Equal Protection Clause when they removed several African Americans from the jury pool during the criminal trial of James Batson, an African American criminal defendant. The Court later extended this principle in civil cases, to cases in which the jurors and the defendant were of different races, and to when a criminal defense attorney also exercised the use of peremptory challenges in a racially discriminatory way. Finally, the Court also ruled that it violated the Equal Protection Clause to remove potential jurors based on their gender.

Are the only limitations on peremptory challenges those that constitute a form of race discrimination?

No, lawyers also may not exercise peremptory challenges in a way that discriminates on the basis of gender. "Certainly, with respect to jury service, African-Americans and women share a history of total exclusion, a history which came to an end for women many years after the embarrassing chapter in our history came to an end for African-Americans," Justice Harry Blackmun (1908–1999) wrote in *J. E. B. v. Alabama ex. rel. T. B.* (1994).

The U.S. Supreme Court has not explicitly ruled on whether it violates the Equal Protection Clause for lawyers to exercise peremptory challenges in a way that violates freedom of religion. However, several lower courts have extended the rationale of *Batson* to religion as well as race and gender.

Blackmun further explained:

> Discrimination in jury selection, whether based on race or on gender, causes harm to the litigants, the community, and the individual jurors who are wrongfully excluded from participation in the judicial process. The litigants are harmed by the risk that the prejudice that motivated the discriminatory selection of the jury will infect the entire proceedings.... The community is harmed by the State's participation in the perpetuation of invidious group stereotypes and the inevitable loss of confidence in our judicial system that state-sanctioned discrimination in the courtroom engenders.

> When state actors exercise peremptory challenges in reliance on gender stereotypes, they ratify and reinforce prejudicial views of the relative abilities of men and women. Because these stereotypes have wreaked injustice in so many other spheres of our country's public life, active discrimination by litigants on the basis of gender during jury selection "invites cynicism respecting the jury's neutrality and its obligation to adhere to the law."

VOTING

Is voting often restricted to U.S. citizens?

Yes, voting is often restricted to U.S. citizens. You must be a U.S. citizen to vote in federal elections, and many states also limit voting to U.S. citizens. Thus, one of the key benefits or rights one has upon obtaining citizenship is gaining the right to vote.

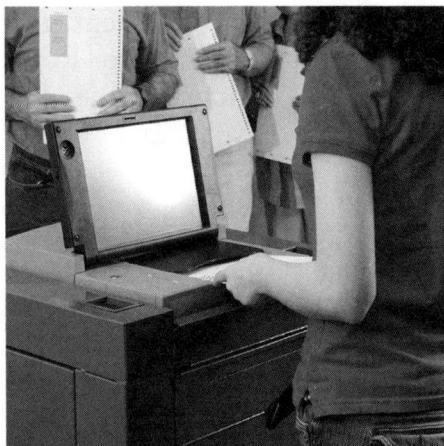

Voting in federal elections is reserved for U.S. citizens only, but some states allow noncitizens to vote in some local elections.

What constitutional amendments deal with voting?

Four constitutional amendments deal with voting—the Fifteenth, Nineteenth, Twenty-fourth and Twenty-sixth Amendments.

The Fifteenth Amendment (effective 1870), one of the three amendments passed during the Reconstruction period, prohibits the denial of the right to vote based on race. The Fifteenth Amendment provides: "The right of citizens of the United States to vote shall not be denied or abridged by the United States or by any State on account of race, color, or previous condition of servitude."

The Nineteenth Amendment (1920) provides that women have the right to vote. It reads: "The right of citizens of the United States to vote shall not be denied or abridged by the United States or by any State on account of sex."

The Twenty-fourth Amendment (1964) prohibits poll taxes, which is a tax applied to someone before they can vote—in other words, charging someone to vote. It reads: "The right of citizens of the United States to vote in any primary or other election for

President or Vice President, for electors for President or Vice President, or for Senator or Representative in Congress, shall not be denied or abridged by the United States or any State by reason of failure to pay poll tax or other tax."

Finally, the Twenty-sixth Amendment (1971) lowered the voting age to 18. Previously, some states had limited voting to those who were 21 years of age. It reads: "The right of citizens of the United States, who are eighteen years of age or older, to vote shall not be denied or abridged by the United States or by any State on account of age."

If the Fifteenth Amendment existed, how did states still engage in racial discrimination in voting?

Unfortunately, the Fifteenth Amendment was circumvented for nearly 100 years. States came up with all sorts of different

Even though the Fifteenth Amendment went into effect in 1870, white opposition to black voters continued, as this 1876 political cartoon graphically illustrates.

tests to deny the franchise to African Americans, including literacy tests, poll taxes, and bizarre qualification tests. In some jurisdictions, prospective white voters would have to pass the easiest test imaginable, but prospective black voters would be asked a bevy of the most arcane and difficult questions about the Constitution.

What famous law finally provided even more protection to individuals to vote free from racial discrimination?

The Voting Rights Act of 1965 was a landmark piece of civil rights legislation that sought to do what the Fifteenth Amendment should have made clear—that states may not engage in racially discriminatory practices regarding voting. The law prohibited poll taxes, literacy tests, and other harassing methods used by state officials to limit the political power and voting rights of African Americans.

President Lyndon Baines Johnson (1908–1973) signed the Voting Rights Act into law, considered perhaps the seminal achievement of his presidency. It had an immediate impact, as African American voter turnout increased substantially after the passage of this law.

What bloody event caused President Johnson to speak to the nation about the need for voting rights legislation?

"Bloody Sunday" was the tragic and awful event that caused President Johnson to speak to the nation about his intent and his urging to Congress to pass voting rights protections. A civil rights

Protestors march across the Edmund Pettus Bridge in Selma, Alabama, as police officers armed with billy clubs prepare to beat them in what is remembered as Bloody Sunday.

march on March 7, 1965, from Selma to Montgomery, Alabama, took place and was met with violent white resistance. The march was designed to draw attention to civil rights abuses and the killing of a young civil rights protestor in Marion, Alabama. State and local police used their billy clubs to repress and abuse more than 600 civil rights protestors who marched across the Edmund Pettus Bridge. These marchers risked their lives and personal safety to the cause of voting rights. Civil rights leaders John Lewis (1940–2020) and Hosea Williams (1926–2020) led the march. Bloody Sunday was televised across the world and seared the collective conscience of fair-minded Americans.

Whose death inspired the Selma march across the bridge?

Jimmie Lee Jackson (1938–1965), a protestor and deacon in a local church, was shot to death behind Zion Methodist Church in Marion, Alabama, by Alabama state trooper James Bonard Fowler (1933–2015). Jackson and others were marching to the Perry County jail to protest the imprisonment of civil rights worker James Orange (1942–2008). Jackson was unarmed, but Fowler claimed that he acted in self-defense, as he alleged that Jackson made a move for Fowler's holster to grab the officer's gun. A grand jury declined to indict Fowler in September 1965.

In May 2007, Fowler was indicted for Jackson's murder. He pled guilty to manslaughter and was released from prison after serving only five months.

What does a citizen need to do to vote?

You must register to vote. There are different ways to register in most places in the United States. You certainly can register in person. This normally takes place at a local voter registration or election office, at the Department of Motor Vehicles, or even at a military recruitment center. You can also register by mail, as there is a National Voter Registration Form. You can obtain this form at the U.S. Election Assistance Commission's website. Some states even allow persons to register online. If nothing else, google for voting and local election office. It generally is not hard to find.

How do I actually vote?

A common place where people vote is at a polling place. It could be at a local school, a local library, or some other public place. You generally show a form of identification, often a driver's license, and then go over to a machine that votes. Generally, there are people there who can assist you with the machine and the ballot.

There are also absentee ballots. These are for when a person cannot get to the polls to vote because they are in military service or out of the country for an extended period. In many locales, there is an early voting period. This means you don't have to vote on the actual day of the election when the lines are long and there could be a possible problem with the voting machines (hopefully, this is quite rare).

Can a state limit a new resident from voting?

A state can impose only a minimal durational requirement on voting because voting is considered a fundamental right. The U.S. Supreme Court established this in *Dunn v. Blumstein* (1972), a case involving a constitutional challenge to Tennessee's durational requirements on voting. James Blumstein (1945–), an assistant professor of law at Vanderbilt, had recently moved to Tennessee, and a month later, he sought to vote. However, election officials denied his right to vote because he had not yet lived in Tennessee for more than a year.

"Durational residence laws penalize those persons who have traveled from one place to another to establish a new residence during the qualifying period," the Court wrote. "Such laws divide residents into two classes, old residents and new residents, and discriminate against the latter to the extent of totally denying them the opportunity to vote." The Court also reasoned that Tennessee's durational requirements violated another fundamental right—the right to travel.

DID YOU KNOW!?

Is voting mandatory?

No; while voting is considered an excellent civic responsibility, there is no law that actually requires someone to vote.

Do states require photo ID?

About 36 states require some form of photo identification to vote. There is a trend over the last decade or so to tighten photo ID laws in some states to combat possible voter fraud. Some contend that these laws are discriminatory. However, it is prudent to check the voter ID law in your state to make sure that you comply.

For example, the state of Alabama requires a person to show photo identification to vote. Alabama accepts the following forms of identification—a valid driver's license or nondriving ID card, a passport, a valid student or employee ID card as long it has a photo, a valid government employee ID card with a photo, a military card with a photo, or a valid photo voter ID card.

Other states do not require photo identification but allow other ways for a person to prove who they are. For example, in the state of Alaska, the following forms of identification are acceptable to vote—an official voter registration card, a driver's license, a birth certificate, a passport, a hunting or fishing license, or a current utility bill, bank statement, or other government document with the voter's name and address.

Can citizens vote online?

Online voting is allowed in some jurisdictions and some federal elections. According to a 2023 article in NPR, in 2020, more than 300,000 Americans voted online in some election. However, cybersecurity experts warn that widespread Internet voting is still not secure enough. This is the primary reason why most states still do not allow Internet voting and those that do limit it to those in the military or for absentee voting. It remains to be seen when more citizens will be allowed to vote online and if cybersecurity can be improved more.

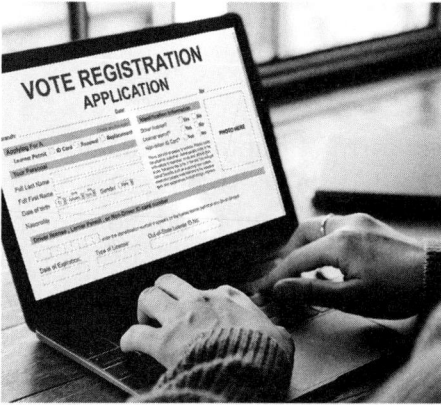

Registering to vote online is fairly simple, and some states allow online voting, but not all do because of fears that voting data is not secure enough.

What other forms of identification in certain states might suffice to vote?

A few states allow an individual to produce a valid handgun carry or conceal carry permit to vote. For example, in Arkansas, one can show a valid handgun carry permit to vote. Other states allow individuals to show a public assistance benefits card. Colorado allows a person to show a pilot's license to vote. Florida allows a person to show a neighborhood association ID. Iowa allows a veterans' identification card as one way to be eligible to vote. Kentucky allows one to show a social security card to vote. Rhode Island allows a government-issued medical card to vote. West Virginia allows a valid bank or debit card.

In states that don't require photo identification, what other ways can a person vote?

Some states might require a person to sign an affidavit declaring who they are under criminal penalty if they make a false statement. In some states, a person may have to provide their signature so that persons at the polling place or election office can compare that signature to a signature on file in the state. Some places may require a prospective voter without a photo ID to provide biographical information.

For example, the state of Oregon does not have a rigid voter identification requirement. There, the prospective voter signs the poll book, and that signature is then compared to signatures on file.

Are there additional requirements for first-time voters?

Yes, there may well be additional requirements for first-time voters over those who have voted previously. The federal law known as the Help America Vote Act requires first-time voters to produce either a photo ID or a government document, utility bill, or paycheck—some type of document that has the person's name and address on it.

Are voter ID laws discriminatory?

It depends on whom you ask. Professor Carol Anderson, a voting rights expert, believes that they are. She writes in her book *One Person, No Vote: How Voter Suppression Is Destroying Our Democracy* (2018): "The goal of all GOP voter ID laws is to reduce significantly the demographic and political impact of a growing share of the American electorate. To diminish the ability of blacks, Latinos, and Asians, as well as the poor and students to choose government representatives and the types of policies they support."

However, others contend that enhanced voter ID laws are necessary to reduce the possibility of voter fraud. For example, Kris Kobach (1966–), the current attorney general and former secretary of state in Kansas, wrote in an opinion column published in the *Washington Post* that voter photo ID laws are a good protection against fraud. "The frequency of voter fraud in Kansas is not unusual," he wrote. "Unfortunately, voter fraud has become a well-documented reality in American elections."

What has the Supreme Court ruled about voter ID laws?

The U.S. Supreme Court in recent years has upheld voter ID laws from constitutional challenges. For example, the Court ruled in *Crawford v. Marion County Election Board* (2008) that Indiana's photo ID law for voting was constitutional. The law required prospective voters to present a photo ID to vote at the polling place. "There is no question about the legitimacy or importance of the State's interest in counting only the votes of eligible voters," Justice John Paul Stevens (1920–2019) wrote in his main opinion for the Court. "Moreover, the interest in orderly administration and accurate recordkeeping provides a sufficient justification for carefully identifying all voters participating in the election process. While the most effective method of preventing election fraud may well be debatable, the propriety of doing so is perfectly clear."

Justice Antonin Scalia (1936–2016), in his concurring opinion, was even blunter. He viewed the requirement of obtaining a photo ID as a minimal burden if a burden at all. He explained: "The universally applicable requirements of Indiana's voter-identification law are eminently reasonable. The burden of acquiring, possessing, and showing a free photo identification is simply not severe, because it does not even represent a significant increase over the usual burdens of voting."

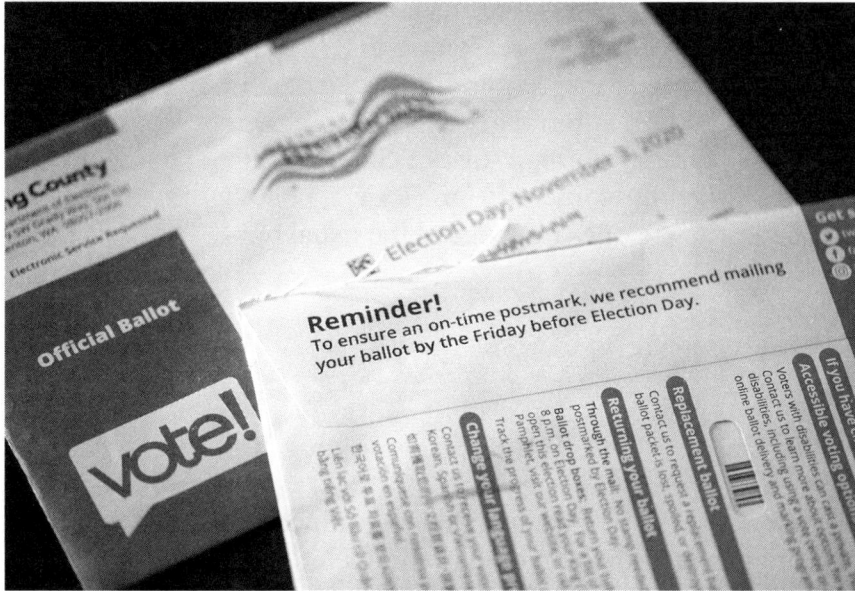

For those who may have difficulty getting to a polling place on election day, voting by mail has become a convenient option. Some states allow any registered voters to do this, while other states require you to provide a reason why you are voting by mail.

What happens if a person does not produce a valid photo ID?

In most places, the person will be allowed to cast what is called a provisional ballot. This means that you still fill out a ballot, but the ballot will not count unless after a specific period you produce a valid form of photo identification accepted by state law.

What happens if I go to vote at the wrong polling place?

In some states, you may not be able to vote, or your ballot will not be counted. The U.S. Supreme Court upheld an Arizona law that required voters to vote in their own precinct. The Arizona law required that voters who choose to vote in person on election day in a county that uses the precinct system must vote in their assigned precincts.

The U.S. Supreme Court upheld this Arizona law in *Brnovich v. Democratic National Committee* (2021), reasoning that "Arizona's out-of-precinct rule enforces the requirement that voters who choose to vote in person on election day must do so in their assigned precincts." In his majority opinion, Justice Samuel Alito Jr. (1950–) added that "[h]aving to identify one's own polling place and then travel there to vote does not exceed the usual burdens of voting."

Can felons vote?

In many states, a felony conviction precludes an individual, even a citizen, from voting even if the person has completed their sentence. These are called felon-disenfranchisement laws. Maine and Vermont are the only states that allow prisoners to vote without restriction. Twenty-two states limit voting to those who are currently incarcerated. These states are California, Colorado, Connecticut, Hawaii, Illinois, Indiana, Maryland, Massachusetts, Michigan, Montana, Nevada, New Hampshire, New Jersey, New York, North Carolina, North Dakota, Ohio, Oregon, Pennsylvania, Rhode Island, Utah, and Washington. Fifteen other states prohibit felons from voting if they are in prison, on parole, or on probation. These states are Alaska, Arkansas, Georgia, Idaho, Kansas, Louisiana, Minnesota, Missouri, New Mexico, Oklahoma, South Carolina, South Dakota, Texas, West Virginia, and Wisconsin.

How has the right to vote been extended since the Civil War?

Before the Civil War, in many states, only white males aged 21 or older and some African American males in certain nonslave states were eligible to vote. Since this time, through a series of constitutional amendments and laws, the right to vote has been extended to other groups. Most notably, the Fifteenth Amendment, which was ratified in 1870, prohibited the denial of the right to vote on the basis of race. The Nineteenth Amendment, ratified in 1920, extended the right to vote to women. The Twenty-third Amendment gave residents of the District of Columbia the right to vote. In 1964, the Twenty-fourth Amendment prohibited the use of poll taxes as a way to limit voting. A poll tax charged individuals money to vote. The Twenty-sixth Amendment, ratified in 1971, extended the right to vote to individuals 18 years of age or older. Previously, some states had limited the right to vote to those 21 years of age or older.

Congress also passed the Voting Rights Act of 1965 during the Civil Rights Movement, which made a significant difference in limiting the ability of states, particularly Southern states, from continuing to deny the franchise to African Americans.

When did African Americans get the right to vote?

African Americans supposedly got the right to vote with the ratification of the Fifteenth Amendment in 1870, but unfortunately, it took later legislation and Supreme Court decisions to ensure that right. The Civil Rights Acts of 1957, 1960, and 1964 and the Voting Rights Act of 1965 suspended literacy tests and other devices that were used to deprive African Americans of the right to vote. For example, in some states, individuals would apply different tests to African Americans and whites to determine whether one was eligible to vote.

In 1975, Congress again extended the Voting Rights Act, enacting a permanent nationwide ban on the use of literacy tests and other similar devices, expanding the act to cover minority groups not literate in English, and requiring affected states and jurisdictions to offer certain types of bilingual assistance to voters.

What devices did these Southern states use to limit voting by African Americans?

Many of the Southern states enacted so-called poll taxes, charging people to vote. The Southern states of Alabama, Arkansas, Florida, Georgia, Louisiana, Mississippi, North Carolina, South Carolina, Tennessee, Texas, and Virginia all passed poll tax laws. Monitors at the polls would apply these poll tax requirements selectively on the basis of race. States also passed literacy tests, requiring would-be voters to read various provisions of the state constitution. Some states also passed so-called "grandfather" clauses that essentially limited the right to vote to individuals whose grandfathers were eligible to vote. Such clauses eliminated African Americans from voting, as their grandfathers were largely enslaved men who had no rights.

When did the Court cast doubt on the use of literacy tests to vote?

The Supreme Court cast doubt on the use of such literacy tests in upholding a key provision of the Voting Rights Act of 1965 in *Katzenbach v. Morgan* (1966). The Court earlier had ruled in *Lassiter v. North Hampton County Board of Elections* (1959) that a literacy test requirement did not violate the Equal Protection Clause. However, the U.S. Congress in 1965 passed the Voting Rights Act of 1965, which essentially prohibited the use of such tests. However, New York had a state law that in effect had denied many persons from Puerto Rico the ability to vote.

Writing for the Court, Justice William Brennan Jr. (1906–1997) penned the following: "Here again, it is enough that we perceive a basis upon which Congress might predicate a judgment that the application of New York's English literacy requirement

President Lyndon Johnson talks to Martin Luther King Jr. after the signing of the Voting Rights Act of 1965, with Rosa Parks standing at right. The act made many of the discriminatory voting laws in southern states illegal.

to deny the right to vote to a person with a sixth grade education in Puerto Rican schools in which the language of instruction was other than English constituted an invidious discrimination in violation of the Equal Protection Clause."

Did the 15th Amendment help African Americans during Reconstruction?

Yes, the 15th Amendment of 1870 immensely helped African Americans during the period of Reconstruction, even leading to the election of African Americans to the U.S. Senate and U.S. House of Representatives. Hiram Revels (1827–1901) and Blanche Bruce (1841–1898), for example, were African American men elected to the U.S. Senate in the 1870s. The Fifteenth Amendment achieved its purpose for a short time, as black voting participation and representation in the South increased rapidly.

However, the Compromise of 1877 essentially ended a federal commitment to ensuring voting rights for African Americans in the South. Federal troops were removed from the former Confederate states. The federal government backed off of federal civil rights enforcement in the South, causing Southern states to institute a series of Black Codes and other laws that segregated African Americans and limited their voting rights.

Thus, more than 20 years after Reconstruction, there were no more African Americans in Congress, and the former Confederate states had rewritten their state constitutions to exclude African Americans from voting.

When did women get the right to vote?

Women finally received the right to vote in 1920 with the ratification of the Nineteenth Amendment. But it took decades and decades of organized struggle for this to happen. The women's rights convention held at Seneca Falls, New York, in 1848 was a significant historical step on the road to slow progress. Suffragettes had to take to the streets to protest to change public opinion on this subject.

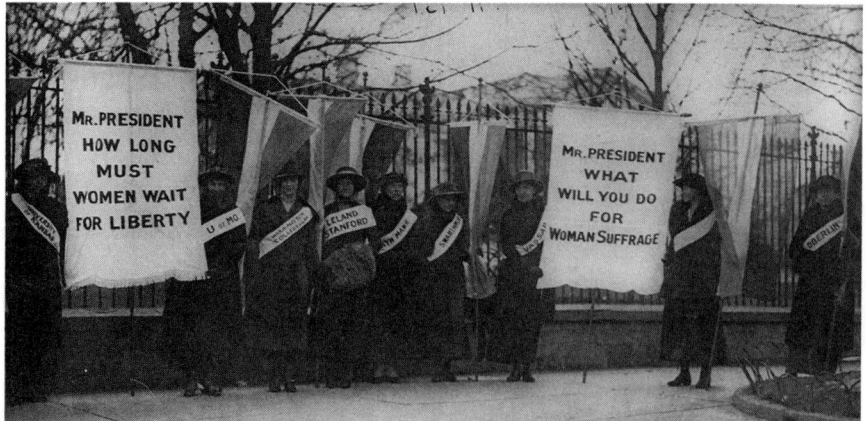

Women suffragists protest in front of the White House in this 1917 photograph. The long struggle for women's right to vote finally bore fruit in 1920 with the passage of the Nineteenth Amendment.

EDUCATION

Do children who are not U.S. citizens have a right to attend public schools in the United States?

Yes, all children in the United States have the right to attend public schools. The U.S. Supreme Court in *Plyler v. Doe* (1982) struck down a Texas law that prohibited a free public education to children of undocumented aliens. "The Equal Protection Clause was intended to work nothing less than the abolition of all caste-based and invidious class-based legislation," Justice William Brennan wrote for the Court. "That objective is fundamentally at odds with the power the State asserts here to classify persons subject to its laws as nonetheless excepted from its protection."

The Court explained that the Equal Protection Clause of the Fourteenth Amendment applies to "any person," not just to citizens. The Court also emphasized the fundamental importance of education to a child's future opportunities in life. Brennan explained: "In addition, education provides the basic tools by which individuals might lead economically productive lives to the benefit of us all. In sum, education has a fundamental role in maintaining the fabric of our society. We cannot ignore the significant social costs borne by our Nation when select groups are denied the means to absorb the values and skills upon which our social order rests."

How is education important to citizenship?

Education may be the most important part to becoming a good citizen. That is because schooling teaches young (and older) people what it takes to become a good citizen, to learn the positive values of society. Kids take classes in American government, civics, world history, and other classes that expose them to various ideas and to the realities of social structures and constructs.

The U.S. Supreme Court recognized the important value of education in its historic decision in *Brown v. Board of Education* (1954), writing:

> Today, education is perhaps the most important function of state and local governments. Compulsory school attendance laws and the great expenditures for education both demonstrate our recognition of the importance of education to our democratic society. It is required in the performance of our most basic public responsibilities, even service in the armed forces. It is the very foundation of good citizenship. Today it is a principal instrument in awakening the child to cultural values, in preparing him for later professional training, and in helping him to adjust normally to his environment.

These words of Chief Justice Earl Warren (1891–1974) ring just as true today as they were when they were written in 1954.

Do states have compulsory education laws?

Yes, every state has a compulsory education law that requires parents or guardians to send their children to school—either public or private—from early years through high school age. This is considered vitally important. In fact, Arkansas law provides that a "free and compulsory education" is a "human right" for children in that state.

Most state compulsory education laws require that children attend school for particular ages. For example, Tennessee's law,

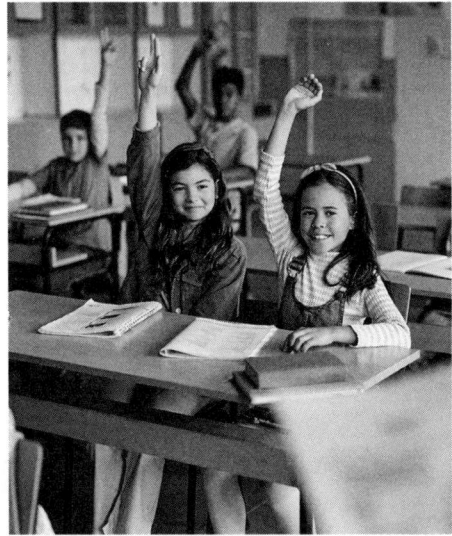

All states require that parents send their children to either a public or private school, including some compulsory classes. When it comes to civics or government classes, only nine states and the District of Columbia still require a year of study in these subjects. That's why the book you're reading can be useful!

codified at Tenn. Code Ann. §49-6-3001(c)(1), provides: "Every parent, guardian or other legal custodian residing within this state having control or charge of any child or children between six (6) years of age and seventeen (17) years of age, both inclusive, shall cause the child or children to attend public or nonpublic school, and in event of failure to do so, shall be subject to the penalties provided in this part."

Do states require the teaching of civic education?

Many states stress the importance of civic education in their state codes. For example, Arizona has a law that mandates that the Center for the Philosophy of Freedom at the University of Arizona shall do the following with regard to civic education:

1. Develop civic education standards that school districts and charter schools must include pursuant to [state law]. The civic education standards must include instruction on:

(a) The original intent of the founding documents and principles of the United States as found in source documents.

(b) The civic-minded expectations of an upright and desirable citizenry that recognizes and accepts responsibility for preserving and defending the blessings of liberty inherited from prior generations and secured by the United States constitution.

2. On or before December 31, 2022, establish and maintain a list of oral history resources to be used along with the civic education standards and social studies standards that provide portraits in patriotism based on first-person accounts of victims of other nations' governing philosophies who can compare those philosophies with those of the United States.

Rhode Island, by contrast, forms a civic education commission that oversees the level of instruction and standards in its schools. The state law defines civic education as "the goal of education in civic and government is informed, responsible participation in political life by competent citizens committed to the fundamental values and principles on American constitutional democracy. Their effective and responsible participation requires the acquisition of a body of knowledge and of intellectual and participatory skills."

Do the states get specific about what must be taught in civic education?

Yes, state laws on civic education generally require that the content taught in the schools meet the state standards for specific subjects. Some state laws get even more specific about content. For example, Tennessee law provides:

Students shall be taught about the formation of the governments of the United States and Tennessee using federal and state foundational documents. They shall also be taught the significance and relevance of those federal and state foundational documents today. This instruction shall include:

(i) The historical and present-day significance of the Declaration of Independence;

(ii) How the United States Constitution establishes the federal government and the characteristics of the republic created by it;

(iii) How the United States Constitution with the Bill of Rights and the Tennessee Constitution with the Declaration of Rights are applicable in today's society;

(iv) How the United States Constitution is changed and the changes that have been made to it since 1787;

(v) Why Tennessee has had three (3) constitutions, the Constitutions of 1796, 1834, and 1870, and how changes have been made to the Tennessee Constitution of 1870; and

(vi) How other foundational documents of the United States and Tennessee aided in the formation of the federal and state governments.

Do states define what is good citizenship?

Some states attempt to define what exactly qualifies as good citizenship. For example, Indiana law provides that for public schools, good citizenship means teaching public school students the following 13 principles:

1. Being honest and truthful.

2. Respecting authority.

3. Respecting the property of others.

4. Always doing the student's personal best.

5. Not stealing.

6. Possessing the skills (including methods of conflict resolution) necessary to live peaceably in society and not resorting to violence to settle disputes.

7. Taking personal responsibility for obligations to family and community.

8. Taking personal responsibility for earning a livelihood.

9. Treating others the way the student would want to be treated.

10. Respecting the national flag, the Constitution of the United States, and the Constitution of the State of Indiana.

11. Respecting the student's parents and home.

12. Respecting the student's self.

13. Respecting the rights of others to have their own views and religious beliefs.

How does citizenship training help young people?

Citizenship training is immensely valuable for young people for many reasons. First, it builds in them a sense of self-confidence. Second, it instills in the people the sense that they are part of something more, a part of a community and a society. Third, it gives the young people a voice, the idea that their ideas matter. It also shows young people how they can make positive contributions to their community, their school, their city or county, and their state.

One technique in inspiring good citizenship is holding parades and special events that motivate people to be helpful and hardworking patriots.

How else do states attempt to foster good citizenship?

States take different approaches to fostering good citizenship. One approach is by recognizing a state holiday that values good citizenship. For example, the state of Wyoming sets aside December 10 as "Wyoming Day." This is a state holiday that the legislature provides: "The day shall be observed in the schools, clubs and similar groups by appropriate exercises commemorating the history of the territory and state and the lives of its pioneers, and by fostering in all ways the loyalty and good citizenship of its people." Wyoming chose December 10 as the day for this civics-minded holiday because it was on December 10, 1869, that Wyoming became the first place in the United States to recognize the right of women to vote.

Other states have created state programs for young people. Under these programs, a select few students from each school are chosen to participate in a weeklong program of learning and civic education that seeks to foster good citizenship and leadership training.

What is the advantage of being a citizen for employment purposes?

There are certain jobs that only U.S. citizens qualify for and, thus, noncitizens cannot obtain. For example, many federal jobs are open only to U.S. citizens. The federal government is a big employer that provides generous health benefits and other perks. Such a job could provide familial stability and income.

Can a state prohibit noncitizens from becoming police officers?

Yes, the U.S. Supreme Court ruled in *Foley v. Connelie* (1979) that the state of New York could limit the employment of state police officers to citizens. The New York law in question provided: "No person shall be appointed to the New York state police force unless he shall be a citizen of the United States." The case involved Edmund Foley, who had emigrated from Ireland and applied to become a New York state trooper. He was denied based on this New York law.

Foley sued, contending that the New York law violated the Equal Protection Clause. A federal district court upheld the law. The case reached the U.S. Supreme Court, which also upheld the law. The Court reasoned that "a State may deny aliens the right to vote, or to run for elective office, for these lie at the heart of our political institutions. Similar considerations support a legislative determination to exclude aliens from jury service."

The Court concluded: "In the enforcement and execution of the laws the police function is one where citizenship bears a rational relationship to the special demands of the particular position. A State may, therefore, consonant with the Constitution, confine the performance of this important public responsibility to citizens of the United States."

SECURITY FROM REMOVAL

How do citizens have an advantage when it comes to removal?

Green card holders, or lawful permanent residents, are not citizens and, thus, can be subject to removal for a variety of reasons

Can noncitizens receive public benefits?

Another major advantage to being a citizen is that a citizen can apply for Supplemental Security Income (SSI). Many people with a disability or the elderly apply for SSI benefits, but you cannot apply for such benefits if you are not a citizen.

identified earlier in the text—such as committing an aggravated felony, committing domestic abuse, or lying on an immigration application. Citizens are free from the fear of being removed. Thus, security from removal is a major advantage to seeking U.S. citizenship.

HOW TO OBTAIN CITIZENSHIP

How does one become a U.S. citizen?

There are two ways to become a U.S. citizen. The first is by birth, and the second is by naturalization. If you are born in the United States or a U.S. territory, then you automatically are a U.S. citizen. The Fourteenth Amendment to the U.S. Constitution reads: "All persons born in the United States, and subject to the jurisdiction thereof, are citizens of the United States and of the State wherein they reside." This birthright principle applies even to children born in the United States to so-called unauthorized immigrant parents. The only persons born in the United States who do not become U.S. citizens are children born to foreign diplomats.

Naturalization is a different process. It refers to the way in which an immigrant legally becomes a U.S. citizen even though they were born into a different country and are a citizen of a different country. The most common way to obtain citizenship by naturalization is to be a lawful permanent resident of the United States for at least five years.

There are other ways to achieve citizenship through naturalization. For example, if you marry a U.S. citizen, you generally can apply to become a citizen after living in the United States lawfully for three years. Another possible path to achieving citizenship is by serving in the U.S. Armed Forces. If you serve at least one year in the armed forces, then you may be eligible for naturalization.

President Donald J. Trump attends a naturalization ceremony in the White House's Cross Hall in 2020.

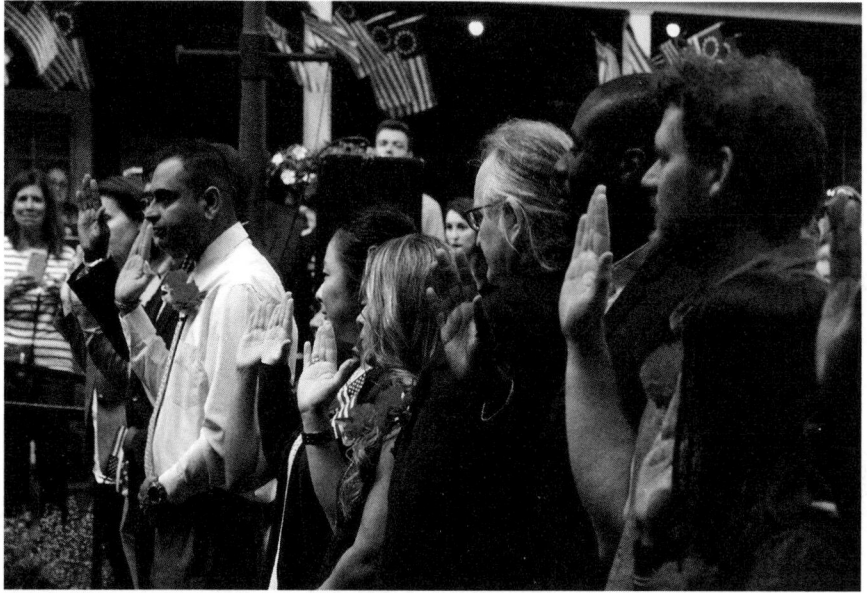

Immigrants swear a pledge of allegiance during a naturalization ceremony. The process of how to become a U.S. citizen is defined by Congress.

DID YOU KNOW!?

What is a conditional resident?

A conditional resident, or conditional permanent resident, is a person who must renew their green card every two years instead of every ten like a permanent resident. A conditional resident is an immigrant who has been married less than two years to their citizen spouse or spouse who is a lawful permanent resident.

What is a lawful permanent resident?

A lawful permanent resident is an immigrant who is legally authorized to be in the United States. A lawful permanent resident is sometimes called a "green-card holder" because they have earned a so-called green card, a document that shows they are lawfully present in the United States. There are many lawful permanent residents living in the United States. According to the Department of Homeland Security, as of January 2022, there were approximately 12.9 million lawful permanent residents living in the United States.

How does a lawful permanent resident become a citizen?

A lawful permanent resident becomes a U.S. citizen through the naturalization process. The lawful permanent resident must meet several requirements to achieve citizenship. They must:

- Be at least 18 years of age;

- Be a permanent resident as mentioned for at least five years;

- Have continuously lived in the United States for these five years before applying for citizenship;

- Must have been physically present in the United States for at least 30 months during those five years;

- Have lived within a state for three months before filing for citizenship;

- Pass an English test and a history and government test;

- Be a person of good moral character.

Must a person be in the United States continuously for a five-year period to apply for citizenship?

No, the requirement is that the person must have a physical presence in the United States for two and a half years—half of the five-year period. In other words, a person could have come to the United States five years ago—but spend some of that time back in their home country or another place—and the five-year period still counts.

This so-called physical presence requirement is there so that a noncitizen's ties to the United States are strengthened. Otherwise, some could have come to the United States briefly five years ago—live abroad for four years—and then still apply for U.S. citizenship. The law does not allow this.

What if a lawful permanent resident takes several short trips out of the country?

This is fine, as long as the person is physically in the United States for at least half of the five-year period. There is an exception to this, however. A lawful permanent resident generally cannot be outside of the United States for more than six months at a time. The lawful permanent resident will have to convince immigration officials that the person really had an intent to stay and become a U.S. citizen.

If a lawful permanent resident is going to have an extended period away from the United States—longer than six months—the resident should apply for U.S. Citizenship and Immigration Services (USCIS) permission to stay outside for that longer period of time.

How does one determine good moral character?

The U.S. legal system and citizenship process considers certain conduct to indicate that a person does not possess good moral character. These include being convicted of a crime of violence; being convicted of a crime that involves fraud; being convicted of two or more crimes that have a combined sentence of five years or more; violating the drug laws; habitual drunkenness; illegal gambling; prostitution; polygamy; lying to obtain U.S. citizenship; failing to pay child support or alimony payments; committing any act of terrorism; or persecuting anyone because of their race, religion, or other protected class.

Those who may have issues involving good moral character should consult with an immigration attorney who may be able to help to convince U.S. authorities that they have good moral character.

Generally, if a lawful permanent resident goes about their business, pays their taxes, and avoids getting into trouble with the authorities, then that is sufficient to show good moral character.

Naturally, having a criminal record or doing anything illegal will disqualify any hopeful immigrant from being accepted into the U.S. as a citizen of good moral character.

What are some examples of conduct that would show a person lacks the requisite degree of character?

There are many examples that would show bad character. Some of these include not paying income taxes, voting illegally in the United States, deserting the U.S. military, lying to obtain immigration benefits, committing crimes, or abusing illegal drugs.

What exactly is an aggravated felony?

An aggravated felony includes serious criminal offenses such as murder, rape, sexual abuse of a minor, drug trafficking, racketeering, and child pornography. It also includes any crime of violence, theft, or burglary that resulted in a prison term of one year or more. Driving under the influence (DUI) is often considered an aggravated felony. If a lawful permanent resident has a criminal record, it would be a good idea for the person to consult with an immigration attorney before applying for citizenship.

How has the definition of aggravated felony expanded?

It used to be that an aggravated felony for immigration law purposes applied only to murder, federal drug trafficking, and unlawful trafficking of destructive devices. However, Congress through the years has greatly expanded the definition of an aggravated felony. It now includes more than 30 different types of offenses. And some of these crimes are not even violent offenses or even a felony. For example, failing to file an income tax return and failure to appear in court are now considered aggravated felonies.

What happens to an immigrant if they are convicted of an aggravated felony?

It depends on whether the immigrant is a lawful permanent resident or someone who entered the country illegally. If the immigrant is not a lawful permanent resident, they may be administratively deported from the United States without a formal hearing or right to an appeal before the Board of Immigration Appeals. If a lawful permanent resident is convicted of an aggravated felony, they too can face deportation, but the government must go through certain steps before effectuating that outcome.

What other negative consequences flow to an immigrant convicted of an aggravated felony?

The immigrant convicted of an aggravated felony becomes ineligible to apply for asylum. Such an immigrant is also ineligible for cancellation of removal—where U.S. immigration officials could deport or remove someone technically but cancel the removal proceedings. Furthermore, an immigrant convicted of an aggravated felony is also ineligible for voluntary departure—where an immigrant who otherwise is subject to deportation and removal is allowed to voluntarily leave the United States without an official deportation or removal order.

DID YOU KNOW!?

What exactly is cancellation of removal?

Cancellation of removal is a form of relief for immigrants in which an immigration judge allows the immigrant to remain in the United States even though that immigrant is capable of being deported or removed from the United States.

Can a green card holder lose the right to remain in the United States if they apply for citizenship?

Yes, a lawful permanent resident can be subject to deportation—what the law calls "removal proceedings"—for a variety of reasons. Some of these include entering into a fake marriage to obtain a green card, helping to smuggle someone into the United States, the commission of a crime of "moral turpitude" for which a judge could have sentenced the defendant to a criminal sentence of at least one year, the commission of what is called "an aggravated felony" (often crimes of violence), addiction to illegal drugs, or the commission of a gun-related crime.

Another reason why a person can be removed—even if they are technically a lawful permanent resident—is if they are convicted of a domestic violence crime or commit child abuse, neglect, or abandonment. The idea here is that the legal system wants to prohibit domestic abuse against a partner or child at all costs.

The reason this can be a real problem is that a lawful permanent resident may have committed one of these offenses, but the immigration authorities never found out or tracked it. But when a person applies for citizenship, it allows U.S. immigration authorities to pore over all your records when considering the citizenship application. In other words, sometimes a person receives a green card in error or receives a green card when they could have been denied.

How does a person achieve citizenship more quickly by serving in the U.S. Armed Forces?

If a person serves at least one year in the U.S. Armed Forces and receives an honorable discharge, then that person can apply for U.S. citizenship if: they are at least 18 years of age; they are a permanent resident at the time they have a naturalization interview; they pass an English test and a history and government test; and they are a person of good moral character.

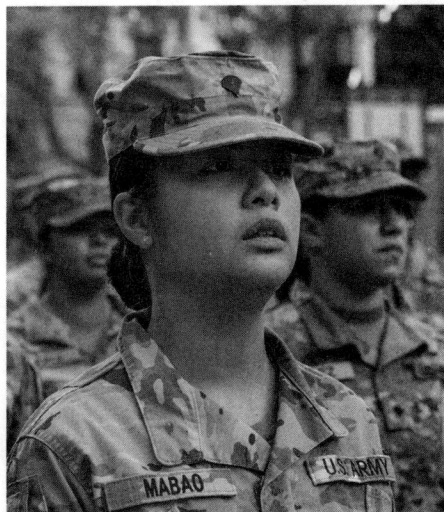

Serving honorably in the U.S. military will create a fast track to American citizenship.

How does a person apply for a green card to become a lawful permanent resident in the first place?

There are two ways that an immigrant can apply for a green card to be declared a lawful permanent resident in the United States. The first way is through a process known as "adjustment of status." This process is available to an immigrant who enters the United States for a temporary purpose—such as a student visa or a tourist visa—and then wants to stay here permanently and lawfully. If the immigrant enters the United States legally and meets certain requirements, they can apply for adjustment of status and become a lawful permanent resident.

The other way to apply for a green card is through consular processing. This is when a person applies at a U.S. Department of State consulate for the opportunity to enter the United States lawfully and obtain a green card. The person applies for

The U.S. Department of State is headquartered in the Harry S. Truman Building at 2201 C. Street NW in Washington, D.C.

an immigrant visa and, thus, hopes to achieve lawful permanent resident status.

What are the steps to consular processing?

The first step is that the immigrant determines their basis to immigrate lawfully to the United States. This determines whether a person is eligible for a green card. Many people have a petition filed on their behalf by a family member or an employer in the United States.

The next step is filing the immigrant petition. There are family-based immigrant petitions, employment-based immigrant petitions, special categories, and humanitarian programs. The next step is waiting on a decision to the petition. If the USCIS denies the petition, the reason for the denial will be stated. The immigrant then has an opportunity to appeal that decision. If the petition is granted, then the approved petition is sent to the U.S. Department of State's National Visa Center.

The immigrant then waits to receive notification from the National Visa Center. The Center then contacts the immigrant for an interview at the consular office. The consular office then determines if the person is eligible. If the consular office approves the person, then the person receives an immigration or "Visa Packet."

Once an immigrant receives approval through this Visa Packet, they can travel to the United States with their Visa Packet. They provide the documents to the U.S. Customs and Border Protection (CBP) officer at the port of entry. An officer with the CBP will inspect the person and determine if the person will be admitted into the United States as a lawful permanent resident. If the CBP officer admits the individual, the immigrant now has a lawful permanent resident status and can live and work in the United States permanently.

What are the English and history/ government tests required for U.S. citizenship?

The English test determines whether an immigrant can read, write, and understand English. The history and government test ensures that the immigrant has a good working knowledge of the United States, its governmental institutions, and how the country works.

What is the history/civics test?

This test consists of a set of questions. There are 100 possible questions that a person could be asked. The USCIS official

What exactly is the English test?

The English test occurs when an official with the U.S. Citizenship and Immigration Services (USCIS) interviews the applicant. The applicant must be able to read English, write English, and speak English. The official asks the applicant to read three sentences in English. The applicant must show the official that the individual can comprehend at least one of these sentences. You also must be able to write at least one sentence in English that demonstrates you understand English. Finally, you must convince the USCIS official that you understand English by your responsiveness to their questions. The USCIS provides free study materials so that applicants can prepare for this English test.

will ask the applicant at least 10 questions related to history and civics. The applicant must answer at least six of those questions correctly to pass the history/civics test.

The questions cover a variety of areas, including principles of American democracy, the American system of government, citizen rights and responsibilities, knowledge of some American history from the colonial period to the present day, geography, symbols, and holidays.

What types of questions are on this history/civics test?

Past questions that have been asked on the history/civics test include the following:

- What is the supreme law of the land?

- What is the form of government of the United States?

- How are changes made to the U.S. Constitution?

- What does the Bill of Rights protect?

- What is one right that the First Amendment protects?

- How many amendments does the U.S. Constitution have?

- What founding document said the United States was free from Great Britain?

- The words "Life, Liberty, and the Pursuit of Happiness" are from what document?

- What is the rule of law?

- Why are there three branches of government?

- Name the three branches of government.

- What part of the federal government writes laws?

- What are the two parts of the U.S. Congress?

- How many U.S. senators are there?

- How long is a term for a U.S. senator?

- How many voting members are in the U.S. House of Representatives?

- Who is one of your two senators?

- How old do citizens have to be to vote in the United States?

- Where is the Statue of Liberty?

- When do we celebrate Independence Day?

- What is the capital of the United States?

What is the Oath of Allegiance?

The Oath of Allegiance is a loyalty oath that a noncitizen must take during the swearing-in ceremony for citizenship.

The Oath reads:

I hereby declare, on oath,

That I absolutely and entirely renounce and abjure all allegiance and fidelity to any foreign prince, potentate, state or sovereignty, of whom or which I have heretofore been a subject or citizen;

That I will support and defend the Constitution and the laws of the United States against all enemies, foreign and domestic;

That I will bear true faith and allegiance to the same;

That I will bear arms on behalf of the United States when required by the law; and

That I take this obligation freely, without any mental reservation or purpose of evasion, so help me God.

At the swearing-in ceremony, the citizenship applicants will be asked to raise their hands and repeat this oath verbally as a group.

Are there other questions on the test that deal with loyalty to the United States?

Yes, several questions on the test are designed to determine whether you will be loyal to the United States of America. This means not being hostile to the U.S. government, believing in representative government, believing in the liberty and ideals reflected in the U.S. Constitution and Bill of Rights, and believing that political change should be carried out peacefully rather than through violence.

What if a noncitizen is a conscientious objector?

Conscientious objectors can still qualify for U.S. citizenship even though they are opposed to war and thus would not defend the United States during wartime. Such persons need to show immigration officials that they are opposed to any type of military service, that they object to such on religious or moral grounds, and that these beliefs are deeply and sincerely held.

What is a tourist visa?

A tourist visa, also called a visitor visa, is what a noncitizen from some countries need to enter the United States for tourism or business purposes. For some immigrants coming to the United States, they must have a passport and their visa to enter the United States.

Foreigners can obtain tourist visas for business and medical reasons. Some visitors need both a passport and a visa to enter the United States.

What are the two different types of tourist visas?

There are B-1 visitor visas and B-2 visitor visas. The B-1 visa is for those immigrants who enter the United States for business purposes. The B-2 visa is for those immigrants who enter the United States for tourist or medicinal reasons.

Does it matter how long a person is staying in the United States?

It does matter. For immigrants from many countries, if they are staying for 90 days or less, the person does not need a visa. Under the United States' Visa Waiver Program, the person can enter the United States with just a passport and not a visa as long as they are staying less than 90 days.

Do some immigrants need a visa to enter the United States even for 90 days or less?

Yes, persons from the following countries need to have a visa to enter the United States even for a short period of time—Cuba, Democratic People's Republic of Korea, Iran, Iraq, Sudan, or Syria. Furthermore, those immigrants who have visited Democratic People's Republic of Korea, Iran, Iraq, Libya, Somalia, Sudan, Syria, or Yemen on or after March 1, 2011, must have a visa.

What is a student visa?

A student visa is for those immigrants who wish to enter the United States as a full-time student studying in the United States. There are two basic types of student visas: F-1 visas and M-1 visas. An F-1 visa is for full-time international students pursuing their academic studies in the United States. The M-1 visa is for those full-time international students entering the United States to pursue vocational studies.

There also is a similar type of visa—the so-called J-1 visa— but it is issued only for international exchange students who come to the United States to take part in work- and study-based exchange programs. For example, visiting scholars, camp counselors, au pairs, and research assistants would need to apply for and receive a J-1 visa to enter the United States.

What is dual nationality?

Dual nationality refers to the concept of a person having two citizenships in two different countries. For example, a person

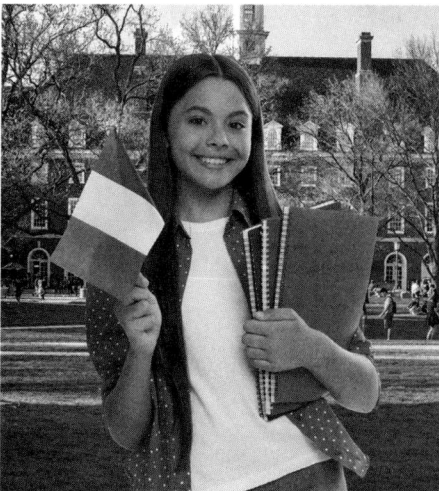

With a student visa, a foreigner can stay in the United States for as long as they are continuing their educational pursuits.

can be a U.S. citizen and a citizen of another country under certain circumstances. A child born in a foreign country to two U.S. national citizens can be a citizen of the United States and the country in which they were born. Or a person may be a citizen of one country and then naturalize to become a citizen of another country. That person may retain the citizenship in the country they were born and become a dual national.

U.S. law does not require an individual to renounce U.S. citizenship when a person becomes a naturalized citizen in a foreign country.

ASYLUM

What is asylum?

Asylum is formal protection from persecution that noncitizens can file to remain in the United States. Every year, thousands of persons apply for asylum when they arrive in the United States. If a person is granted asylum, the person can legally remain in the United States and even get started on the path toward citizenship.

How can a person obtain asylum?

A person can obtain asylum if they are able to convince immigration authorities that they have been persecuted or are likely to face future persecution because of their "race, religion, nationality, membership in a particular social group, or political opinion." The asylum applicant generally must show that they have a credible fear that such persecution will take place. At times, persons seeking asylum are called refugees, referred to as persons seeking refuge from persecution.

What are the different methods of applying for asylum?

There are essentially three different categories: (1) affirmative asylum; (2) defensive asylum; and (3) expedited asylum. Affirmative asylum covers those instances in which immigrants who are not in removal proceedings affirmatively apply for asylum. Defensive asylum refers to situations in which an immigrant who is in removal proceedings then decides to apply for asylum as a defense of sorts against possible deportation. Finally, expedited asylum refers to a situation in which a UCIS officer determines within 14 days of an immigrant's entry into the United States whether they are entitled to asylum.

What is the deadline for applying for asylum?

Generally, a person must apply for asylum within one year of entering the United States. Asylum cases often can take several years to be concluded.

DEPORTATION

What is deportation?

Deportation is the term in immigration law used for when the government decides to remove, or deport, a noncitizen from the United States. Immigration law generally allows the government to file so-called removal proceedings when a noncitizen has committed a serious crime or what is called "an aggravated felony" or

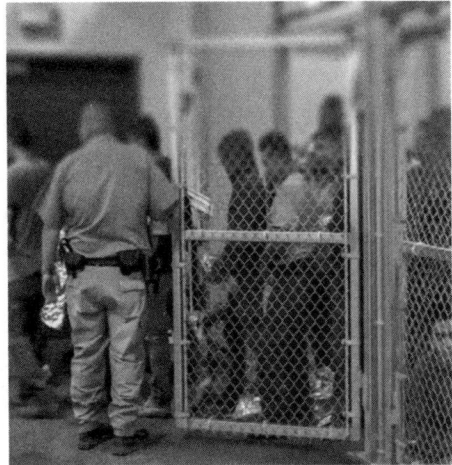

Illegal immigration and the subsequent flow of deportation has been a huge political issue on America's border with Mexico for decades.

has shown bad character or even has been found to have entered the United States illegally.

The process of deportation begins when the government—usually Immigration and Customs Enforcement (ICE)—initiates so-called removal proceedings. The government generally must prove that deportation is necessary.

How does the deportation process begin?

It generally begins when ICE sends a notice to appear before an immigration judge to the noncitizen. The government must include in the notice to appear the government's stated reasons for seeking removal of the noncitizen.

The noncitizen will then need to appear at the hearing. Normally, the immigration judge will then ask the individual if they need time to hire an immigration attorney to represent them. If the individual says yes, then the immigration judge will set another hearing.

If the judge determines the individual can be deported, what can the noncitizen do?

The noncitizen can file a motion for withholding of removal.

Further Reading

Amar, Akhil Reed. *The Words That Made Us: American's Constitutional Conversation, 1760–1840*. New York: Basic Books, 2021.

Bowen, Catherine Drinker. *Miracle at Philadelphia*. Boston: Little, Brown, 1966.

Bray, Ilona. *Becoming a U.S. Citizen: A Guide to the Law, Exam & Interview*. 8th ed. San Francisco: NOLO, 2016.

Brinkley, Douglas. *American Heritage History of the United States*, New York: Viking Penguin, 1998.

Catt, Carrie Chapman, and Nettie Shuler *Woman Suffrage and Politics: The Inner Story of the Suffrage Movement*. New York: Scribner's, 1926.

Chemerinsky, Erwin. *Constitutional Law: Principles and Policies*. 6th ed. New York: Wolters Kluwer, 2019.

———. *We the People: A Progressive Reading of the Constitution*. New York: MacMillan, 2018.

Collier, Christopher, and James Lincoln Collier. *Decision in Philadelphia: The Constitutional Convention of 1787*. New York: Ballantine Books, 1986.

Das, Alina. *No Justice in the Shadows: How America Criminalizes Immigrants*. New York: Bold Type Books, 2020.

Driver, Justin. *The Schoolhouse Gate: Public Education, the Supreme Court, and the American Mind*. New York: Pantheon Books, 2018.

Ellis, Joseph J. *Founding Brothers: The Revolutionary Generation*. New York: Vintage Books, 2000.

Foner, Eric. *The Story of American Freedom*. New York: W.W. Norton, 1998.

Friendly, Fred, and Martha J.H. Elliott. *The Constitution: That Delicate Balance*. New York: Random House, 1984.

Ginzberg, Lori D. *Elizabeth Cady Stanton: An American Life*. New York: MacMillan, 2010.

Gjelton, Tom. *A Nation of Nations: A Great Immigration Story*. New York: Simon & Schuster, 2015.

Goldwin, Robert A. *From Parchment to Power: How James Madison Used the Bill of Rights to Save the Constitution.* Washington, D.C.: The AEI Press, 1997.

Haass, Richard. *The Bill of Obligations: The Ten Habits of Good Citizens.* New York: Penguin Press, 2023.

Hirsch, E. D., Jr. *How to Educate a Citizen: The Power of Shared Knowledge to Unify a Nation.* New York: Harper, 2020.

Hudson, David L., Jr. *The Bill of Rights: The First Ten Amendments of the Constitution.* Updated edition. Murfreesboro, TN: The First Amendment Press, 2021.

Irons, Peter. *The Courage of Their Convictions: Sixteen Americans Who Fought Their Way to the Supreme Court.* New York: Free Press, 1988.

———. *A People's History of the Supreme Court.* New York: Viking, 1999.

Kluger, Richard. *Simple Justice: The History of Brown v. Board of Education and Black America's Struggle for Equality.* New York: Alfred A. Knopf, 1975.

Knight, Alfred H. *The Life of the Law.* New York: Crown, 1996.

Lee, Erika. *America for Americans: A History of Xenophobia in the United States.* New York: Basic Books, 2019.

Monk, Linda R. *The Words We Live By: Your Annotated Guide to the Constitution.* New York: Hatchette Books, 2015.

Rodell, Fred. *55 Men: The Story of the Constitution, Based on the Day-by-Day Notes of James Madison.* Harrisburg, PA: Stackpole, 1986.

Schwartz, Bernard. *The Great Rights of Mankind: A History of the American Bill of Rights.* New York: Oxford University Press, 1977.

Spiro, Peter J. *Citizenship: What Everyone Needs to Know.* New York: Oxford University Press, 2020.

Tocqueville, Alexis de. *Democracy in America.* Trans. ed., with an introduction by Harvey Mansfield. Chicago: University of Chicago Press, 2000.

U. S. Citizens and Immigration Services. *Welcome to the United States: A Guide for New Immigrants* (rev. 2015). M-618.pdf (uscis.gov).

Ward, Geoffrey C. *The Civil War: An Illustrated History.* New York: Knopf, 1990.

Weiss, Elaine. *The Woman's Hour: The Great Fight to Win the Vote.* New York: Penguin, 2018.

Williams, Harry T. *Lincoln and His Generals.* New York: Vintage Books, 1952.

INDEX

Note: (ill.) indicates photos and illustrations